HOPE AMONG US YET

HOPE

DAVID P. PEELER

AMONG US YET

Social Criticism and Social Solace in Depression America

The University of Georgia Press   Athens and London

NEXT TIME TRY THE TRAIN

RELAX   Southern Pacific

© 1987 by the University of Georgia Press
Athens, Georgia 30602
All rights reserved
Designed by Sandra Strother Hudson
Set in Caledonia with Franklin Gothic and
Graphique display
The paper in this book meets the guidelines
for permanence and durability of the Committee on
Production Guidelines for Book Longevity of the
Council on Library Resources.

Printed in the United States of America

91 90 89 88 87   5 4 3 2 1

Library of Congress Cataloging in Publication Data

Peeler, David P.
    Hope among us yet.

    Bibliography: p.
    Includes index.
    1. United States—History—1933–1945. 2. United
States—Social conditions—1933–1945. 3. Depressions—
1929—United States. 4. American literature—20th
century—History and criticism. 5. Social problems in
literature. 6. Journalism—United States—History—20th
century. 7. Social realism. 8. Photography, Documentary
—United States—History—20th century. I. Title.
E806.P447 1987   973.917   86-16016
ISBN 0-8203-0902-8 (alk. paper)

British Library Cataloging in Publication Data available.

For Paula Marie Woodward

Contents

Illustrations

Chapter Four

Chapter Five

Chapter Six

Acknowledgments

Several institutions and individuals have given me important support in this project. The State Historical Society of Wisconsin provided a productive environment for much of the early research, and Wilma Thompson of the Society's Library was particularly helpful. The Midwest Area Center of the Archives of American Art was another essential work place. Financial support came from the Research Fund of the University of Science and Arts of Oklahoma, and important intellectual contributions from the members of the Works in Progress Seminar, Department of History, United States Naval Academy. Tom Mullen of the Academy's Computer Services Department provided generous assistance during preparation of the manuscript. John Collier, Jack Delano, Theo Jung, Russell Lee, Carl Mydans, Beaumont Newhall, Arthur Rothstein, and Marion Post-Wolcott all gave permission to use their oral interviews housed in the Archives of American Art. Bernarda B. Shahn allowed me to use Ben Shahn's interviews from the Archives, and Paul S. Taylor likewise granted access to Dorothea Lange's materials. I also wish to thank Garnett McCoy of the Archives of American Art for permission to quote from the Edith Bry, Ben Shahn and Philip Evergood Papers. Kendall Taylor has helped me locate several of Philip Evergood's works. My special thanks goes to the museums, libraries, galleries, and individuals that have granted permission to reproduce photographs and paintings.

Long discussions with Mike Starr helped provide some of the initial direction and focus to this project. Charles T. DeShong, Mary Wyer, and George Lipsitz have provided insightful readings and intelligent comments. David Lovejoy and John Cooper have been sounding boards for my ideas and critical readers of my prose. Milton Cantor's enthusiasm for the project has sustained me for many years, and James Curtis's suggestions on organization and his photographic interpretations have been invaluable. Zora Sampson's eye and insights, as well as her labor and love, nurtured this project through its early formation. Paul Conkin has given his rigorous attention to many of my arguments, and his superb advice on matters of structure and logic. My greatest intellectual sustenance has come from my friend Dan Rodgers. He has been a challenging teacher and a demanding critic. But above all else, Dan is a terrifically exciting thinker, always brimming with intellectual excitement. My gratitude to Dan is immense.

My greatest thanks is to Paula Marie Woodward. Her contributions have been essential to the final shaping of this book, and her dedication to clear thinking has been an inspiration to me. But above all else I am indebted to her wisdom and love. Thank you, Paula.

HOPE AMONG US YET

ONE

Introduction

The times were awful. Or so the Great Depression seemed to many American artists and writers. Beginning with a severe economic downturn that followed the 1929 stock market crash, the Depression reached its depths in the harsh winter of 1932–1933 and never fully abated until war spending commenced prior to Pearl Harbor. Twenty-five percent of the nation's work force was unemployed by 1933, and another twenty-five percent underemployed. In some industrial cities ninety percent of the working population was laid off. Businesses failed, banks closed, and investment virtually ceased. Personal incomes plummeted, millions lost their homes, and hunger and poverty ranged beyond their usual haunts among the lower classes to stalk the previously secure ranks of the middle and upper classes. Even the weather seemed to turn against Americans, bringing floods to the West and Midwest, and the infamous Dust Bowl to the Plains. Overseas conditions were little better. Japanese militarism was on the rise in the Pacific, and European fascism was steadily spreading outward from Italy and Germany.

But things were good, too. Or so it seemed to many of these same artists and writers. Despite the terrible conditions, creative Americans found reasons to temper their despair with optimism. There was strong evidence that capitalism was dying, and given the Soviet Union's economic health, it appeared that socialism might replace it. Working-class Americans demonstrated spunk and class-consciousness, marching on Washington to demand their veterans' bonuses, and later fighting more successfully to organize new industrial unions. Even President Franklin Roosevelt's New Deal was a comfort to some, signaling as it did a further departure from laissez-faire government and a movement towards the welfare state. Perhaps most gratifying of all was that the Depression offered a bonanza for art and literature. Subjects were everywhere, dramatic action abounded, and scores of injustices needed rebuking. There was a world for art to limn, if not win.

For these reasons, the Depression's social artists and writers thought that the times were *both* good and bad. Initially sorrowful and angry over the decade's crises, they eventually became sanguine. Their first impulses led them to produce art that criticized contemporary conditions and belittled the capitalist institutions apparently responsible for those conditions.

Yet accompanying such criticisms was an ever-growing inclination to discover and celebrate some thing that could lead humans through the calamity, and that would guide them past the destitution almost automatically. This response emerged among documentary photographers like Dorothea Lange, who sought to prove that people possessed a buoyant dignity that would sustain them through the devastation. In a similar way, social novelists such as John Steinbeck portrayed humans as riders upon the currents of fate, drifting through the Depression's storms and toward safe shores. Traveling reporters like Nathan Asch thought that if they could only discover hard facts in the midst of the decade's uncertainties, then solutions to the Depression's problems would quickly follow. For their part, social realist painters such as Philip Evergood believed they had established a community with the common people, one that could almost spontaneously conquer the Depression. These were grand hopes, each of which envisioned an end to hunger, homelessness, and despair. They were, however, hopes without much objective basis, desires springing from the writers' and artists' desperate need to see the times as improving. James Agee realized this and made it a theme in his 1937 poem "Summer Evening,"[1] where he described the atmosphere among such social artists and writers of the Depression:

> There is hope among us yet.
> Hope can cut the roots of reason:
> And the sorrowful man forget.

These Depression intellectuals managed to cultivate an optimism that functioned as Agee suggested, cutting "the roots of reason." Terribly distressed over the decade's suffering, these women and men sought some escape from the pain. They found it in their various forms of optimism, all of which were based more upon wishful thinking than upon any reasoned set of alternatives to the Depression's dilemmas.

By no means was social art and literature the only type of cultural activity during the Depression. Flocks of writers and artists were engaged in quite different exercises. Margaret Mitchell's *Gone with the Wind* (1936) and Edward Weston's photographs of nudes were no less products of the thirties than were Steinbeck's migrant stories or Dorothea Lange's photos of dispossessed farmers. But in Scarlett O'Hara's story or in the pictures of sun-bathed models there is little of the contemporary social scene. Since my intention has been to examine creative responses to the Depression by concentrating upon those who grappled directly with thirties conditions in their work, I have excluded the likes of Weston and Mitchell from this study. The combination of social criticism and social solace was a recurrent refrain in the Depression's social art and literature, but especially in complementary yet distinct echoes in certain genres: the social novel, documentary photography, travel reportage, and social realistic painting. Besides their common concern with solace and criticism, social artists and writers working in these fields shared other characteristics. They were mostly young, middle-class people who were at the thresholds of their careers when the Depression struck, and they were often political leftists who stopped short of embracing Communism. They used realistic, rather than modernistic, forms of expression in their works and had a decided preference for depicting people from the nation's lower classes. Finally, these artists and writers constituted an artistic community. They were friends and frequently neighbors, sharing more than topics and styles: painter Ben Shahn and photographer Walker Evans were studio mates, novelist Josephine Herbst and painter William Gropper jointly attended Soviet conferences, and travel reporter James Rorty shared more than one picket line with novelist John Dos Passos.

Social art is didactic, seeking to deliver messages about the objective world by representing objects and scenes from that world. Nonrepresentational art forms such as music and architecture lack the vocabulary for delivering explicit social messages, and even their implicit ones require a well-trained audience.[2] One may design a modest house for working families or weave folk melodies into a composition, and one may do so with the most finely tuned of social consciences; but neither product can advocate mine safety or lament malnutrition in the same explicit manner that a novel or photograph can. Accordingly, I have not concentrated upon music or architecture. Painting and prose *are* capable of examining the outside world. but many painters and writers chose not to produce representational or social pieces, and I have likewise not dwelt upon them. An analysis of Georgia O'Keefe, for example, belongs elsewhere, for she worked primarily upon abstractionist canvases during the 1930s, and even when she turned to her representational paintings of bleached cattle bones, O'Keefe's emphasis was more upon the problems of shape and texture than upon the problem of drought on the ranges. Similarly, although Henry Roth's 1934 novel *Call It Sleep* contains magnificent descriptions of New York City, it is primarily a psychological exploration rather than a social one, and I have excluded it.

If there are few social messages to be found within the works of a Henry

Roth or a Georgia O'Keefe, this is hardly the case for the Depression's social plays or its documentary movies. Stage productions by the Group Theatre were as steeped in protest as were the decade's social novels, and film makers such as Pare Lorentz and Ralph Steiner likewise shared Dorothea Lange's sympathy with oppressed peoples. There was even some commercial potential on the stage or in film for social art, for Erskine Caldwell's novel *Tobacco Road* became a Broadway success, and the movie version of Steinbeck's *The Grapes of Wrath* did well at the box office. The Depression environment influenced young playwrights and movie makers in much the same way that it did their counterparts among painters or still photographers. Film makers Steiner and Lorentz were drawn into their craft by a sense of responsibility for the tragedies they daily encountered. Similarly, playwrights Clifford Odets and Elmer Rice did not come to political drama from any pre-existing radicalism or carefully weighed political decisions; it was more that they breathed this activism from the air that they shared with other artists who came of age in the Depression. The dramatists were also like the photographers or novelists of the Depression in that they created their works relatively late in the decade. To many of John Steinbeck's readers, *The Grapes of Wrath* seemed to be *the* novel of the thirties, encapsulating much of the decade's atmosphere; yet the book appeared only at the tail end of the decade, in 1939. Similarly, a contemporary heralded Odets's play *Waiting for Lefty* as "the birth cry of the thirties," even though the play was first produced in 1935, long after the decade's birth.[3]

Despite these characteristics of the Depression's social film and plays, I have chosen not to focus upon them in this study, for my goal is to chart the creative process during social crisis. To show most clearly the growth and shaping of that creativity, I have concentrated upon *individual* social artists who wrestled with the Depression. Of course, even a novel by a single author involves a web of editors and publishers; but still that web is considerably less extended for a novel than for a movie. By their very nature, film and theater are corporate, not individual, enterprises. The director or producer might be a dominant force in a moving picture, but the efforts of dozens of collaborators are necessary for his intention to emerge on the screen. While a novelist or painter most likely executes his work and then makes his revisions in solitude, the production of a film or play happens amidst a welter of voices and suggestions. Even if the various contributions occur sequentially rather than all merging at the moment of shooting or rehearsal, each adds a key dimension to the final product. Where, for example, does one find the creative center of the film version of *The Grapes of Wrath*—in John Steinbeck's original novel, John Ford's direction, Nunnally Johnson's screenplay, Greg Toland's photography, or Henry Fonda's rendition of Tom Joad?

Drama may be somewhat different from film, for there the playwright's voice is undeniably strong, and within the tradition of drama as literature—"armchair" drama—the script itself often has a degree of independence from the production company. But that independence was seldom the case for social drama of the Depression. Clifford Odets, for instance, was unquestionably the author of *Waiting for Lefty*, a play he wrote while a member of the Group Theatre. But the Group Theatre was more than just a production company; it was a virtual commune in which members shared living quarters, collectively selected plays, and mutually agonized over the political and moral content of their works. The Group Theatre and other drama or cinema production collectives developed their material as much by consensus as by any other method, and their products bore the imprint of numerous creative contributions. Among film groups like the Film and Photo League, this shared creativity helped to isolate the film makers from the Depression's social novelists or still photographers. Constantly reinforcing each others' views, the members of these film collectives accepted Soviet cinematic esthetics and consequently interacted little with social writers and artists who, like Steinbeck, insisted upon independence from Moscow.[4]

My emphasis upon the creative process has also led me to concentrate upon artists and writers rather than upon critics and commentators. Furthermore, I employ more than an artist's or writer's single major work. A major novel or painting *can* reveal much about the maker's thinking, but I use other sources—secondary works, letters, autobiographical materials—to chart the Depression experiences leading up to or away from those major pieces. Within each genre, I give extended discussion to one or two individuals, not to suggest that they are *the* "typical" figures within each art form, but because their careers provide particularly revealing combinations of the criticism and solace that their colleagues echoed. Since the decade's esthetic debates influenced the efforts of artists and writers, I employ a genre-by-genre treatment in examining the ebb and flow of those debates.

Depression artists and writers like Lange and Steinbeck were neither completely like nor completely distinct from their contemporaries. Many thirties intellectuals searched for an organic American *culture* that remained permanent and untroubled beneath a Depression-plagued American *civilization*. The people whom I examine here shared this concern to find some continuum that remained unmarred beneath the Depression's surface. But the continuum that they sought was more of a universal *human* entity rather than a peculiarly *American* one, for their primary intention was not some sort of cultural nationalism in which they aimed to cultivate a unique American art in the midst of the crisis. Inclined to be internationalists, artists in this crowd sometimes found leftist politics alluring. But ideology, leftist or otherwise, was of secondary concern for them, and emotional quandaries, particularly their own searches for a pathway from despair to solace, were much more important to them than political doctrines.[5] There was a certain intellectual softness, an unwillingness to employ ideology, among American thinkers of the 1930s. In this aspect at least, Steinbeck, Lange, and the others were like their contemporaries. Had they been more concerned with reason and less absorbed with emotions, their art may well have been the better for it. But that was not the case, and they embraced a hope that cut the roots of reason.

Before going on to examine social criticism and social solace in Depression America, we should pause to place these creative efforts in some relation to the immediately preceding cultural period. One of the more enduring American myths is that social art of the thirties, with all its intensity and commentary, was completely divorced from a frivolous and self-indulgent twenties culture. The myth of a hedonistic and escapist 1920s was a product of the 1930s, and Malcolm Cowley contributed as much to its forging as did any other Depression intellectual. Generations of undergraduates have read Cowley's *Exile's Return* (1934) and have come to think that the principal cultural experience of the 1920s was expatriation, an exile that ended when artists and authors finally matured and returned from Europe to their work in their native land during the 1930s. As Cowley looked back, it seemed as though "the 1920s had been like a long party," either a forgetful binge in Paris or a salesman's spree at home. But with the Depression, Cowley's overzealous revelers were ready to wash away their sins and hoped "to bury the corrupt past and be reborn into a new life."[6] There had been art during the besotted decade, but it was cultivated for all the wrong reasons. Mable Dodge, epitomizing art patrons of the 1920s, seemed to Cowley like "a species of head-hunter" who collected writers as one would collect so many hunting trophies.[7]

Edmund Wilson, Cowley's friend and fellow critic, shared these sentiments and likewise described the twenties as a benighted era. In contemplating "the literary consequences of the crash," Wilson's interpretation of the immediate cultural past became a recurrent *mea culpa* that
echoed through social art and literature of the 1930s. As Wilson described
it, art of the twenties had been marked with the gentility of critic H. L.
Mencken, a grudging appreciation for business, and a distinct intellectual
aloofness. This orientation "involved compromises with the salesman and
the broker," producing so much guilt and shame among artists and writers
that "the stock market crash was to count for us almost like the rending of
the earth in preparation for the Day of Judgment." Wilson granted that
the Depression brought pain and woe, but still "one couldn't help being
exhilarated at the sudden unexpected collapse of that stupid gigantic
fraud" of American capitalism. Saved from that capitalist barbarianism,
thirties artists and writers set about the invigorating task of making a true,
unblemished culture.[8] Others repeated Wilson's art history, and almost
all divided the recent past into three periods. The first stage had been a
time before the World War, when American culture had seemed set on
the right path, and many social artists of the thirties felt closer to that
generation than to their immediate forebears. But then had come a second period, lasting from the war's conclusion to the Crash, when the sins
of the twenties were committed. Finally, and graciously, a present third
stage ensued, and American culture was purged of its earlier Bohemian
infection.[9]

Thus, to Cowley, Wilson and other thinkers of the thirties, the Crash
and subsequent crisis formed a sort of cultural filter, a barrier through
which little of the twenties' corruption passed to pollute the purged and
pure thirties. While this perception reveals a good deal about Depression
intellectuals' sense of relief and their esthetic egotism, it contains no small
number of errors. That crowd of prewar radicals whom Depression artists
and writers so admired is a case in point. Earlier radicals like John Reed
lived in Bohemias from Davenport to Greenwich Village, contributed articles or drawings to *The Masses*, and joined various socialist movements.
But those prewar Bohemians possessed a desire for spiritual liberation
that they believed must accompany any political revolution, and they
were determined to lead their lives in open flaunting of the Philistines'
way. John Reed reported on the Industrial Workers of the World with a
fervor that Cowley or Wilson might have approved, but he also had
gloriously good times at Mable Dodge's New York salon, where the guests

denounced sexual inhibition as well as capitalism.[10] If thirties social writers and artists sometimes saw too great a dissimilarity between themselves and the prewar generation, they were also inclined to overlook important similarities between themselves and the generation of the 1920s. Some esthetic and ideological continuities managed to transcend the barrier of the Crash. Depression painters often considered their social-realist canvases to be at odds with the abstractionist innovations that seemed part of a twenties Bohemianism. But *both* modern and realistic art were parts of an artistic avant-garde assault upon the stuffiness of art academies.[11] In another similarity, white intellectuals of the twenties evinced a fascination with "primitives" that led them to Taos, Harlem, and Kiowa art shows, a fascination bearing strong resemblance to the pursuit of "natural" warmth and honesty that led their thirties counterparts to seek out "the people." Nor were the twenties as complacent as they might have seemed from the thirties. Excessive talk of Bohemia and ivory towers doubtlessly led many to forget that the twenties had given rise to Sinclair Lewis's *Babbitt* (1922) and John Dos Passos's *Airways, Inc.* (1929), or that the "typically thirties" periodical, the *New Masses*, was first published in 1926. Furthermore, intellectuals of the twenties were no less willing than their counterparts of the thirties to engage in forceful political criticism. Many, for example, took to the streets to protest the Sacco and Vanzetti case. In the midst of the supposedly apolitical decade, these demonstrations against the railroading of the two Italian anarchists began in 1921 and reached a fever pitch in 1927, when it became evident that Massachusetts was determined to execute the two men.

For all these continuities, some important differences did exist in the temper of the two decades. In comparison to intellectuals of the thirties, those of the twenties were more likely to be cultural radicals than political ones. Consider two outstanding critiques issued in the 1920s. Harold Stearns's 1922 collection, *Civilization in the United States*, brought together thirty essays by authors such as H. L. Mencken, Lewis Mumford, Van Wyck Brooks, and Stearns himself. In the preface Stearns summarized their assessment of American civilization. They found it wanting, but not because people were starving or poor—that critique would be more prevalent ten years later. Instead, America was too commercialized a place, full of "emotional and aesthetic starvation," and beset with what Stearns called "spiritual poverty." At the conclusion of the 1920s, Joseph Wood Krutch offered a similar indictment in *The Modern Temper* (1929). But Krutch believed that American (and Western) materialism was even more deadly than Stearns and his contributors had thought. Skepticism and science had taken mystery out of the universe so that people were worse than hungry; they had lost all craving for emotion and beauty. In a world where science explained everything, people could only exist, not transcend, so that, in Krutch's summation of the human condition, "ours is a lost cause."[12]

Krutch, Stearns, and others of the twenties found that the United States shortchanged the inner person. Artists and writers of the thirties were inclined to grant some of this, but thought there was a more immediate problem: with the Depression it was the physical human who was swindled. Minus its tinsel, capitalism's economic and social injustices seemed more obvious than ever, and simple commercialism appeared to be one of its lesser evils. Unemployment, hunger, and dispossession were rife, and capitalism seemed determined to drag millions of innocents along with it as it sunk into the grave. Social writers and artists of the Depression witnessed this not only with anger but also anguish, and their acute despair over Americans' physical condition was a distinguishing mark of the thirties artist. Steinbeck, for example, battled his own poverty and yet managed to stay in pretty good spirits. But when he met migrant Californians who were in even worse condition, he changed, for "what I found horrified me." Steinbeck and his friends "had been simply poor, but these people were literally starving," and Steinbeck's heart was broken. Such suffering also distressed Harold Clurman, and as he observed intellectuals and others in his New York neighborhood, "my own bleak state seemed to be reflected in thousands of faces." That bleakness would become a hallmark of the photographs, novels, essays, and paintings of the Depression. As critic Anita Brenner reported upon seeing a 1933 painting exhibition, artists of the Depression manifested both anger and panic, and the tone of their work ranged "from nervous depression to shrill despair."[13]

Accompanying the pain and anger there was also an exhilaration that was another part of living in the thirties. Social artists and writers exhibited much the same feeling as would young activists living in the Vietnam era. To both groups it appeared for a time as though history's continuum had suddenly broken, and although horrors such as the Southeast Asian war or the Depression accompanied that break, the world had begun moving toward greater justice. Critic Alfred Kazin demonstrated this mood during the 1930s. Even though the decade's crises gave the appearance that "the planet had locked in combat," it still seemed as though the forces of righteousness were winning and that "history was going our way." Thus, if the times were terrible, they were also thrilling, with the excitement and the hopes centering around social issues. No wonder then that creative people of the thirties so frequently gave a social or political slant to their works, an emphasis that set thirties efforts apart from those of the twenties. Sometimes the social preoccupation became a virtual parody of itself, as in a love song in the 1937 edition of the International Ladies Garment Workers Union's musical review, *Pins and Needles*. Here the women singers admonish their male admirers:

> Sing us a song with social significance,
> Or you can sing till you're blue.
> Let meaning shine from every line,
> Or we won't love you.

The Depression led intellectuals to social interpretations of even the most unlikely circumstances. This happened to Edmund Wilson when he considered a late-night drinking match involving himself, Ernest Hemingway, and F. Scott Fitzgerald. Well into the evening, Hemingway announced (with characteristic frankness) that Fitzgerald was plagued by fears that his penis was too short. Hemingway's solution was equally in character—Fitzgerald's problem was simply a matter of perspective. If Fitzgerald would confront the matter directly by facing a mirror, rather than examining himself over his whiskey-filled belly, he would see that his penis was no smaller than any other man's. It remained for Wilson, the member of the party most at home in the thirties, to provide the social analysis: "Ideas of impotence were very much in people's minds at this period—on account of the Depression, I think, the difficulty of getting things going."[14] Given the habits of these authors, a drinking session such as this was likely to happen almost any time the three were together. But Wilson's analysis of Fitzgerald's concerns was something peculiar to the 1930s. Worries about penile length or impotence may or may not have been on people's minds any more during the Depression than during any other times, and yet social readings of such concerns *were* very much on the minds of American intellectuals. The times were momentous, and artists and writers weighed the social influence of those times on all manner of things. Much of what they saw seemed to them both lamentable and worthy of protest, but they also spied just enough evidence to give them the solace that happier times were to come.

Walker Evans, "Sunday Singing, Frank Tengle's Family," Hale County,
Alabama, Summer 1936. (Library of Congress.)

TWO

Empirical Errands:
Traveling Reporters in
Thirties America

ometime in 1940, Erskine Caldwell pulled into a Missouri gas station. As had been his habit for the past six years, he asked the attendant not for gas or oil, but for an analysis of the state of the nation. With events in Europe on his mind more than the fading Depression, Caldwell asked the attendant whether or not Americans would rise to repulse a foreign aggressor. The attendant knew Caldwell's type. For years writers had been stopping and asking him "all sorts of fool questions" without buying anything. Well prepared, he silently handed Caldwell a neatly printed card describing his life and thoughts, ridiculing with its detail the questions that writers asked him. He smoked a pack a day, drank an occasional beer, visited his in-laws once a year, wore 9 1/2 shoes and 7 1/4 hats, liked rice and pork sausage, disliked the aggression of Hitler and the Japanese, voted for Franklin D. Roosevelt, favored the New Deal, and most importantly, was in the business of selling gas and oil, not answering questions. Taken aback, Caldwell could only look sheepish, drive on, and abandon "the filling station circuit."[1]

There were others like Erskine Caldwell. Confused and dismayed in the midst of the Depression, literary figures from novelists to exposé writers abandoned their former genres for the travel report. The country seemed in a terrible jumble, and they angrily criticized those conditions. But even more distressing was their own ignorance of the exact nature of the nation's condition. They craved sure knowledge of the Depression's destruction, together with some sense of American responses to the devastation. Personal observation seemed the only way to wrestle that consoling certainty from the surrounding confusion. Likewise, the only literary effort that seemed to meet their need was an unembellished reporting of fact and detail, for the crisis left no room for the imprecisions of artifice or elaboration. Distressed over the tragedies about them, they thus abandoned poetry for reportage. Their despair had its limits, however. For all their other uncertainties, the Depression's social reporters were sure that "the people" in the nation's heartland could provide unclouded views of the present crisis, and maybe, just maybe, the human warmth that could assuage a writer's loneliness.

Nathan Asch: Long Rider

Nathan Asch (1902–1964) was as inquisitive and as ardent as any of the traveling reporters of the 1930s. Son of Sholem Asch, a prolific Yiddish novelist, the Polish-born Asch immigrated to the United States in 1915. His brother, Moe Asch, was an accomplished folk musicologist active in the same circles as Woody Guthrie and Pete Seeger. The family lived in New York and was financially comfortable enough to send Nathan to Syracuse and Columbia Universities. During his youth, Asch decided to become a writer, and after leaving college, he achieved his goal when he moved to Europe and wrote several novels. In the late 1920s he returned to the United States, joined several artists' colonies, and became good friends with social novelist Josephine Herbst, to whom he eventually dedicated his travel report. Throughout the twenties, Asch continued with his writing and produced stories about loneliness and missed communications. By the beginning of the thirties, he had moved to Hollywood, where he held a lucrative position as a screen writer.[2]

But early in 1932 Asch abandoned his earlier work and began to explore the world in nonfiction prose. As he examined Depression America, Asch concluded that the country had become a horrible place. Amidst the confusion of a collapsing economy, Americans appeared in terrible shape— homeless, out of work, and hungry. Their lack of food was particularly distressing to him, for he too had had bouts with hunger during the 1930s. Asch was a man who dearly wanted to keep track of things around him, and so for him one of starvation's worst aspects was its ability to fog the mind. Without food, a person's vitality goes first, then concentration, and finally "reality turns into hallucination."[3] Asch's personal encounters with hunger were brief, and thanks to screen writing they were few. But these experiences and the larger social crisis left their marks upon him and helped inspire his most significant work of the 1930s. Although he won his own fight against deprivation, Asch wanted a better understanding of the foe that continued to hold so many Americans at bay.

Asch traversed the country in pursuit of that understanding. By the mid-thirties he had decided to leave his security and move physically closer to the crisis, abandoning those activities and locales that seemed increasingly frivolous or remote. He wanted to discuss the Depression with as many people as possible and hoped to find both warmth and a sense of the future in their replies. To accomplish this, Asch made two transcontinental bus trips. The first, a cross-country ride from Los Angeles to New York in 1933 or 1934, was a flight from his Hollywood job. Like playwright Clifford Odets and other talented young writers of the thirties, Asch worked there without completely accepting the movie business, and agonized over the compromises it demanded from an author. In Hollywood, Asch complained, "nothing seemed quite lived, firsthand, actually real." Not even those tragic human consequences of the Depression, the "marooned homeless men" who littered Los Angeles' streets and doorways, seemed real. The industry jaded one's perceptions, for in writing scripts one had to ignore life's tragedies and make everything into "a gag, a situation." Feeling trapped in this "oblivion to reality," Asch fled Hollywood "to shake the nightmare off" and rode straight through to New York. There he plunged into work with the Film and Photo League, one of the many Communist-affiliated artistic groups to emerge in the early 1930s. League members rebelled against Hollywood by producing stark documentary films of Depression conditions, and Asch did his part by writing a screenplay and helping to raise funds.

But with his League activities, he *still* felt too far removed from actual occurrences. Although these New Yorkers discussed contemporary events more readily than did Hollywood movie people, there was still too little direct news about Depression conditions outside the city. When he read some of the few reports available, ones written by social travelers Erskine Caldwell and John Spivak, Asch said it was "a relief to get some news about America." Seeking even more of that relief, he again set out to make contact with the "reality" of the Depression. Once more traveling by bus, this time he boarded with a ticket that was yards long and then spent four months circling the entire country. This second trip was different from the earlier one not only in its duration but also in its intention, for it was less a flight than the first one had been. Instead, it was a search for some pattern in Americans' responses to the Depression and an attempt to get closer to their suffering. When the time came to describe his experiences, Asch found that his message was so full of "reality" that fiction could no longer convey what he had to say. Now the only acceptable form was the factual report, which he first published as a series of articles during 1936, and then later as his only major nonfiction piece, *The Road: In Search of America* (1937).[4]

During his travels, Asch developed a method for finding the "real" America. The other passengers on his first bus trip (the flight from Hollywood) had been mostly open and friendly as he traveled eastward, until he reached Pittsburgh. But from there on into New York, those who boarded the bus were brusque, taciturn, and, unlike the matter-of-fact heartlanders, almost ashamed of their Depression reverses. In charting his longer trip, Asch decided to leave the Northeast out of his plans. It seemed that other regions held his quarry, for there at least people were willing to talk. He was certain that lower-class people would be most in touch with the "reality" he wanted, and so he decided to travel by bus once more; the bus was more personal and more crowded than either a train or an automobile, and, as the cheapest transportation, promised to hold more of the Depression's ambulatory wounded. When it came to conducting his interviews during the trips, he planned to shun community leaders and "big shots." Instead, he hoped to poll a variety of people from working-class America: bootleggers, sharecroppers, loggers, pimps, sheep herders, and radical workers.[5]

It was a complex bundle of motives that led Asch into his second bus trip of the Depression. But his need to meet new, plain people, together with an almost masochistic desire to share in their suffering, was clearly one of his more compelling drives. Although he loved his native New York, he already knew the city and its people; the countryside was full of others whom he hoped to make even more familiar. Striving for more than just empathy with his subjects, Asch wanted to "reach inside" those he met and actually share their lives, almost as though his writer's life had a deficit of experience. "Deeply and tenderly" he "wanted to feel birth, life and death," the joys, pains, and monotony of the lives he encountered. (Transcontinental bus travel doubtlessly provided considerable monotony, and probably no small amount of pain.) To know the Depression's "realities" and lessen the distance between himself and its victims, Asch hoped to "place inside me the want" of those people and "make it my want." Certainly he had had his own encounters with deprivation, but Asch felt no small amount of guilt because others suffered even more. He was determined to redeem himself by taking their agonies for his own.[6]

In addition to these yearnings, there was also an empirical impulse behind his trips. The Depression's chaos seemed to have made trustworthy reports very scarce. Desiring certainty, wanting to know the exact state of affairs in the country, Asch decided to go out and collect the unblemished facts for himself. So important was it for him to uncover the *normal* evolution of events, that he carefully distinguished his task from the journalist's search for *news*. Some documentary film makers of the 1930s, such as the producers of *The March of Time* newsreel, saw themselves as journalists and hoped to report the most recent news. But rather than news, Asch "wanted facts" and therefore "wanted to see what was so typical to the natives it was almost banal." At one point this pursuit of the typical became dangerous. Near Marked Tree, Arkansas, the Southern Tenant Farmers Union was organizing among black tenant farmers. Property owners and the rest of the white community violently opposed not only the organization but also any authors who proposed to write about it. Asch believed that the Union's effort was not an extraordinary push or an unusual piece of news, but that it was instead another example of an oppressed people's everyday struggle toward their eventual liberation. The owners sensed that Asch would not take their side in the contest and shot at him when he came to Marked Tree. But he braved their gunfire to get the facts, not the news, about the struggle at Marked Tree.[7]

Although concrete details were his immediate goal, Asch hoped ultimately to discern a general pattern in the course of Depression events. When he began, he was certain that if he just made enough observations, he would eventually reach a satisfactory understanding of the crisis-ridden country and the spirit of its people. The process started with the collection of small building blocks or facts about a subject, and then, "after a week, a month, a year, or most of your lifetime, you get enough of these facts, and they begin to form a pattern in your mind." Finally, Asch believed, all those blocks would fall into place and form themselves into an enlightening edifice. Confident in this general epistemological process, he set out thinking that one region of the country would help him explain others, and that certain individuals would become symbols for many people. At the moment he achieved some critical mass of observations, those bits of information "would stand in my mind and glowing in my imagination would fuse, synthesize into a clarifying whole." When that happened, when he had "found the key" to Depression America, then he would be able to sit down and write a book that would be "absolutely objective."[8]

He further promised himself that he would describe things precisely as they were, "with no wish fulfillment." Otherwise, he might just as well have stayed in New York "and argued what I wanted America to be." All such denials aside, Asch was no different from most other people who investigate a given subject; he had a notion of the pattern he would find, and specifically looked for it. He expected to discover Americans in deplorable conditions and was primed to castigate the long-festering economic inequalities and social injustices that he believed had finally come to a head in the Depression. He hoped to find Americans engaged in a dignified, courageous struggle against their want, a fight that, since it was virtually universal, united people in a struggle against suffering until they had left it "vanquished." A political liberal inclined to acknowledge the legitimacy of the Russian experiment, Asch believed he would discover Americans working toward the same equality he thought the Soviets had managed to achieve.[9]

For all his expectations, Asch found neither pattern nor valor in American responses to the Depression. Instead of discovering some sense of order or a comprehensive vision, he returned from his second trip with "nothing but isolated images and phrases." Explanations refused to form from the evidence, symbols did not emerge, and nothing fused or glowed in his mind. Nor did people appear to be meeting their plight with courage; unlike the folks whom photographers like Dorothea Lange located, Asch's Americans were cowering victims rather than proud fighters. Young country women came to the cities and fell into prostitution with little protest. People in the Ozarks seemed humbled, destitution having dulled their responses. Feelings of "dread" and "awful doom" pervaded displaced Minnesota farmers. A sheep rancher on the plains was not the glamorous and crusty character that photographer John Vachon pictured, but instead stood broken and defeated in the midst of the stinking carcasses of 10,000 sheep that had died in the drought.[10]

If "the people" in general were so devastated, the thinkers among them were no better off. The homespun intellectuals Asch encountered in his travels were as bewildered as he was, so impotent that they could not help him find a pattern in Depression America. In North Dakota, he looked up a local dentist who had spent his life writing a book that just might explain the country. What Asch discovered was a manuscript in cipher, and the philosopher, gone blind, unable to reconstruct his arguments. Nor did the next generation of intellectuals seem any more promising. The son of a Finnish logging family wanted to be a writer, but to Asch's dismay, the boy did not write straightforwardly about the world before him, but instead prattled on in florid prose about "nightingales and of the English heath." In Denver, Asch met the Miltons. The father was an established architect and the son was preparing to join his father in the profession. Surely these designers, Asch hoped, were people with constructive projects and plans for the future. But no, they were content to drift into the destruction of the brewing world war, the father approaching it with blasé objectivity, while the son reveled in its promise of violent action. The Miltons took Asch for a drive, not into Denver, where the future was a-making, but into an empty past, the ghost town of Central City. In his retelling of the episode, Asch exploited the metaphorical potential of the road in the same way that another American novelist, Jack Kerouac, would do in the 1950s. With little concern for their peril, the Miltons went much too fast over the treacherous mountain roads, careening dangerously close to the precipices. The wife and mother sat in the back seat, blinking unconcernedly like a hen on her nest, the father gave a nonchalant history lesson, and all the while Asch sat terrified in his seat. At the wheel was the son, still representing a dark future. The boy thought he lived only "to plan houses no one will ever build," and he pathetically envied Central City's former inhabitants who had "lived for gold, for danger, they lived to get killed."[11]

Asch encountered others who seemed just as impotent and isolated, and he developed a broader metaphor of the road to describe thirties America. Living in the Depression was like riding a bus, and human relationships during the crisis were like those among its passengers. When traveling, or living in America, one tried to look down the road and make out some pathway into the future. "But facts were forced into the mind; the present jerked one back inside the bus." No matter how great the effort, "one never saw the milepost ahead, one never saw the moment that was coming." The trip that he had thought would bring him enlightenment showed him only "a mad darkness" outside his bus window, a confusing country where people bustled about at random and crashed into each other, sometimes getting up to hurry on, and sometimes getting "crushed" where they lay. The only discernible "unity of thought and desire" was the impulse to flee the decade's calamities, just as he and his companions in a California-bound bus were temporarily united in their desire to escape the Dust Bowl. Along the way, passenger-victims gave each other a few small comforts: a stick of gum or a little conversation.

Fundamentally, though, Americans were isolated and comfortless, and not even they, much less Asch, could tell where their bus or their country was going.[12]

Just as he failed to derive insights from those people, so he failed to find emotional ties with them. In Minnesota he briefly registered the suffering of a Swedish farm family, but that was the only time he managed to share the agony of the Depression's victims. Much more typical was his experience outside Texarkana. There he decided to stay with tenant farm families, the same idea that occurred to James Agee the following summer in Alabama. But Asch was unable to bridge the gap between himself and the tenants, finding he could only stare in awe at their tremendous suffering. He asked one tenant how he and his family could possibly live in such circumstances, and the man replied, "We don't live here. We're just here." Asch gave up, deciding that he could not stay with people who merely existed, for it seemed impossible "to live with people who don't live." Before taking his second trip, he had witnessed a mastectomy during which he experienced no empathy with the patient, only "the objective strain" of watching an unfamiliar process. As he traveled cross-country, he found himself plagued with the same objectivity, acquiring a set of disparate descriptions of individuals' plights, but only once achieving the deep sympathy and shared sorrow he so intensely desired.[13] The very objectivity that he hoped would replace his confusion with certainty had instead deprived him of the warmth he also craved. A middle-class writer surveying largely unfamiliar tragedies, he found himself a cool note-taker rather than a caring sympathizer. Upon his return, Asch was aloof where he hoped to be compassionate, and confused where he had hoped to reach understanding. His venture was almost completely without success. Yet in the end, he refused to be disconsolate and allowed himself one small ray of hope: at least Americans did not think it was right that they should suffer.[14]

Other traveling reporters of the thirties were much like Asch. Like him, they perceived the decade as a disorderly time, so full of confusion that one could not be certain of events unless he actually witnessed them. Hungering for certainty, they also strove to collect verifiable bits of information, and they hoped that those collected pieces would eventually reveal the true pattern of Depression America. Like Asch's Hollywood writing, their former work seemed ill suited for conveying those facts, and so they either abandoned fiction and poetry for a reportorial motif, or else changed the scope of their writing to examine the Depression's effects upon Americans. In a period and place that appeared confused, where events befuddled and even impeached the usual sources of enlightenment, these authors were confident that "the people" in the hinterland would provide the "truth" about the crisis. Shunning the isolation of their desks and the intellectuals' Northeastern home pasture, the social reporters ranged instead over the countryside to ease their sense of confusion, looking not within themselves for the patterns they hoped to find, but instead turning to those whom they met along the way. Although their searches resembled Nathan Asch's, most of them returned home considerably more content than he with their results, and without his sense of bitter disappointment.

Travelers

A host of Depression Americans took to the road with the intention of writing about their travels. Estimates of the number of traveling authors vary. To dramatist Harold Clurman, looking back from the perspective of 1945, it seemed as though in the years "from 1931 through 1935 all America's young writers were going on bus and motor trips through the country." Doubtlessly Clurman exaggerated, and in the absence of precise numbers, it is best simply to accept art critic Anita Brenner's 1936 assessment that "there were quite a lot of us riding around the country in buses or flivvers." When they got out of their cars or stepped off their buses, they approached ordinary Americans and asked question upon question. To some of those ordinary folks, it seemed as though far too many inquisitive writers were loose upon the land. Erskine Caldwell's gas station attendant preferred to print up cards rather than respond directly to questions from writers, and a prostitute complained to novelist Edward Newhouse that he was like her other 1930s customers—rather than using her usual services, "all they do is talk." The writing that emerged from these conversations was sometimes odd, for authors were not always adequately prepared for the midland's vernacular; author Jack Conroy pointed to one English major who had heard men of the Ozarks refer to their wives as "the old lady" and who therefore concluded that the men realized that their poverty forced women to grow old before their time.[15]

But in this crowd of writers, there was a smaller community of authors who possessed more discerning ears. These women and men composed the decade's most significant travel reportage. In reaction to the Depression, they made significant departures from their earlier careers as they set out to travel in and write about America of the 1930s. Their works are analytical, going beyond mere local color to examine critically the Depression's breadth and depth. Most of these reporters had attended college, and their literary reputations were usually established before they began their treks.

Like Asch, many in this group came to their idiom from traditional literary backgrounds. To these writers, it seemed that art could not suffice in the Depression, that the times called for reportage more than poetry. Theodore Dreiser was one of their number. All of his earlier novels had been chock-full of social reportage, but with the Depression, Dreiser dropped the facade of fiction from his work and produced rambling investigatory reports. Sherwood Anderson likewise left behind fiction in the early thirties and gave himself over to traveling and writing about his findings. Similarly, Ben Appel took time off from his novels about New York's Hell's Kitchen to traverse the nation and describe the ways in which its people spoke. In the mid-thirties Erskine Caldwell stopped writing fiction, launched into traveling and reporting, and eventually produced a series of books in collaboration with photographer Margaret Bourke-White.[16] James Rorty had earned his living in advertising while writing poetry, but during the thirties, he stopped publishing poems and wrote about his travels around the country. James Agee had likewise been interested in poetry but, under the Depression's economic pressures, he took a journalistic job at *Fortune* magazine and became increasingly interested in actual events rather than in the symbolic events of his early poems.[17]

In addition to traveling and writing, these poets and novelists were active, for a time, in the many radical causes that flourished in the decade. Rorty was a principal author of *Culture and the Crisis* (1932), a pamphlet urging writers, artists, and professionals to support the Communist Party's 1932 presidential ticket. He and Anderson joined a delegation of authors that assailed the White House in protest of President Herbert Hoover's hard-line attitude toward the Bonus Army, a group of World War I veterans who converged on Washington in 1932 to demand early payment of their authorized war bonuses. Other writers worked to achieve a united political voice among artists. Caldwell, Dreiser, and Asch joined with novelists like Josephine Herbst and James T. Farrell to sign the call of the Communist-backed League of American Writers for a 1935 Writers' Congress. Though Dreiser was considerably older than the rest, he too was politically active, leading an investigation of coal mining in Harlan County, Kentucky, working for Spanish Civil War relief, and eventually joining the Communist Party.[18]

For a second, smaller group of authors, the Depression also inspired a new set of projects. But these writers came into the thirties from reportorial rather than literary backgrounds, and they made less dramatic shifts in their writing than did Anderson or Rorty. Anna Louise Strong, for instance, had a lifelong interest in radical politics, a dedication that took her to Ireland, China, Soviet Russia, and eventually into the Communist Party. With the Depression, she interrupted her international exploits to come home for a tour of her native land. John L. Spivak's case was similar. He had made a career of writing exposés about Georgia prison corruption or American anti-Semitism, but by mid-decade the scope of his interests had broadened, and he turned to assessing the potential for revolution in the entire country. Others took leaves from more traditional journalistic enterprises. Mauritz Hallgren left his desk at *The Nation* to see the country, and Jonathan Daniels, editor of the *Raleigh News and Observer*, took off to tour the South. Hallgren and Daniels were joined by Lorena Hickok, one of the few women journalists of the interwar years; for a time, she left journalism and became a traveling investigator reporting Depression conditions to Eleanor Roosevelt and New Deal administrator Harry Hopkins.[19]

Finally, there were some social reporters who were not journalists, poets, or novelists. For example there was Gilbert Seldes, who surveyed the Depression's psychological impact upon Americans. Prior to the Crash, Seldes had been an art and movie critic, and he was unlike other social reporters in that he chose not to travel to gather his material. Or there was Louis Adamic, an emigrant from Yugoslavia whose literary career was a lifelong effort to wrestle the American experience into a comprehensible form. During the thirties, he traveled thousands of miles in this effort and composed a frequently anguished chronicle of his journeys. J. Saunders Redding had a similarly personal quest. A college teacher who received Rockefeller Foundation support to travel among and examine the beliefs of his fellow southern blacks, Redding's trip became a mirror in which he studied his own values.[20]

Most of these authors made their trips in the mid-thirties, choosing routes and timetables that allowed them to survey large segments of the country and yet have time to reflect upon their observations. Before bringing out completed books about their travels, they usually published portions of their accounts in magazines such as the liberal *New Republic* or the more radical *New Masses*. Such journals gave the authors an important institutional framework, providing a forum for the writers while simultaneously fulfilling subscribers' appetites for firsthand reports of the Depression. (The public's desire to know about itself was considerable—pollster George Gallup prospered during the decade by providing objective, nongovernmental data on the nation.) Though the travel reports appeared in journals like the *New Republic,* the essays were more the reflections of the authors' own creative efforts than of some editor's assignment. Most of the writers worked on a free-lance basis, peddling their wares to the magazine or book editor who would have them, and those among the travel writers who were directly connected with journals held positions that afforded them considerable independence.[21]

The Depression stimulated the production of other prose materials based on firsthand observation and recording. But the social scientists and guidebook writers of the thirties were engaged in enterprises quite different from those of the social reporters, and an analysis of their work belongs elsewhere. Contemporary sociologists shared many of the reporters' interests in poverty, tenantry, and vagabondage. Yet scholars such as Robert and Helen Lynd, Arthur Raper, and Thomas Minehan were unlike the traveling authors in that they were engaged in projects closely akin to their normal pursuits, were more dedicated to detail, and had considerably stronger allegiance to the rules of evidence and inference. Several products of the Federal Writers' Project (FWP) were also superficially similar to the literary reports. Volumes of the *American Guide* series described what one could see while traveling through the United States, but such guides were essentially travel aids for the automobile tourist and, as work relief projects, intended to provide economic support for their authors rather than platforms for creative expression. There was more room for creativity in other FWP projects. In some of the Project's efforts, such as the life history narratives, the folk music collection, or the narratives of former slaves, Project employees did exercise some license in showing how Americans were faring in the straits of the Depression. But for all this, these collections were still much more exercises in straight recording than any of the social reporters, save Agee and perhaps Apple, ever attempted.[22]

Despair, Truth, and "The People"

N o single motive compelled these writers to leave their earlier work, travel about the country, and write about Depression conditions. Instead, a combination of dismay and confidence pulled them away from their desks and into the field. Able to hold within themselves a complex bundle of contradictory emotions, they were simultaneously angry and assured, upset and hopeful.[23] After their initial brushes with the Depression, many authors were as troubled as Nathan Asch had been. The distressing prevalence of unemployment and homelessness left the writers bewildered, perturbed, and eager to find some pattern in the course of events. But, again like Asch, they were confident that the cure for their dismay lay in confronting the very crisis that so upset them, for although the Depression would not go away once they comprehended it, they were confident that a certain amount of factual information would end their confusion. This desire for certainty, along with their faith that they knew where to find certainty, drew writers into their travels.

These authors had little difficulty determining the origin of the Depression and no qualms about handing out blame for it. America's distress appeared a predictable consequence of its capitalism, and they readily condemned the economic system. In hindsight, it seemed that the nation had headed straight for a precipice that Americans could have avoided if only they had chosen a path other than capitalism. Gilbert Seldes described the collapse as the "natural outcome" of the corrupt and greed-ridden American economic system, a sentiment Sherwood Anderson echoed when he told a correspondent that "America is being caught up with." Anna Louise Strong was more descriptive when she called the thirties a "high wilderness," located just where she expected to find a barrens, at the end of the tortuous capitalist trail. In one way or another, they all shared James Rorty's belief that the Depression was "a fatuous and seemingly unnecessary chaos," the tragic though logical consequence of the flawed economic system.[24]

But this retrospective perception of the Depression as a "natural" event did little to assuage the authors' despair over the present. Hard times could sap the very will to live so that to them suicide seemed a sad but understandable solution to a person's problems. Dreiser could not bring himself to condemn a man who committed suicide after a long, unsuccessful search for employment, and Erskine Caldwell sympathetically retold the story of another desperate worker who allowed his father to kill himself. For James Agee, suicide was more than just a social phenomenon; it became an alternative to his own despair. In 1932 he wrote to one of his former teachers, saying that the era had the darkest and most forlorn spiritual tone in centuries and that the country appeared caught in an "*epidemic* of despair and weariness." By August Agee himself had become a victim of the epidemic and said that he had "felt like suicide for weeks now." Although others did not become quite so despondent, the environment of those early years of the Depression deeply disturbed them. Looking back upon that period before he had begun his journeys, a time when he had seen "American working men eating out of garbage cans," Anderson described himself as having been "pretty wrought up." As Rorty listened to Americans and to himself in 1931, the only voices he could hear were like those coming from a tumultuous madhouse where the inmates could only "beat on the bars, / and count the idiot sum / Of Chaos." No matter where he searched in the early thirties, whether in the broad mass of people, his fellow writers or within himself, all Rorty could find was a collection of "bewildered souls."[25]

The Depression's calamities were peculiarly distressing to Louis Adamic. He had come to the United States, he said, not for wealth, but in pursuit of excitement that was not to be had in Yugoslavia. America provided abundant excitement, but also more confusion than he wanted. In grappling with the new land, Adamic resembled other thirties intellectuals in that he drew upon Van Wyck Brooks for help. He borrowed the title of one of Brooks's essays and described the United States as a vast "Sargasso Sea." Like the real Sargasso Sea, America was clogged with a welter of organisms randomly drifting upon uncharted currents in a manner which Brooks likened to "that of the first chaos." The only difference, according to Brooks and Adamic, was that the floating bodies in America were humans rather than clumps of sargassum seaweed. When the Depression struck, things only became worse, for Americans were now hungry and homeless; more than simply drifting, they were "lost in a fog."[26]

Twice Adamic found such confusion too much to bear. The winter of 1931–32 was perhaps the decade's worst; mounting unemployment, dwindling savings, and harsh weather combined to push large numbers of Americans into ever more desperate circumstances. Although there would be plenty of hard times throughout the remainder of the thirties, these few months were the Depression's darkest period for many people. It was a disturbing time, and Adamic's diary is a catalogue of the bewildering events. During February, children rang his doorbell asking for food. A destitute man had resorted to robbery, been convicted, and sentenced to Sing Sing; his wife told Adamic the rest of the family would be better off dead. Other people almost matter-of-factly predicted a revolution. Adamic found it impossible to keep calm in this country that had become *too* exciting, and though he had once been drawn by its fast-paced life, he now decided that he would "like terribly to get away from America." He got his wish the next month when a Guggenheim fellowship allowed him to visit Yugoslavia, and he lost little time fleeing to the old country. When he returned, Adamic managed to retain his composure for a while. But by late 1936 he once more became overwrought, this time over ferment in the labor movement. There had been little labor militancy during the 1920s, but in the 1930s worker activism grew as the concept of industrywide organization emerged to challenge the traditional craft union ideal. This electric development suggested that workers might lay aside the petty differences dividing one craft from another and achieve a power equal to their numbers within a given industry. In the steel industry, the Congress of Industrial Organizations (CIO) launched an organization campaign marked by a series of long, bitter strikes, and in a similar effort, automobile workers adopted a dramatic new tactic: the sit-down strike. Intense excitement surrounded the news reports from these strikes, and in this charged atmosphere, Adamic developed what he called "something very akin to a neurosis." He rushed out every hour to buy the latest newspaper and, in his sleepless excitement, thought himself "on the border of a breakdown." Again he fled the United States for a more languid pace of life, this time to Guatemala.[27]

Where Adamic took occasional flights from the suffering and turmoil of the 1930s, other writers strove to make firsthand examinations of those conditions. Although their initial assessments of the crisis were no brighter than his, they designed trips not as flights from Depression America but as encounters with it. Just as they believed that the crisis called for direct confrontation, they also thought it demanded a literature that was equally direct, stripped of all embellishments down to a narrative of actual occurrence. Unsatisfied with anything less than the complete "truth" about the "reality" of the situation, they rejected the imprecision of secondhand reports, promotional literature, and fiction. Like a contemporary, critic Edmund Wilson, they held that "the place to study the present crisis and its causes and probable consequences is not in the charts of the compilers of statistics." Instead, one should study the replies of the people one interviewed, and then publish the results to satisfy an insistent American hunger for information. Since that appetite was so demanding, it seemed to Wilson that the 1930s would produce mostly factual accounts and only a very few "long-range works of literature."[28]

Gilbert Seldes thought unelaborated facts were necessary for the country's mental health. On his title page, he gave a version of the same Francis Bacon quotation that photographer Dorothea Lange had tacked on her darkroom door: "The contemplation of things as they are, without substitution or imposture, is in itself a nobler thing than a whole harvest of inventions." After some years of contemplating the Depression, Seldes offered up his conclusions. Writing in 1933, he observed that the years since the 1929 collapse had been terrible ones for Americans' physical condition. But their emotional condition was even worse. National leaders, especially those in the Hoover administration, kept telling people that prosperity was just around the corner, giving groundless assurances and keeping Americans from confronting *"the reality of our situation."* Seldes's goal in writing his report was to tell the truth, all of it, about the social and economic tragedy, and to prepare "a fever chart" of Americans' despondency as they piecemeal learned the *"reality"* of their situation. In giving that truth, he would be administering a strong and bitter medicine, but the treatment could only help the patients, for knowing the actual state of affairs was "an essential thing for the health of the community."[29]

James Rorty called for the same tonic. To him, the past under capitalism had been one gigantic "flight from reality." America had been a dream society with a dream economy, especially during the booming twenties; people had kept their eyes focused on a phantasmal future that seductively promised to be better. Some invested in hopes of future profits, while others toiled patiently in hopes of future security. With their attention on an illusory world just over the horizon, Americans became so oblivious to the present that they had nearly lost "all instinct for reality." So pervasive was this damage to instinct that, even in the midst of the Depression, many people continued to believe that life would be better just around the next corner. Rorty felt more than a touch of responsibility for the deplorable situation, and in what became something of a ritual for thirties intellectuals, he denounced his earlier role. As an advertising man during the twenties, Rorty had helped perpetuate the dream, skillfully composing advertisements that, like Bourke-White's photographs for Buick or Pare Lorentz's magazine for General Electric, fed the baseless hopes by promising happiness if only consumers would buy a given product. Before the Crash Rorty had written a booster pamphlet about California, promoting the state with all his skill and technique. But, like any advertising, it had a spurious veracity and was at best a collection of "half-truths only." The facts he had written had been "true facts—as far as they went." By 1936 Rorty found that he could no longer write in that manner, for with all its turmoil, "the intervening decade had done something to me." Taking the pamphlet title and adding a new subtitle—*Where Life is Better: An Unsentimental American Journey*—Rorty began to compensate for his earlier sins and pledged to tell the whole truth this time, to give his readers "a straight story" about the country and its crisis.[30]

Others felt that falsehoods so thickly blanketed America that virtually all existing accounts were suspect. Theodore Dreiser had studied economic statistics and heard a number of people speak out on conditions of the day. But he needed "to see for myself," to take a firsthand look at what he called "definite examples of life under our present economic regime." Accordingly he traveled to Pennsylvania to examine miners' lives and to New Jersey to examine conditions in an industrial city. Particularly dubious were official assessments of conditions, products of the same reality-obscuring system for which Rorty had worked. John Spivak complained that official unemployment statistics, which should have given some idea of the Depression's suffering, were horribly incorrect, and he believed such errors only proved that few officials really cared about the workers' plight. Seldes echoed the complaint but more gently suggested that inaccuracies arose from a widespread emotional inability to face suffering. In 1931, Mauritz Hallgren went to South Bend, Indiana, to see how a representative American city was faring during "the panic." He found the community's official voices, its newspaper, chamber of commerce, leading citizens, and labor leaders, all in agreement: despite some minor discomforts, things were fine. Suspicious of that analysis, Hallgren went knocking on doors in working-class districts and found actual conditions far from acceptable. The workers, he discovered, were in sad shape, "facing the future with despair." Much like Rorty's victims of advertising, those confident people of South Bend were optimistic about the Depression only because they had "not been allowed to know what it means."[31]

Once these authors had gathered their information, they faced the question of how to present their material. Each concluded that he could not continue to write in the same manner that he had used prior to the 1930s. Louis Adamic thought that the "play of the Depression" upon his "mind and emotions" had enhanced his inclination toward social, economic, and political subjects, leaving him "a different writer from what I would have been had there been no Depression." The crisis had a similar effect upon Erskine Caldwell, Sherwood Anderson, and Theodore Dreiser. Caught up in the tragedies of hunger, displacement, and despair, they came to believe that their earlier form of writing, fiction, was inappropriate for the thirties. Caldwell had been something of a wanderer most of his life, growing up the son of a roving minister and spending his college weekends riding freight trains. As an adult, he continued traveling, and in the belief that his characters should be as close as possible to "real people," he turned out stories closely based upon his experience. Beginning in 1935, however, Caldwell diluted the gloss of fiction on his writing and produced books that more directly reported his journeys. He told the readers of *Some American People* (1935) that he had written the book to show them "what can be seen and experienced in America today." Later he made the trip upon which he based *You Have Seen Their Faces* (1937) with the twin intentions of writing "a factual study of people in cotton states living under current economic stress," and of proving that real-life counterparts existed for the characters he had created in his novel and play, *Tobacco Road* (1932).[32]

Like Caldwell, Anderson had composed novels that fit well within the tradition of American literary realism. But shortly after the Crash, Anderson came to believe that even the realism of his early fiction was not sufficient to meet the challenges of the thirties. In all of his writing, he wrote a friend, he had tried to avoid actual events "and to concentrate on pure storytelling." Given the drift of things in the 1930s, though, he found that "it can't quite be done now." No matter how he tried, Anderson could see no way back to fiction. Simply put, "right now the reality of life is more fantastic than any imaginary life." Like Anderson, Dreiser also decided to give up fiction. Explaining his decision to write about economics, Dreiser said that the country's conditions made any other "literary achievements" completely "ridiculous." Hoping to make his writing more compelling, Dreiser buttressed his arguments with repeated examples, all to show his readers that he was "not talking without the machine guns of fact at my elbow."[33]

With such antipathy toward fiction and such preferences for straight renditions of the world, these writers shared a larger thirties fascination with photography. They found the camera an appealing tool in their work, and photography an attractive metaphor for their idiom. Appearing to capture the world without bias or embellishment, the photograph seemed more suitable to the epoch than did fiction. Both Caldwell and Spivak thought that if audiences were to believe their messages, then their words had to have accompanying photographs. When Spivak went to Georgia to gather material for his exposé of the state's prison camp system, he felt that Americans would not accept the veracity of his message unless he could "prove it with visual evidence." He took along a Kodak, surreptitiously snapped pictures of the atrocities he found, and smuggled the exposed film out of Georgia for safe processing. In hopes that "the realism of photography would support the disputed realism" of his words, Caldwell hired photographer Margaret Bourke-White to accompany him on his 1936 trip through the South. To Asch and Agee, photography provided a handy metaphor for the objective, unadorned reporting they wished to accomplish. Asch thought that his first bus trip had been a "snapshot of America," capturing things as they were without undue embellishment. Agee not only took along photographer Walker Evans when he went to Alabama, he thought photography unable to produce anything but "dry truth," achieving with the release of a shutter what he struggled to accomplish in his writing.[34]

But merely possessing the means for recording truth was not enough. There had to be some source of truth in order for an instrument to record it. Observing someone in his search for truth or reality usually tells us what the searcher accepts without question, what he takes on faith. Such a quest involves authorities, signposts that the seeker trusts as guides to, or sources of, the truth. Even the skeptic believes that his disbelief is well founded, reserving the ultimate authority, and faith, unto himself. The

Depressions's literary reporters distrusted fiction as a tool for reaching truth, and instead embraced a reportorial motif represented in the camera metaphor. In doing so, they retained a measure of faith in themselves, an assurance that their perceptions would remain unclouded so that they in effect would be properly functioning cameras. But when they sought a source of truth, they did not point their cameras at themselves to make self-portraits, but instead looked outside themselves.

Depression intellectuals often distinguished between an urban-industrial American civilization (apparently repudiated during the crisis) and a more enduring set of values or culture (that would, they hoped, survive the crisis). Traveling reporters shared the view, and James Rorty made precisely the same distinction when he contrasted an "older, more organic American culture" with a newer "hard, arid culture of acquisitive emulation." Rorty and the other reporters much preferred the organic, enduring culture and believed that it lay embedded in the broad masses of the country, in "the people." Repeatedly they set forth to glean truth from "the people." Since the usual channels of communication were not open for "the people" to express themselves, the traveling authors had to go directly to them, avoiding those leaders who suppressed the masses' voices or sought to speak in their stead. Ben Appel found what the people had to say so worthwhile that he entitled his book *The People Talk* and gave over the bulk of his 502 pages to simple transcriptions, word snapshots, of the conversations he heard. When Mauritz Hallgren wanted to know the true condition in South Bend, he sought out the workers, not the community's official voices. Sherwood Anderson thought Presidents Hoover and Roosevelt would benefit from talking with "workers, men out of work, country lawyers, farmers, bums," and invited each president to take time off and go riding around the country with Anderson in his car. Middle-class blacks seemed indifferent or snobbish to J. Saunders Redding, but among their lower-class counterparts (whose company Redding preferred anyway), he found a "strength in their utter lack of sophistication." Though artless in the usual sense, such people were not gullible; beneath a union hall banner proclaiming that American workers were free, Redding found "a drawing of a horse's hindquarters dropping dung."

James Rorty discovered the same sentiment and was likewise pleased. As Rorty looked out on the wasteland of capitalism and on the works of its handmaiden, advertising, he could find only one bright spot. He, too, placed his faith in "the people" but, unlike most of the other reporters, saw in them not so much a glowing dignity as a scowling skepticism. He thought it best to avoid the utterances of "reasonable people," and go instead to such places as cheap restaurants, beer gardens, and police stations. *There* one would find those whom the oppressive culture had virtually destroyed, a set of isolated and pulverized women and men. They were America's discarded victims, and they possessed "anarchic voices" that were "truthful, and wise with a kind of bleak factual wisdom." They cried out against the emptiness of the acquisitive society, and in their own blunt words, they described its hollowness: "Fake. Baloney. Bunk. Apple sauce." Rorty listened to such voices not only for their truth, but also because their characterizations of the system gave him some hope that "the human essence is indestructible." Nothing profound, that essence was the will to give a raspberry.[35]

However the commoners dispersed truth, literary reporters were determined to consider each representative of "the people" as a unique individual. Warmth and human-to-human contact were essential antidotes to the coldness and anonymity that accompanied the Depression, and it seemed important to provide that personalization through the details of individual tragedies and triumphs. They shunned the broad generalization and statistical average for the case history. In Rorty's survey of the country, he intended to note some of the larger trends he found but hoped to convey "not so much the statistics as the people whose current dilemmas the statistics fail to express." Adamic did not want to tell the general story of the Depression, but rather the particulars of peoples' lives. He toiled as a welfare worker and then filled his book with the case histories he had collected. Lorena Hickok also wanted to understand the individuals who composed the general trends and, at the start of her travels, lamented that the unemployed millions "were not really people at all. They had no faces." Yet over the months and miles, they acquired an identity for her, "they emerged—individuals. People, with voices, faces, eyes." Anderson was not so bothered by statistical anonymity at first, and when he went to St. Louis to get stories on absentee ownership and a New Deal program, he was "determined to write giving facts and figures." But instead of getting his statistics, Anderson spent his time getting drunk with two men, a father and son, for he discovered that the most important thing about St. Louis lay not in the information he had come to gather. It lay instead in the much smaller story of how these once distant men had grown together during the crisis, and Anderson managed to share both their fellowship and their bottle.[36]

This pursuit of "the people" suggests more than an aversion to statistics and a respect for the common person's authenticity. It displays the authors' loneliness. Behind Anderson's St. Louis drinking spree and Asch's wish to share "deeply and tenderly" his subjects' lives, there was a profound desire to reach out for human contact. Hoping for wider networks of friends and acquaintances, Anderson and the others chose not to approach people who were close at hand, but instead sought those further afield. For Anderson, isolation was a sort of illness particularly prevalent in "times like this." The cure, which he prescribed for presidents and for himself, was to travel and make contact with other people, especially hitchhikers. Each time he picked up a hitchhiker and talked with his passenger, Anderson gained "a kind of reward" that lessened his loneliness. Rorty was also concerned with loneliness and frequently described Americans, including himself, as atomistic, drifting individuals. Part of Rorty's goal was to reestablish community in the land; he wrote his travel book to argue others out of their isolation and took his trip to forge his own new ties. During his travels, new friends emerged from among the warm people he met, people like a woman in a Detroit bar or his fellow prisoners in a California jail. Rorty and Anderson certainly craved companionship, but compared to Anna Louise Strong, they had only minor cases of loneliness. As Strong told her life story, her struggle to overcome alienation had carried her into a series of causes, wars, and revolutions. She remembered that as a young girl she had felt "cut off from the world" and that she "painfully wanted to get back" in touch with others. When she matured, Strong was attracted to radical ventures, particularly the Communist Party and the Russian Revolution; they seemed able to assuage her loneliness by bringing her into the masses and to overcome her alienation by directing history toward collective goals. Thinking that the class struggle had finally come to the United States, she returned in 1939 to tour America and pursue the camaraderie of her new partners in the struggle.[37]

This search for fellowship along the road was one of the brighter elements in the mixture of hope and despair that produced travel reports of the 1930s. To the authors who composed those reports, the Depression appeared to have left the country in a dismaying shambles, with its social structure shaken, its economy fallen, and its people adrift. The crisis pressed so harshly and events moved so bewilderingly that only the firmest of literary handholds, the description of unembellished fact, seemed capable of sustaining a writer's equilibrium. Yet accompanying their confusion was a confidence about where they could find the "truth" about the Depression. It lay in the hearts of "the people" out in the provinces, and it could be had by recording their stories. As a bonus, the writer might come to feel less lonely in the process.

How to Search

There is a persistent perception of these writers as a shell-shocked crew, the stunned victims of a confusing era. Supposedly plagued with paralysis of the imagination, they numbly collected facts, shouting down their uncertainties by loudly romancing a set of nationalistic values.[38] But there was no uniform American celebration among these reporters, and they were far from numb as they went about their projects. Largely internationalists rather than nationalists, they were optimistic about apparent global trends toward socialism and distressed over the proclivities in some nations (including the United States) toward fascism. Though disturbed over contemporary circumstances, they went about the collection of their facts with unparalyzed minds or imaginations.

On the surface, such empirical errands seem simple enough. One *merely* observes, and then reports what one has seen. The project also apparently involves little of the observer's intellect, being a description of things witnessed and not the fabrication of scenes a novelist might produce. An ordinary, everyday activity, it is like going to the window to check the weather and then reporting back to the household, something any normal adult and most children should be able to do. But that very familiarity may lead us to forget Sergeant Friday's lesson, that while getting "just the facts, ma'am," is all in a day's work, it is not such a simple task. Which window does one look out of to get the weather? Does a quick look accurately represent the entire day's conditions? How much of the vast detail revealed in even the briefest glance should one report back? Far from a quiescent activity in which the observer goes out "empty" and comes back "filled," the job is loaded with questions requiring a good deal of mental activity to answer, no matter how automatic the process becomes with practice.

How should one observe and analyze the outside world? This was the greatest single issue dividing social reporters as they made their observations of and wrote their reports about Depression America. Should the investigator approach his material with certain preconceived notions of what he will find, concentrating his quest in those areas at the expense of others? Or should one drift along in the material, hoping, as Nathan Asch did, that some pattern will emerge from it, looking first here and then there but avoiding any theoretical predictions for fear that they would prejudice the findings? The same issue arises in making one's report. One can run the risk of distorting events for the sake of rendering them into a comprehensible pattern. Or one can report the bulk of what one has seen with great fidelity, neither sifting nor arranging the material for fear that doing so would falsify the report. Thirties reporters divided along such lines, some taking a more active role and striving to confirm their predictions with observations, while others were less active and disclaimed any role for theory in their work.

Closely aligned with these attitudes toward observation and analysis were their notions on activism in the world. To some, the flow of history was largely beyond human control, and they strove to float along with it as best they could, trying to steer around the worst snags and sandbars. Others thought that it was a fairly pliable thing, and they struggled to bring it into line with their theories. Both personal and public factors coalesced to make leftist political thought the most prevalent ideology in the social reporters' discussions. Many believed that the tragedies of the Depression were the product of a capitalist crisis resembling the one Marx had predicted. Social reporters divided into three groups over the role of theory, particularly Marxist theory, in data collection and report writing. Some were like Anna Louise Strong in that they granted it a large role, others resembled Sherwood Anderson in their eventual rejection of it, and those in yet a third group had James Rorty's mixed feelings about its function in their work. But when it came to giving their conclusions about the future of America, these differences mattered little, for they all slanted their verdicts to suit their inclinations. At heart they all dearly wanted to see a better world just over the horizon. Time and again they weighed their hopes against the ponderous evidence that dark times lay ahead, and even the gloomiest managed to tip the scales in favor of a brighter tomorrow.

Revolutionary Reporters

Anna Louise Strong, John Spivak, and Mauritz Hallgren were no less upset over Americans' suffering than were other traveling reporters. But these journalists understood the meaning of that suffering, for they believed that the Depression presaged a Marxist revolution. Convinced of this, they burnished and molded the facts they uncovered to bring those facts in line with the higher truth of the approaching revolution. Confident of what they would find, the revolutionary reporters were not so much concerned with discovering a pattern in Depression events as they were concerned to uncover the manner in which events fit their preconceived patterns.

Attracted to Communism's promise of universal community, Strong had initially "hated all these theoretical discussions" that the comrades conducted incessantly. Itching to get to work, she nevertheless decided to be a good comrade and reluctantly resolved that "if theories had to be swallowed," she would swallow them somehow. But after a time she came to believe that a clear theoretical position was essential. It turned out that "Marx's analysis gave a weapon," just the right one for blasting out her own niche in the struggle, pushing the course of events into the right pathway, and arming her with a reassuring knowledge of the future. Marx's analysis also helped her know how to tell the truth. She thought that Soviet Russia's fight against hunger was a heroic struggle, one made all the greater by its battles with inefficiency, sabotage, and corruption. But a Russian comrade would not let her write of how the Soviets had overcome such setbacks, and censored her material. Of course, the comrade said, her obligation was to tell the truth. But telling the truth had a special meaning in Soviet circles. It meant giving "a clear description of the general line of our struggle," and was certainly "not to give away sensational unanalyzed 'facts' from which no good can come."[39] To give the larger truth that Marx had seen (i.e., the Party line), a writer could and should withhold any inconsistent smaller truths, telling about the

Soviets' victorious war against hunger, but not about the battles that they lost along the way.

Strong adopted the comrade's analysis and brought it to her work. In traveling from one revolution to another, she remembered, it was "the chaos that drew me, and the sight of creators in chaos." Like a good house-keeper who wanted to tidy things up, Strong disapproved of disorder and had little tolerance for those folks who were content to live in a mess. Having discovered theory as a means for taming confusion, it now gave her "a pain in my heart" to see the theory-less but well-intentioned American reformers, "drifting, drifting to disillusion after disillusion" because they still refused to let Marx guide them. One of those drifters may well have been a traveling companion during her Russian travels, novelist John Dos Passos. He shared only a portion of her enthusiasm for Communism or Russia and was even less well disposed toward Strong, whom he called a "big busty self-centered spinster." But such disapproval seldom deterred Strong, and when she returned to the United States, she brought her new-found vision with her, traveled throughout America during the later part of the 1930s, and wrote a Communist report so that Americans like Dos Passos could see the proper, Marxian fulfillment of their destiny.[40]

As a boy in the years before World War I, John Spivak listened to radical speakers on New Haven's city green. From the assorted socialists, anarchists, and Wobblies, he absorbed leftist affinities that eventually led him into a number of liberal or radical organizations. Before the Depression he had assumed that there was an objective and discoverable truth in the world, which when aired would be a swift cure for social or political injustice. But in the midst of background reading for his trip to Georgia's prisons, he came to realize that historians who wrote about identical events often gave quite different interpretations of those events. Until then, Spivak claimed, he "had taken it for granted that a fact is a fact and history is a series of facts." With his growing realization that facts were flexible in accordance with an author's predilections, Spivak came to think of writing as "more to me than just a trade I liked; it was a weapon." He unleashed that weapon in his travel report, bent the facts as needed, and proclaimed that the class struggle was at hand.[41]

Mauritz Hallgren also looked to the left, and he hoped that a general uprising would topple American capitalism. Like many other progressive

Americans, he looked to the American Communist Party for leadership and direction because only the Communists had the sufficient theoretical basis to carry off any revolt. His journeys of the early 1930s were essentially one long search for that insurrection. In South Bend, he kept pressing until he at last found people turning toward the Party, enduring police repression to attend clandestine Communist meetings. Traveling about the rest of the country, he worked just as hard to locate similar "seeds of revolt" and through his writing hoped to sow more. [42]

Like the other social reporters, these radical journalists examined the nation's emotional and physical status. Americans' physical condition, particularly as Hallgren and Spivak found it early in the thirties, was pitiable. This only strengthened the authors' loathing for capitalism, and they vividly described the scenes they encountered in hopes of evoking similar outrage from their readers. Spivak, for example, began his book with an open letter to Roosevelt. He told the story of a fifteen-year-old Mexican migrant cotton picker who wanted the president to keep the lights on in her waterless, scarlet-fever-ridden cabin; she was scared of giving birth in the dark. Spivak went on to say that the only group aiding such victims was the Communist Party, which had managed to win a slight pay raise for the migrants. *This*, Spivak told the president and his other readers, was "why people are beginning to listen to 'red agitators.'" Similarly, Hallgren told of the hunger and poverty he had seen in places like South Bend and Philadelphia, and Strong showed her audience that capitalism had only worsened the lives of Montana miners. [43]

Strong, Hallgren, and Spivak wanted to do more than simply denounce capitalism. They hoped to find Americans would tolerate it no longer. But the three writers discovered little evidence that Americans were on the verge of boiling over into a popular revolution. Instead, Americans seemed as beaten psychologically as they were physically. In this, the authors encountered one of the saddest aspects to the Depression, for Americans repeatedly felt that they had brought destitution upon themselves and were accordingly ashamed over what seemed to be personal, not social, failures. Strong found that the unemployed had difficulty developing the initiative they needed to help themselves because they had been robbed of the necessary self-esteem. Capitalism laid off people and then let them believe that *they* had failed; it was a system "devilishly efficient for destroying their natural self-respect." In North Carolina, Spivak likewise discovered that working-class whites had been oppressed so long that they were incapable of rising up against the men who kept them chained to the textile mills. Having acquired "the psychology of those fated to be walked upon," the southern worker was a pathetic sight, "accepting whatever crumb is thrown to him and clinging to a sense of loyalty to his employer." Hallgren also reported few signs that the obviously hungry masses of people would rise up in revolt; instead they were markedly apathetic considering the gravity of their situation.[44]

Strong, Spivak, and Hallgren managed to remain buoyant, nonetheless, maintaining their hopes in the face of such testimony and managing to make the best of what evidence they could muster. Despite the frequency with which capitalism destroyed initiative and wrecked character, Strong could still look at organizations like the CIO and find some confirmation of her belief that "the people" were "not passive, not stupid, inattentive." Similarly, Spivak came back from his tour convinced that a revolution was not imminent and that American workers would remain quiescent if their creature comforts were met; but he also said that when conditions got worse, as they probably would, then "sooner or later" those workers would revolt. Hallgren was the least optimistic of the three. Given the inertia of the masses, he doubted there would ever be a proletarian revolution, and he hoped instead for a Communist coup d'état. Although he found even those prospects a little slim, he nonetheless remained confident that capitalism would fall, and he maintained just enough faith in the Communists to warn them that the Party had better get busy.[45]

Strong, the only one of the three actually to join the Communist Party, was also the most persistent in her radical commitments, continuing to write on liberation movements up through those of the 1960s in Southeast Asia. Hallgren kept a friendly but critical perspective on the Party while looking for his "seeds of revolt" in the early thirties. But by 1940 and 1941, he had turned away from radical social change to write about stamp collecting and civil liberties. Spivak also moved away from his earlier radical position, and he was able to pinpoint the moment his faith in Marxism collapsed. On August 24, 1939, he learned that Soviet Russia and Nazi Germany had signed their mutual nonaggression pact, and, as were countless other leftists, he was overcome with "a sense of personal betrayal." In spite of all his criticism of the Soviet Union, he had still believed that Russia's ultimate goal was "to realize that rosy dream of a brotherhood of man I had first heard about on New Haven's green." But there, staring up at him from the headlines was the news that the Soviets had made common cause with his greatest symbol of evil, the Nazis. It was the end of his faith, for "if the Soviet Union could sign a pact like that, then no government and no ideology could be trusted."[46]

New Deal Drifters

Sherwood Anderson, Louis Adamic, Gilbert Seldes, Lorena Hickok, and Jonathan Daniels were considerably more chary of theory than the radical reporters. Though they indicted the unthinking social and economic drift that seemed to have produced the Depression, they were leery of efforts to replace that drifting with social designs like Communism. When the severity of the Depression abated in the later thirties, these writers eventually rejected all such designs. Anderson and the others retained, however, a distaste for the worst aspects of laissez-faire economic and social development and preferred instead a moderate amount of loosely coordinated planning. This preference made them ready and even enthusiastic supporters of the New Deal and its notorious absence of theoretical or ideological consistency. When it came to writing travel reports, they were no more sympathetic toward theoretical constructions than they were in the political arena. For them, the world was full of anomalies and inconsistencies, moving only very slowly and circuitously toward a probably brighter future. Accordingly, they thought that the writer should not place a preconceived pattern upon events; he should instead depict the world as it actually was—an often confusing, always complex, and, despite the Depression, usually benign place. This world view was, of course, just as much a theory as any of Strong's Marxist projections, and their writings constituted a similar but considerably less self-conscious effort to bring the outside world into conformity with their conception of it.

Of the five, Sherwood Anderson left the most detailed traces of his thinking. Already beset with marital problems, his distress only increased with the Depression's onset. By December of 1930, he was certain that the deprivation he saw would be intolerable for Americans and that great social changes, perhaps even the coming of a Communist revolution, were at hand. He had a few reservations, however. Communism's economic and social equality seemed fine, but there was a narrow moralism Anderson thought he detected among Communists. Having protested against the restraints of prudishness in *Winesburg, Ohio* (1919), he worried that Communism might prove to be "only a new sort of Puritanism." He was willing to put these worries aside for the time being, though. Since he believed that those early days of the Depression were ones in which story-telling would not do, he reluctantly concluded that at the moment the writer's job was to aid the struggle, composing "what might be called propaganda for the masses." Anderson wrote one such piece for the *New Masses*, a Communist magazine, saying that if the needs of the masses required the end of literature and the submergence of his own generation of writers, then so be it: "Let us be submerged. Down with us." But despite such carryings-on, his enthusiasm for Communism was not wholehearted. When his signature appeared a few months later on James Rorty's pamphlet endorsing the Communist presidential ticket, it was there only because Edmund Wilson had secured Anderson's proxy to put his name to anything Wilson himself was willing to sign.[47]

Even this less-than-enthusiastic support for Marxism soon faded. In October 1934 Anderson admitted that for a while he "did rather go over to something like a Communist outlook" but stressed that those days were behind him now. By the time his travel book appeared, Anderson comfortably called himself "an individualist," claimed he could "no longer believe in mass good," and held that one simply had "to take the world of man as it is." Accompanying this change of political views was a shift in his idea of the writer's duty. Where he earlier called upon the writer to be an ideologue and servant of the revolution, he now outlined a different job for the author. Anderson believed that his friend Dreiser was "wet" in his "notion of the writer being also thinker, philosopher, etc." Instead, an author should narrow himself and tell only "the simple story of lives." In short, Anderson came to believe that writers should work in something like his pre-Depression style, in which he claimed to have composed *Winesburg, Ohio* with "no social theories."[48]

Louis Adamic also admitted that a Marxist analysis might possibly apply to the United States in the early thirties. People around him were saying that a revolution was imminent, claiming like songwriter Florence Reece that there would be only two sides in the upcoming battle, and demanding to know "on which side of the barricades will you be?" He wanted to disregard such talk but could not quite do so: "It sounds all crazy to me; yet—." Adamic did not spend much time wavering, however, and soon decided against Marxism, or any other theory for that matter. He disliked Communism because it seemed to take the admirable goal of equality and then "tie it to some definite plan" of political action. America may have been a Sargasso Sea, with perhaps only the gentlest of currents toward equality, but Adamic decided that he liked it that way, drifting along by *"instinct,"* constantly and correctly "torn by inner contradictions." The trouble was that the Depression had so shaken writers and intellectuals that they were no longer brave enough to be uncertain in the drift of world events. In one of his own courageous moments (when the urge to flee America was not upon him), Adamic proudly wrote, "I *am* confused," and said that anyone who was not bewildered was "either an intellectual superman . . . or a damn fool kidding himself with a convenient formula like Marxism." Marxism might apply to some place like Russia, but America was different, and Adamic decided his job was "to keep America different." The United States was a place beyond formula, where the unfolding of events "cannot be caught or imprisoned in words of finality, and he wrote to confirm that tenuousness."[49]

Gilbert Seldes and Jonathan Daniels also elected to drift rather than accept the direction of any theory. In the early thirties, Seldes found it disturbing that Americans simply coasted along in the same habits even after the Depression had exposed the hollowness of capitalism. By 1936, however, when he had looked more closely at Communism and particularly its Russian manifestations, Seldes decided that he was one writer in favor of America, which meant "to be in favor of uncertainties." As such, he decided that he would reject "all finalities and perfections." Daniels shared this sentiment and complained that the Communists were too rigid in their thinking and plans. While he believed America should have a moderate amount of economic planning, Daniels continued to believe that social development came more from people's unpredictable "itching," rather than any theoretical forecasts.[50]

What the country needed to help it get through the Depression was not ideology, but leadership. Anderson, Adamic, Seldes, Hickok, and Daniels thought that Franklin Delano Roosevelt provided just the right brand of leadership. Anderson wrote that what Depression Americans wanted most was a president whom they could trust, for they had "a hunger for belief, a determination to believe." It seemed more important to trust the leader than to know where he intended to take the country, and after examining the New Deal, Roosevelt's massive but uncoordinated recovery program, Anderson believed that Roosevelt had captured Americans as his willing followers. Adamic agreed that this capability was important and found it at many levels of FDR's administration. He liked Tennessee Valley Authority (TVA) administrator Arthur E. Morgan, for Morgan argued that the nation needed "not dogma, not isms, not rigid ideologies or social programs, but character in men and women." In Adamic's judgment, Morgan and other New Dealers were not only doing good jobs, they were also people of good character. Hickok was similarly enthusiastic, particularly about the New Deal's rural resettlement programs and the TVA, a program for flood control and electrification in the South. She thought they were pragmatic, nonideological projects and urged their expansion into other regions. Daniels admired the TVA, too. As a southerner, he felt TVA administrators represented a new breed of federal officials, noble outsiders who came as the South's true servants rather than as mere carpetbaggers. Seldes added his voice to the chorus. By 1936, he too claimed that Roosevelt was just what America needed. FDR not only had strength of will, he was also an undogmatic, pragmatic leader who understood that "capitalism was never an abstraction," and who rescued *American* capitalism, "an exceptionally experimental, audacious and flexible" subspecies.[51]

This faith in New Deal leadership influenced the writers' reports in much the same way that the leftists' beliefs had shaped *their* observations. Anderson, for example, discounted the incredibly dismal disposition that he discovered among Americans. They frequently reacted to their Depression plights as did a man to whom Anderson gave a ride; the man had lost his farm in the Depression, and he interpreted the loss as a personal failure, a sign of his worthlessness. Another hitchhiker told Anderson that the only logical solution to the Depression was to execute the poor and unemployed who had proven themselves so unworthy, and the hitchhiker counted himself among those who would have to die. Like Anna Louise Strong's workers, Anderson's passengers had so internalized capitalism's equation of economic success with human worth that the Depression caused "the breaking down of the moral fibre of the American man." But Anderson always found New Deal projects that restored Americans' respect and gave them hope. Millworkers were able to organize under new federal regulations and experienced "a kind of religion of brotherhood." In the Civilian Conservation Corps, workers eagerly planned the future use of natural resources, and among the once-despondent miners of Harlan County, Roosevelt's leadership had aroused "a sort of vast neighborliness." Despite the frequency with which he found dispirited hitchhikers, Anderson could look back on his travels and say, "I have heard amazingly little whining."[52]

The other writers shared Anderson's penchant for optimism. Hickok's Americans were in terrible condition; Nebraskans had resorted to eating a soup made of Russian thistles, and others had lost all resolve. One former teacher, now working as a domestic, had completely internalized her Depression failure; she told Hickok that "if, with all the advantages I've had, I can't make a living, I'm just no good, I guess. I've given up ever amounting to anything." These people were "bewildered, apathetic," yet in her final report to New Deal administrator Harry Hopkins, Hickok described them as "terrifyingly patient," "willing to work," and salvageable under Roosevelt's leadership. Adamic also found Americans in sad shape. The thirties had left the average worker without "the spunk and character of a muskrat," which when similarly "caught in a trap" would at least *do* something, "gnaw off his leg to remain a muskrat and be free." But Adamic concluded that certain men would release Americans from their traps, men like TVA official Morgan who understood the course of the "long road" to political and social equality, and whom the nation could confidently follow. Likewise, Daniels remained confident that New Dealers would replace the cowering men he had found throughout the South, and Seldes thought New Deal leadership had cured America.[53]

In hindsight, this faith in leadership, occurring as it did in the decade of fascism's flowering, has a tragic air about it. Keeping no ideological criteria with which to judge their leaders, relying on something as elusive as character, Anderson and the others seemed on the verge of the unquestioning devotion to leaders that afflicted so many Europeans during the thirties. But the European example was familiar enough to them, and the others joined Anderson in an unconvincing effort to distinguish *their* sort of leader from such despots. Anderson reckoned that men who had deep faith in Roosevelt "could be made into brown or black shirts easily enough." But, he insisted, Roosevelt and other New Dealers were good people who would never allow such a thing to happen.[54]

A Role for Theory

U nlike the New Deal apologists, other traveling writers respected theory. James Rorty, Erskine Caldwell, Nathan Asch, J. Saunders Redding, and Theodore Dreiser thought it should play a role in their observations and reports. Rorty was perhaps the most explicit in his position, holding that "no science and no art begins and ends with fact finding . . . some sort of social philosophy must guide the collection of facts and control their interpretation and use." He found academic sociologists too enamored with "objectivity," forever collecting descriptive material, holding no testable hypotheses, and refusing to draw any conclusions. Nor would the academics see themselves as persons who could direct as well as observe the course of events. Forever gathering but never analyzing their data, their efforts were the opposite of what he hoped to accomplish. Rorty intended to discover the patterns of capitalism's former hegemony and its current decline and then to share that story with readers so that they could cease being capitalism's passive victims and become its informed adversaries. When he failed to achieve this, Rorty thought he had fallen into the same trap as the sociologists, oberving rather than analyzing, traveling "to substitute physical motion for the motions of the mind."[55]

Even with Rorty's strong respect for "social philosophy" as a guide, he nonetheless feared that writers too frequently bent facts to fit theory, a fear that grew as his dissatisfaction with the Communist Party increased. Rorty eagerly worked for Communism early in the Depression, and he claimed that the effort improved his poetry. (Maybe the commitment did enhance his work; critic Malcolm Cowley heard two of them at the Cooper Union and thought they "were pretty good poems.") Beginning the thirties with the faith that capitalism would eventually fall, he continued to hope this throughout the decade. But the early enthusiasm that led him to endorse the Party's 1932 presidential ticket and to accept its leadership of progressive forces had evaporated by 1935 or 1936, when he became more critical of the Party and its ideology. He came to think that too many intellectuals accepted "the new gospel" of the Party line with "an uncritical unction" similar to that of religious converts. Reviewing Spivak's travel report, *America Faces the Barricades*, Rorty detected an unacceptable correspondence between parts of the book and the Party line; he lectured Spivak and other intellectuals, telling them that "to misrepresent facts" was to do a grave disservice to their radical hopes. Rorty believed that his ultimate responsibility as a writer was "to tell the truth as I see it." The task was to maintain one's own integrity while balancing between, but never succumbing to, the ideology of "an existing revolutionary party," and "the implicit bribes" of capitalism's publishing industry.[56]

The other social reporters thought much like Rorty. Dreiser and Asch shared his respect for theory and his unwillingness to shape their findings for theory's sake. Asch believed the travel reporter should "write from a point of view," yet insisted that the final content of a report should not come from one's preconceptions. Instead, it should emerge when one had enough "facts so that they form a pattern in your mind." Dreiser had been theorizing that forces beyond human control determined the human condition since the turn of the century. But with the thirties, he altered the role for theory in his writing, abandoned determinism for a gentler evolutionary theory, and insisted upon the doctrinal independence of his work.[57] Redding's mission was somewhat different from the others, yet he shared their belief that one must search systematically. The only black among the travelers, Redding had for years been casting about for some sense of his place within the larger white society. But his earlier searching had been unorganized and left him "in a bewilderment"; he commenced his Depression travel with a carefully planned itinerary in the hope that he could compensate for those "years of planless seeking." Caldwell was the most circumspect in admitting that he wrote "from a point of view." Indeed, he insisted that he "had no philosophical truths to dispense" and no desire to alter "the course of human destiny." His job was "simply to describe to the best of my ability" the things he saw. At one point, he even called his writing an effort "to hold a mirror up to nature," giving the reader as undistorted an image as possible. But the images in his mirrors belied his assertions, for Caldwell's reflections of the thirties almost invariably portrayed poverty and destitution in an effective critique of the system that had produced the Depression. Caldwell himself hoped his work would "have some effect on many lives," leading people to eradicate the tragedies he mirrored.[58] Rather than simply presenting his material, he arranged it to convey his point of view and sway the attitudes of his audience.

Caldwell and the others uniformly described Americans as hungry, ill-clothed and poorly housed. They portrayed Americans' psychological condition as equally devastated. The hitchhikers Rorty picked up were "garrulous with bewilderment and half-confessed terror." They talked readily, as had Anderson's hitchhikers and Strong's workers, and they had likewise internalized the values of capitalism. But Rorty's riders still believed, despite their present failures, that they would soon become successful "according to the Horatio Alger Theory." So strong was the "Rotarian rhetoric" of a better tomorrow that his riders refused to listen to their hungry bellies and continued to dream of a bountiful future. These were a decimated yet beguiled people, and Redding found the same phenomenon among American blacks. He encountered one elderly black woman who was worried lest she not have a proper burial place, and who clung desperately to the false hope that her only remaining possession—a dollar pocket watch—would purchase a plot upon her death. This was hardly clear thinking, and Caldwell and Asch shared the assessment that Americans were befogged. Asch found them inured to their malnutrition, dispiritedly sliding into prostitution, and so isolated and terrified that they could not possibly forecast or plan the future. The Americans whom Caldwell encountered gave him no reason to believe that two reports of mental collapse in the badlands were at all atypical. In one tale, a service station owner who had not sold any gas for weeks began pumping imaginary gas into an equally imaginary car; in the other story, a banker, formerly the wealthiest man in town but now destitute, stood alone in the street and began pitching in an illusory baseball game.[59]

In spite of all such evidence of a devastated nation, Rorty, Asch, Redding, and Caldwell managed to convince themselves that the future had just enough promise to make it worth seeing. Lacking Anderson's trust in leadership or Strong's belief in the Party line, their faith was in a future that somehow just *had* to be better, and "hope" became a byword among them. Caldwell's catalogue of the plights of southern tenant farmers showed that the present generation was beyond rescue. With little indication that the youngsters could avoid the traps that had ensnared their parents, Caldwell nonetheless placed his faith in the section's youth who, with no more than "hope and a dream before them" would somehow "change hell into a living paradise." Asch could see no direction emerging from Americans' responses to the crisis, but nonetheless he managed to "still feel there is hope, there is a future." Redding, in his search for identity, encountered so many distinct world views that midway through his journey he felt "mired in abysmal futility." Nevertheless, by the end of his trip he claimed that all those positions were simply parts of a larger Afro-American value system: "integrity of spirit, love of freedom, courage, patience," and, as the other writers found among whites, "hope." Rorty came to what he called "a certain stoic optimism." Even though the slumber and dreams of capitalism continued during the Depression, all the hardship at least made it more difficult to sleep soundly and dream undisturbed; some of the futility and silliness of the years before the Crash would fade and Americans would "be *worthier*—at least I find myself able to hope this."[60]

James Agee

James Agee's relationship to the other social reporters is as full of paradoxes as is *Let Us Now Praise Famous Men*, his travel report. Though he shared their concerns with the role of ideology in observation and writing, Agee's rejection of theory was at once more sophisticated and more equivocal than their attitudes toward it. Drawn to commoners as were the other writers, he sought out "the people" not so much as unimpeachable dispensers of truth, but as examples of existence at its most basic level. Originally as ill at ease with the uncertainties of the thirties as were his fellow travel reporters, he came to accept uncertainty as they never did. An existentialist among reformers and radicals, Agee granted with them the need for some action in the world but never attained even Nathan Asch's slight faith that humans could make the world a better place.

For Agee, there were two basic modes in which the human mind functioned. One was "merely deductive, descriptive, acquisitive." In this mode, the mind captured the outside world in complete fidelity and without any elaboration. It was a state of pure beholding, and he metaphorically described this process as like that of a good camera, which seemed "incapable of recording anything but absolute, dry truth." The other activity of the mind produced what he called "works of the imagination," including science, art, and ideology. Here the mind was creative rather than transcriptive, bringing into the world something "which has never existed before." In its first mode, the mind only collected data, but in this imaginative mode, it placed some pattern upon the data, forcing "an opening in the darkness," and bringing light and order to a dim, chaotic world. The imagination helped to "advance and assist the human race," giving birth to beneficial new products and processes, such as the telephone or pasteurization, and encouraging social progress with ideas like democracy or socialism.[61]

Although works of the imagination might have some relationship to those things the other side of the mind recorded, imaginative products were not necessarily true to things in the actual world. Under Agee's scheme, for example, the atomic theory was a work of the imagination that had no necessary connection with the actual structure of any atom, even though the theory might inspire new insights that do not contradict the known properties of the world. Agee granted that works of the imagination were useful in such ways. But he thought that as interpretations of reality they were "quite as capable of muddying as of clearing the water" and suspected that they actually did both at the same time, "clouding in one way the thing which they are clearing in another."[62] Consider again the atomic theory example. By keeping scientists' perceptions centered on certain predicted (and usually occurring) outcomes, it is quite possible that the theory manages to blind them to inconsistent phenomena they might otherwise have seen.

Where the camera was his instrument of the descriptive mind, language was Agee's tool of the imagination. Adaptable to all sorts of imaginative works (stories, concepts, prayers, and more), Agee thought that language was the most plastic of art forms. But when it came to recording the objective world or to communicating ideas, words seemed bankrupt, for no matter how many qualifiers one added, they could never to his satisfaction represent *completely* the thing or notion intended. Unlike the simple, direct camera which (he thought) attained representation with ease, words managed to convey actuality or ideas only through a "Rube Goldberg articulation of frauds, compromises, artful dodges and tenth removes."[63]

Agee's writing reflected this growing discontent. During the course of the 1930s, he left behind an earlier interest in symbolic works and became increasingly fascinated with describing experience as purely as possible. Agee had the narrator of a 1931 short story try to utilize his mental tools to find some pattern to life. But the narrator failed because of his "weakness and diffuseness of mind and the fearful unarrangement of life." In 1932 the unarrangement of the Depression and his personal life overwhelmed Agee, and he considered suicide.[64] He managed to shake his suicidal inclinations but three years later was still wrestling with the relationship between actuality and his representation of it. He was distressed that his writing seemed too "tied up with symbols and half-abstractions," products of the imagination that he had "better steer clear of now." In the struggle that took him most of the decade, he continually found himself coming up short of what he believed "the real job of art is: Attempt to state things as they seem to be, minus personal opinions of any sort." It was not until the publication of *Let Us Now Praise Famous Men* (1941) that Agee felt he had attained his goal. Only then could he assert with confidence that "nothing here is invented." He accepted the confusion of experience without the aid of abstraction and wrote a book that often *is* confusing.[65]

Throughout this transformation, Communism both attracted and repulsed Agee. On the one hand, its theories gave a comprehensible order to the flux of events; yet on the other hand, its constructions violated "reality" as did any other imaginative construction. As early as 1936, he thought the Communist explanation of events was more compelling than any other and, as late as 1941, would describe himself as "a Communist by sympathy and conviction." But in 1937, he made plans for an "anti-communist manifesto." Rather than their politics, it was the arrogance of the Communists that most irritated Agee; to him, it was impossible to believe, as they seemed to, that an ideology could fully and adequately explain the vast complexity of experience. Agee scolded the Communists for their assumed attitude of omniscience. They seemed to feel that Marxism made humans wise and mature, that the perceptual waters were no longer muddy for good Marxists. To Agee this was preposterous. He thought that humans were much more humble, with no such level of understanding, having "scarcely entered the post-diaper stage of our development."[66]

Like the other traveling reporters, Agee also sought out "the people," spending eight weeks among three Alabama tenant farm families. During his stay he became fascinated with *existence,* something even simpler than what the other reporters studied. In the dust and heat of a southern summer, Agee located something that seemed to him worth describing—pure, simple being. He came back to the North and eventually wrote up his description as *Let Us Now Praise Famous Men.* He insisted that the book would be truthful, and *not* journalism, for "the very blood and semen of journalism . . . is a broad and successful form of lying." While Agee was involved in the project, he told a correspondent that his central concern was with "the whole problem of the nature of existence." He eventually gave his readers the same message, telling them that the ulti-mate, "true meaning" of any character in the book would be "that he *exists*, in actual being, as you do and as I do, and as no character of the imagination can possibly exist." Innocent, unsophisticated people at-tracted Agee, and the tenants were the strongest of lures. He quoted beatitudes over them, blessing not the suffering that Jesus had conse-crated in the original sermon, but their stature as pure lumps of human-ity, so lowly that they had only in the crudest forms any paraphernalia of the imagination such as pride, hope, or even a sense of justice.[67] Nathan Asch had found it impossible to stay with other, equally poor tenant farm-ers, who had said, when describing their situation, "We don't live here. We're just here." In contrast, it was exactly that rudimentary state of being in the Alabama tenants that drew Agee's attention. To him, they were "profoundly members in nature," living amidst household furnish-ings and human relationships "as scarcely complicated 'beyond' nature as such things can be." Esthetically drawn to the simple, Agee found their existence a thing of great beauty and gave himself over to simply describ-ing it.[68]

Agee admired the plainness of his tenants but, at the same time, pitied and protested their poverty. Their furniture, diet, and dress constituted "a steady shame and insult." A tenant house, striking in its almost classical simplicity, was as much an "abomination" as it was beautiful. The only weapons these tenants (or anyone else, for that matter) could use against the world's onslaughts were "understanding, and action proceeding from understanding." But the world had bombarded these people so long that they had become "profoundly anesthetized," hardly realizing the severity of their plight. Their rudimentary existence, the attribute that made them so beautiful, at the same time left them incapable of saving themselves, for they lacked the mental equipment "to handle an abstract idea or to receive it." Agee acknowledged this dilemma: the very simplicity that made the tenants so worth describing also doomed them to deplorable conditions. Another conundrum, which he admitted just as readily, was that the same understanding or consciousness that was the tenants' (or humanity's) sole weapon against the affronts of the world was also the "deadliest enemy and deceiver." Because understanding was part of the imagination, it could only ravage and distort the actual world, muddying the water while clearing it.[69]

The only hope was the imagination, and the imagination did as much harm as good. Agee had built himself a neat paradox. He appreciated the complex as well as the simple, declared them incompatible, and was unwilling to do without either. Like the other reporters in his fascination with empiricism, he was unlike them in that he did not temper his observations with his notions of the way the world ought to be. Indeed, the outlines of the future were not among Agee's concerns as he wrote *Let Us Now Praise Famous Men*. He noted his dilemma, acknowledged its severity, and then went on to write what he wanted, a didactic exercise in esthetics. His purpose was to show the public and his fellow artists, through a preponderance of example and an occasional direct lecture, that the simplest forms of human existence had a unique beauty all their own. Concerns about the course of human destiny, about understanding, and about social justice were all important, Agee granted. But he thought the time had come to consider simple existence.

Empiricism

I t was a pursuit of solace and fact that drew the Depression's social reporters into the field. Confused and bewildered, they were nonetheless confident that they could uncover the facts about Depression America and maybe even a touch of fellowship in those Americans whom they met along the way. They shaped their observations and molded their reports in accord with their expectations and their attitudes toward theory, especially Marxist theory. Apart from James Agee, they all forecast a brighter future, frequently in spite of considerable evidence to the contrary. Theirs were empirical errands, conceived in a mixture of dismay, confidence, and protest, and executed according to each author's notion of the proper relationship between speculation and observation.

These errands illustrate two pitfalls awaiting those who likewise study the outside world, be they reporters, physicists, or historians. The first, and more widely recognized, is the lure of allowing one's theories to color and direct observation so that the conclusions resemble one's expectations more than the objective circumstances. The second, a less widely recognized but more frequently troublesome snare, is the temptation to ignore the mind's necessarily active role in empirical exercises. Nathan Asch's efforts were a prime example of this problem, for he was determined to bring as little as possible to his observations, hoping that once he had collected enough facts they would fuse together by themselves to produce a sense of understanding. His frustration when this failed to happen underscores the lesson that no understanding comes to the passive intellect. Asch and the others could have benefited from the counsel of a contemporary, historian Charles A. Beard, who realized that "facts . . . do not select themselves or force themselves automatically into any fixed scheme of arrangements in the mind."[70] Meaning and order are not products of the outside world. They are original creations that, at best, do not contradict what we can see of that world. In a sense, any empirical report resembles a photograph in the way that Asch and the others thought, for in varying degrees such reports strive to be depictions of an external world rather than self-portraits of the investigator. They strive to be windows showing others the world rather than mirrors in which the investigator examines himself. But just as every photograph is partially a self-portrait revealing the photographer's imprint in its framing and composition, so even the most objective of observations mirrors an investigator's biases and inclinations. We correctly demand that such factors be unobtrusive, but to insist upon their absence ignores the nature of understanding and postpones forever the job of comprehending the flow of events. Too much timidity, too much insistence that all pattern come from without, will leave us like Nathan Asch, hopelessly wailing over our inability to discern any pattern whatsoever. To collect, collect, and collect information but neglect its analysis for fear of damaging the material is, as James Rorty saw, to substitute physical motions for motions of the mind. It is a poor substitute.

Overleaf: Dorothea Lange, "Ruby from Arkansas," 1935. (Dorothea Lange Collection, © 1982 Oakland Museum, City of Oakland.)

THREE

Rendering Order From
the Chaos:
Documentary Photography
of the Thirties

Y oung John Vachon chanced upon a fine school for learning documentary photography. A specialist in Elizabethan poetry, Vachon found himself fresh out of graduate school and unemployed in the midst of the Depression. But with some luck, he located work as a messenger in the federal agency that employed many of America's major documentary photographers. Vachon advanced within the agency, came to have charge of its immense file of photographs, and eventually decided that he, too, had a talent for photography. He studied the older photographers' work, practiced his own camera techniques, and finally earned an assignment to photograph the Great Plains. The assignment was everything Vachon hoped it might be. During the days he could make pictures modeled upon the works of his documentary teachers, and in the evenings he passed the time in contemplation of his teachers' ideas. On one of those evenings, Vachon wrote to another young documentary photographer, suggesting "a game we might play" in their correspondence. The name of his game was "definition of a good photograph." Drawing upon his photographic education and his own experiences, Vachon offered an orthodox documentary definition as the game's first move: "A good photograph is a false or exaggerated composition or design which symbolizes a true or typical situation."[1]

Vachon had learned his lessons well. Documentary photographers of the 1930s believed that one of their tasks was to portray thirties America. But like Vachon, they insisted that the truth about the Depression was not something that simply appeared in front of a photographer. Instead, the "true or typical situation" was what Vachon or any other photographer *believed* it to be; the scene before the camera was a pliable one that the photographer could arrange according to his own notion of just what the truth should be. America stood before them as an infinite set of images from which the photographer could pick and choose according to his inner vision, and if the country did not cooperatively provide scenes corresponding to that vision, then it was up to the photographer to arrange the setting properly.

Photography has exercised considerable dominion over subsequent images of the past, and at times, it has served as a record of actual experience.[2] Of course, the camera *can* capture the world in ways that drawings and paintings do not. Yet as John Vachon's game suggests, photography is as full of interpretation as are painting and drawing; it is no more free of the tricky relationship between truth and art than any other form of visual expression. If we somehow ascertained that photographers were unbiased in their sampling and that they truly depicted the 1930s, then we *might* be able to use their photographs to make some broad generalizations about the decade. But interpretation is an inescapable element in any photograph, and we can more directly face that element if we ask how a photo came into being, rather than if it is objectively true. It is by exploring the intentions of people like John Vachon, and not by probing the fidelity of their images, that we can move to an understanding of the creative mind in the Depression years. Accordingly, the focus here is not upon the subject that happened to be before a released shutter at a given instant, but upon the photographer's reasons for releasing it at that moment.[3]

Although documentary photographers of the 1930s operated within the traditions of twentieth-century American photography, world events had a greater influence upon them than upon either their photographic predecessors or contemporaries. As Vachon and his teachers surveyed their America, it appeared to them that the Depression had thrown the country into a terrific jumble. In the midst of such confusion, their earlier styles seemed inadequate, and they turned to documentary photography of ordinary people in their everyday settings. Most of the photographers made significant changes in their work as they moved into this new genre, and they embraced it in hopes of rendering comprehensible images from the surrounding chaos. They struggled to arrange the Depression's vistas and to bring some pattern to its flow of time. The Depression's suffering appalled them, and they hoped to ease that misery with pictures intended to move government officials and others to help its victims. Documentary photographers were also keenly interested in Americans' emotional ability to weather the decade's challenges, and they employed their cameras to diagnose the country's spiritual well-being. What they discovered was that Americans bore their trials with apparent dignity and courage, which to the photographers seemed reassuring evidence of an emotional stability somewhere beneath the decade's confusion. As the thirties passed and the pressures of the Depression gradually eased, documentary photographers increasingly left behind criticism for solace. They turned away from making complaining pictures of suffering people and more frequently explored the cheerful idiosyncrasies and resilient spirits of those Americans who rode out the storms of the 1930s.

Dorothea Lange
and Margaret Bourke-White

The careers of Dorothea Lange and Margaret Bourke-White exemplify the concerns that brought American photographers to the documentary idiom during the 1930s. Dorothea Lange (1895–1965) grew up in suburban New York City at the turn of the twentieth century. She commuted into the city each morning with her mother, Lange going to school and her mother to work as a librarian. Early in her life, Lange suffered an attack of polio that permanently crippled her right leg, but even as a child she displayed a characteristic vigor and curiosity, roaming the city alone and developing habits of observation that served her until her death. While still young she decided to make a career of observing things and set out to become a photographer. She devised her own course of training, studying under photographer Clarence White for a period, working with a series of "lovable old hacks" for a longer time, and independently sharpening her techniques all the while. Finally satisfied with her skills, she set out to travel and photograph her way around the world. She headed west but got only so far as San Francisco, where a pickpocket stole her money and forced an early end to the trip. Lange found work in a photofinishing business, began settling into the city that would become her lifetime home, and eventually became the owner of her own portrait studio. Her friends included other San Francisco photographers such as Ansel Adams and Imogen Cunningham, and her studio developed into a gathering place for the Bay Area's artistic and Bohemian set. She married Maynard Dixon, a western painter and member of that crowd, and by 1928, their family had grown to include two sons. Although the marriage never developed into a happy one, Lange devoted herself almost exclusively to raising her family and photographed only a little during the mid- and late twenties.[4] The few pictures she did produce were strikingly different from her later photographs of the 1930s. Like her 1928 portrait, "Mrs. Kahn and Child" (Figure 1), these works were often carefully composed studio arrangements lit with a gentle side-light that captured the texture of clothing or accentuated facial details. Images of contented, frequently well-to-do families, these softly focused romantic depictions have a relaxed, contemplative mood missing from Lange's later work.

Then the Depression struck. At first Lange fled from the crisis. In 1930 and 1931, when she felt that "the outside world was full of uncertainty and unrest and trouble," Lange, Dixon, and the boys made off to the tranquility and obscurity of Taos, New Mexico. In many ways this was a withdrawal from the thirties, a flight to the town that during the twenties had become an oasis for artists and writers eager to abandon Main Street and live among New Mexico's fashionably "primitive" Indians. At the center of that Taos community was the long-standing cultural rebel, Mable Dodge, who had married Tony Luhan, an Indian; it was she who took in Lange and her family, loaning them a house that also served as Dixon's studio. In this mountain retreat, they heard little of the world below; Dixon painted his canvases, the boys played in the snow, and Lange kept house. But the idyll did not last, for the tensions that eventually led to divorce plagued the family, and they all returned to San Francisco. Life in the city seemed even more unsettling than before, because, as Lange put it, they were "confronted immediately with the horrors of the Depression." The widespread unemployment and displacement were distressing, and other people appeared to share Lange's dismay, for the entire city seemed "shocked and panicky." The present was confusing, and the future appeared no more certain, because in all the confusion, "no one knew what was ahead." Under the economic pressures of such tumultuous times, and out of a desire to be independent from her husband, Lange agonizingly placed her sons in a boarding school and reopened her studio. No longer the traditional homemaker, missing her sons very much, and distressed over confusion in the larger society, Lange felt "under personal turmoil to do something" and began reevaluating her photography.[5]

A seemingly insignificant event helped draw her away from studio pictures of comfortable clients and into photography of Depression victims. While working at a window one day, she happened to look out toward the San Francisco waterfront. A young workman stopped at a street corner and stood in obvious indecision. Behind him were the wholesale and waterfront districts, to his left was the financial district, to his right were the flophouses, and ahead were Chinatown and city hall. He could not stand on that corner all day and had to move in one direction or another. But the Depression had rendered all the alternatives equally unpromising. The waterfront offered no work, he had no money for a meal in Chinatown, and city hall offered no welfare. In that young man's lingering confusion, Lange saw "an image of the dilemma which had captured a whole country." The nation had to do something, yet there was no obvious direction for it to take. Lange's desire to comprehend and delineate this dilemma brought her to documentary photography. As she later explained, "I was compelled to photograph as a direct response to what was around me."[6]

Lange took her camera outside the studio and began making pictures quite unlike her earlier romantic portraits. "Man Beside Wheelbarrow" (1934; Figure 2) was one of her first efforts. Five years earlier, Lange believed, she "would have thought it enough to take a picture of a man, no more." But now in the depths of the Depression, when the social environment affected so many so adversely, the isolated individual would not do; she "wanted to take a picture of a man as he stood in his world." Always one to capture an apt visual metaphor, Lange found this particular man in a condition all too typical during the 1930s. He was a person "with his head down, with his back against the wall, with his livelihood like the wheelbarrow, overturned."[7] Other artists followed Lange, and the bowed figure became a standard symbol among Depression photographers and painters, repeated more often than the corner apple-seller whom later generations more often associated with the Depression. This photograph is also an early example of a trait that characterized much of Lange's work in the 1930s. Not only did she achieve a good set of symbols to explain the sociology of how this man stood in his world, she also managed to convey the psychological consequences of that standing. The viewer *sees* the facts of the man's life and *feels* the dismay conveyed through his stooped shoulders.

During the early thirties, Lange also portrayed other people who were considerably angrier than her wheelbarrow man. There was in this early work a political dimension that would fade later in the decade but that manifested itself in pictures such as "White Angel Breadline" (1933; Figure 3). The bewhiskered man here has been driven to accept a breadline dole. Yet he stands apart from the others who likewise wait for their handouts, his glowering expression and grim jaw hinting that he may soon compel society to give him more than charity. Lange sensed a tension and explosive potential in the breadline crowd and took her brother along to act as a bodyguard during this venture into the streets. She managed to incorporate that tension into the photograph as part of her own social critique—a message that charity cannot buy off anger, and that society might soon pay a great price if it failed to meet the needs of people like this man.[8] By 1934, the hostility present in "White Angel Breadline" had spread to other San Franciscans, who pressed their demands upon the city's capitalists and organized a general strike. The strike was short-lived, and ultimately ineffective, but still one of the more contentious episodes in a time that saw no shortage of militancy. Police, strikers, and spectators were wounded in bloody confrontations that cost two lives and that San Francisco's business community took to be the start of a revolution. Lange ventured forth to photograph rallies for better wages and conditions and returned with angry images of placard-bearing crowds and haranguing speakers.

This was documentary photography, but Lange did not fully embrace it until later that same year. The friends and customers who saw "White Angel Breadline" were not supportive of the new direction in her work, and Lange herself found it difficult to shed old ways of seeing. Unwilling to make a complete break quite yet, she went to the mountains for a vacation in the summer of 1934, and there tried to photograph some of the natural forms she liked—young pine trees, skunk cabbage, and stumps. But her efforts failed; try as she would, Lange could not capture those shapes. She thought back to the general strike and realized that such human events, rather than the forms of nature, were her subjects. As she recalled with exaggerated hindsight, this revelation came to her in the middle of a mountain rainstorm, properly dramatized "with the thunder bursting and the wind whistling." But despite the exaggeration, Lange had indeed reached a turning point. From that time forward, her subject was "people, only people, all kinds of people, people who paid me and people who didn't." Thus launching her career in documentary photography, Lange believed that she had single-handedly discovered a new genre—an easy mistake to make, for there were few documentary precedents and her contemporaries were a far-flung lot. Unaware of her photographic progenitors or the other people who were also independently developing documentary photography, Lange took up her camera, left behind both nature and studio work, and "went out just absolutely in the blind staggers."9

Gradually supporters emerged, people who sensed the innovations in Lange's work and encouraged her to continue. Willard Van Dyke, a documentary movie maker, arranged a 1934 show of her prints. In 1935, Paul Taylor, an economist directing a division of the California Emergency Relief Administration, hired her to make photographs of migratory agricultural workers. Lange and Taylor worked well together, married later the same year, and eventually teamed up to produce a book about displacement upon the plains, *An American Exodus* (1939). The federal Resettlement Administration also learned of her work in 1935 and offered her a position in its photographic section. She accepted the job and remained with the agency on an on-and-off-again basis until 1942, when she transferred to other government agencies concerned with the war effort.

Lange came to documentary photography with a sense that the world was suddenly disordered and with a feeling that neither her former studio pieces nor nature photography were germane to such a world. As she embarked upon this new work, a deep concern for other people helped shape her vision. One pattern Lange thought she could make out amidst all the confusion was that suffering people needed assistance, and she condemned their plights with eloquent photographs of the very faces of misery. She took picture upon picture showing desperate people in urgent need of help and found it comfortable to work within a government bureau charged with lessening such misery. This melioristic impulse lay behind Lange's most famous photograph, "Migrant Mother" (1936; Figure 4). Returning home from a trip in March of 1936, Lange first drove past the soggy camp of some migrant pea pickers; but then she succumbed to an eerie attraction and retraced her tracks some twenty miles to photograph this homeless, starving mother and her children. Recognizing these people as powerful symbols that might move the rest of the country to aid other destitute people, Lange found herself pulled to the mother and children "as if drawn by a magnet." This poignant picture is probably the single most enduring visual image to emerge from the Depression and was part of a series that Lange took in the hope that "my pictures might help her." (And need help she did, for depending upon which of Lange's versions one reads, the woman had just sold either her tent or the tires from her car in order to buy food.) Continually pressing in upon the woman, Lange made one photograph after another until in the final frame she captured this pained expression and apprehensive gesture that have become iconographic classics.[10]

In addition to helping Americans, Lange also wanted to understand the spirit with which they met their problems. During her travels about the crisis-ridden land, she discovered that people were far from beaten. Impoverished, hungry, and uprooted, they still faced the times with "real courage. Undeniable courage." This courageousness was especially heartening because it suggested that at least *something* had remained solid and unshaken amidst the decade's pandemonium. Lange sought out this fortitude and, in short order, "learned to recognize it." Indeed, Lange became uncannily adept at presenting down-and-out people as courageous, determined, and even a bit transcendent. Her "Drought Refugees from Oklahoma Camping by Road" (1936; Figure 5) is only one of many such photographs. It has a companion picture, made just before this frame, in which the same Oklahomans appear much more complacent in their poverty; but that companion image scarcely fit Lange's vision of a courageous people, and she favored the present photo. This steely-eyed woman stares back at the world with a look full of determination, her expression announcing that she is undefeated despite her ragged clothes. She is a strong person, and yet Lange managed to portray her as being kindly as well as brave, for the young mother tenderly feeds her child. The nursing infant served Lange perfectly as a symbol of hope for the future, for he absorbs his mother's courage and strength and is a promise that those qualities will endure. With such images, Lange demonstrated that Depression Americans continued to have hope, a hope that flourished in spite of their current conditions. Lange came to believe that human emotions like this were universal and that photographs portraying emotions had a much broader audience than pictures of natural shapes or abstract forms. Ironically, she even held that photography should go beyond immediate circumstances such as the Depression that inspired her; it should instead tackle timeless themes like human courage, for they seemed the very essence of good pictures. Speaking in a sort of proto-language, the best photography would overcome the accidents of time and place and speak "in terms of everyone's experience."[11]

Margaret Bourke-White (1904–1971) was born into a family of more comfortable means than Dorothea Lange's. But like Lange's mother, Bourke-White's suburban New York parents urged their daughter to explore the world rather than pursue the domestic life so frequently prescribed for girls of the time. Her mother was an outgoing and eccentric woman who encouraged her daughter's interests in pet snakes and insects. Her father was a more retiring person, but he may have helped Bourke-White develop an interest in photography, for he was an inventor who frequently tinkered with lenses. One day he took his young daughter to a foundry where she saw molten metal explode in a darkened room, a visual experience that at the time seemed to her "the beginning and end of all beauty." Together with a desire to share that beauty with others, "this memory was so vivid and so alive that it shaped the whole course" of her career.[12]

Bourke-White went to college, married a graduate student, and followed him to several more schools until their marriage dissolved. Like Lange, she briefly studied with Clarence White at Columbia University. But most of Bourke-White's academic work was in zoology, and she only started making photographs while at Cornell, her last school, in order to earn money. By 1928 or 1929, she abandoned zoology for photography, moved to Cleveland in hopes of selling her pictures as architectural illustrations, and continued a program of self-training through trial and error. Architectural photography provided a living, but Bourke-White's heart lay elsewhere. Her childhood fascination with foundries drew her to Cleveland's industrial district, where she photographed the scenes of factories and smokestacks (Figure 6) that she found so appealing. Like many other Americans during the 1920s, Bourke-White's fascination was more esthetic than economic, for she found machines "sincere and unadorned in their beauty," and her work echoed the industrial scenes of contemporary precisionist painters such as Charles Sheeler. She managed to convince the president of a Cleveland steel mill that plants like his were at "the very heart of industry with the most drama, and the most beauty," and so gained permission to photograph his mill's interior. On the basis of such industrial photographs, publisher Henry R. Luce in 1929 added her to the staff of his new business magazine, *Fortune*, and for the next several years she contentedly worked away in the heart of New York's business community, photographing half-time for *Fortune* and half-time on commission for advertising agencies. She also made several trips to Russia between 1930 and 1932, trips that were not so inconsistent with her business interest as they might at first seem. Unlike leftist writers such as Anna Louise Strong who also visited the Soviet Union, it was the spectacle of a country first coming to industrialization, and *not* the socialist experiment, that drew Bourke-White. At this stage in her career, it seemed to Bourke-White that "politics was colorless beside the drama of the machine."[13]

Bourke-White's photographs of foundries, cogs, and smokestacks seemed to her a necessary antidote to the emphasis earlier photographers had placed on soft-focus renditions of romantic themes. With its sharp delineation of nonallegorical subjects, this industrial work "was an advance toward realism, and, as such, was good." But in 1936, she came to feel that this single-minded focus upon industry "was not enough." By then the crisis had penetrated even her posh Chrysler Building studio, and Bourke-White, who could be remarkably imperceptive, began to see the Depression about her. She realized that if the pursuit of what she called "realism" was to be successful, she had to take into account those forces that could bring her beloved factories and mills to a halt during the economic slump. This belated but growing awareness of the Depression opened her eyes to what she called a disturbing "lack of order" in the land, the chaotic side of capitalism that she had previously missed and must now depict if she was to be true to her realism. Eager to move on to this new work, Bourke-White was elated to receive a *Fortune* assignment to photograph the drought on the plains. The country's dusty interior was an important center of the Depression, and the assignment seemed "an opportunity to show what was really going on—a chance to get close to the realities of life."[14]

As had Lange, Bourke-White became increasingly interested in people as photographic subjects and began examining their human responses to the Depression. But Bourke-White was decidedly less empathetic than Lange, and she saw Americans as neither courageous nor determined. She described Dust Bowl victims as "numbed like their own dumb animals," struck with "the very paralysis of despair," and it seemed ever more important to capture that numbness and despair on film. In her earlier work, she had included an occasional person only as "a figure put into the background of a photograph for scale," and many of her industrial pictures, like Figure 6, have barely discernible people in them. But once she came face-to-face with the drought-ridden farmers, "suddenly it was the people who counted."[15] Photographing people was something new for Bourke-White, however, and her habits subverted her intentions. She went into the Dust Bowl to get pictures of drought-ridden people and returned with pictures of dust-drifted buildings. The ebullient celebration of American prosperity was now absent from her plains pictures, yet it was some time before she managed to bring to her portraits of the Depression those people whom she said had become so important to her. Having been a photographer of buildings, she remained a photographer of buildings.

Bourke-White's interest in Depression "realism" continued to grow after the Dust Bowl experience, and she persisted in moving away from her earlier themes. When she came back from the plains and returned to her advertising commissions, she found none of the earlier harmony between her own social vision and the perspectives of her corporate clients. The advertisers' only human concern was to convince people to purchase products, and having determined that people mattered more than products, Bourke-White no longer found creative satisfaction in her clients' connivances. As she tried to photograph a tire purposely distorted to make its qualities more obvious to potential customers, Bourke-White's dissatisfaction reached a critical point. She "longed to see the real world which lay beyond the real tire, where things did not have to look convincing, they just had to be true." Preferring truth to salesmanship, she quit advertising. Like Lange with her mountain storm, Bourke-White's recollection of her own moment of commitment to documentary photography has a suspiciously dramatic air. Yet beneath her exaggeration, there is more than a hint of how out-of-place advertising had come to seem in the social crisis, and of the tremendous relief she felt after deciding to change photographic styles. According to Bourke-White, her conversion came with a haunting nightmare: the Buicks she had been photographing for an advertisement chased and tried to devour her, and upon waking, she resolved to abandon advertising for documentary photography.[16]

Erskine Caldwell and *Life* magazine gave her places to display her newfound style. Caldwell felt that the public had never fully understood that there were plenty of real-life people corresponding to the characters in his novel, *Tobacco Road* (1932). So he hired Bourke-White, put her and her cameras in his car, and launched an expedition to the South in hopes that "the realism of photography would support the disputed realism" of his words. This project, which Caldwell and Bourke-White published as *You Have Seen Their Faces* (1937), brought her once more into close contact with the Depression's grim "realities of life." Caldwell's emphasis helped Bourke-White accept people as legitimate photographic subjects, and, not too surprisingly, her pictures resemble the verbal portraits in his *Tobacco Road*—Bourke-White's poor white Southerners frequently seem defeated and fatalistic, and the jointly composed captions in *You Have Seen Their Faces* convey a benighted despair similar to that of Caldwell's characters (Figure 7). Her Depression portraits are thus markedly different from Dorothea Lange's. Where Lange believed the camera should not prey upon people who have lost their pride, Bourke-White had no such compunctions and willingly rendered her subjects as a set of grotesques riddled with poverty and disease. *Life* magazine liked this sort of photography, however. It began publication while she was organizing the Southern expedition, and Bourke-White soon joined its staff. She found that the magazine's editorial policies allowed her to photograph sufficient quantities of her own brand of "reality," and *Life's* circulation doubtlessly benefited from her often sensational coverage.[17]

Taken together, the careers of Lange and Bourke-White succinctly illustrate those impulses that gave rise to American documentary photography and guided its growth during the 1930s. Like Lange, those who became documentary photographers were often distressed over the extensive suffering they witnessed, and hoped that, with sympathetic portraits of the downcast, they could protest the circumstances of stricken Americans while moving others to ease that suffering. This inclination made the New Deal's social agencies agreeable work places for Lange and other photographers. Besides an ameliorative impulse, documentary photographers also exhibited a desire, much like Bourke-White's, to bring their work closer and closer to "realities" like those of the Depression. The world of the thirties seemed disorderly, with previously solid subjects such as industrial forms now gone weak, and with the country figuratively standing at the intersection of many paths, uncertain about which one to take. Photographers hoped to discover some pattern within that disorder, and one constant they frequently saw was that the Depression's victims faced their trials with remarkable bravery. Documentary photographers like Lange and Bourke-White set out to take the pulse of the nation, and their diagnoses more often agreed with Lange's than Bourke-White's, for they usually found the country's heartbeat quite strong. Concentrating on "people, only people," these photographers came to feel that the decade's victims were also repositories of the courage and strength that would enable America to endure the Depression.

The Photographic Scene

Documentary photography emerged from broader trends in American culture of the late nineteenth and early twentieth centuries. In the visual arts, as in literature, there was a general movement away from romantic or allegorical presentations and towards greater verisimilitude and concreteness. Photography participated in the movement. Up until the turn of the century, the most pressing question in American photographic circles had been whether or not photography was art. Unable to shed the visions that prevailed in "accepted" art forms such as painting, photographers produced pictorial photographs that resembled old-master prints, landscape paintings, or the works of impressionistic painters. Using blurred focusing, extensive staging, and models representing mythic figures, photographers produced pictures that were scarcely distinguishable from romantic paintings. Taken to its extreme in the work of photographers such as F. Holland Day, pictorialism became a loose parody of painting. In 1898, Day produced a picture of Christ suffering on the cross (Figure 8) and gave the picture a soft-focus rendition. Of course, there were no cameras in Jesus' day that might have made an actual photograph of the crucifixion, and so he had to find a substitute; using himself as the model, Day arranged this self-portrait so that he would resemble the hackneyed Christ of Western art tradition. But as painting moved toward greater abstraction, and as the 1913 Armory Show and other forums fostered American awareness of such innovations, photographers came to recognize their medium's limited ability to reproduce the effects of painting. They moved away from fuzzy renditions of mythical topics and toward "straight" photography—glossy prints, sharp focus, and an absence of painterly scenes. Pictorial representations like Holland Day's crucifixion scene had fallen from popularity by the 1920s, and photographers such as Alfred Stieglitz and Edward Steichen abandoned softly focused metaphorical subjects to compose sharply defined studies of shapes and common objects. Straight photography so dominated the field that only a few diehards continued to produce soft-focused romantic images.

By the middle years of the Great Depression, two distinct schools had evolved within straight photography. There were important differences between the two, but practitioners in both schools saw their work as Bourke-White viewed hers—reactions against, and antidotes for, pictorialism. Those in the first branch of straight photography were inclined to concentrate upon formal or abstract themes, and many of its practitioners were associated with a loose organization of California photographers, Group f/64. This group took its name from one of the smallest camera openings then available, symbolizing the extreme sharpness and clarity possible with a lens adjusted to f/64. These photographers were interested in depicting beauty, timelessness, and, above all else, natural forms—nudes, mountains, or even vegetables. The group's central figure was Edward Weston, a Californian who made pictorial photographs until the early 1920s and then turned to sharp-focus images. Perhaps best known for his close-up pictures of vegetables (Figure 9), Weston emphasized depth and detail in his work and shunned any tampering with negatives or prints. Like most photographs, this is a picture *of* something—in this case a bell pepper in a dime-store funnel. But there was a decidedly modernist bent to photographers such as Weston, and the true subjects of their photographs often lay below the surface of things. While Figure 9 is a picture of a particular bell pepper, for example, it is also a study of the fantastically convoluted shapes nature can assume and of the swirling interplay of light and dark produced by those shapes. Weston was an influential figure who helped inspire and direct other Group f/64 photographers like Ansel Adams, whose breathtaking images of western mountains were also preoccupied with shape and form. The other branch of straight photography was documentary photography, and in contrast to their Group f/64 counterparts, documentary photographers like Lange and Bourke-White focused on the day-to-day, which was frequently far from beautiful. They were more concerned with people than natural forms, and with people's faces more than their bodies. Unlike Group f/64, documentary photographers concentrated on the temporal more than the timeless, and often took a critical or ironical approach to their subjects rather than the almost reverential emphasis found in the works of Adams and Weston.

Documentary photography did not flower until the Great Depression, even though a number of earlier photographers had used pictures to record historic events and, in doing so, had foreshadowed documentary photography's development in the 1930s. In the 1860s, Mathew Brady (and the other cameramen whose works bore Brady's name) created a large body of material showing the preparations for and consequences of American Civil War battles. Similarly, Jacob Riis recorded New York

City's slums during the late nineteenth and early twentieth centuries, and in the first decades of the twentieth century, Lewis Hine photographed workers and newly arrived immigrants. But Riis and Hine considered themselves writers primarily and saw photography as chiefly an adjunct to their prose. Hine once complained that if he could only improve his writing and completely "tell the story in words," then he "wouldn't have to lug a camera." Only later, during the Depression, would people who made pictures similar to Riis's and Hine's come to employ photography as their primary means of expression. Indeed, documentary photographers of the 1930s resembled Lange in that they came to their idiom with very little knowledge of their photographic forebears and with little exposure to each others' work. Nor were they drawn by the lure of wealth, for whether still or moving, documentary photography was seldom commercially successful.[18] Maturing within the tradition of straight photography, documentary photography developed during the 1930s as an independent genre of social commentary when people like Lange and Bourke-White abandoned their earlier motifs and used their cameras to wrestle with scenes of the Depression.

Photographers' Roots and Work Places

Besides Lange and Bourke-White, there were others who took documentary photographs, considered themselves documentary photographers, or achieved recognition as documentarians during the 1930s. Some came to the genre from backgrounds in painting, others moved into it from different types of photography, and still others came to the idiom from backgrounds other than the visual arts. Like Bourke-White, most of these people were from fairly comfortable families, homes that could provide them with some education past high school. They found markets for their work in the New Deal's Resettlement Administration (RA, later Farm Security Administration—FSA), other government agencies and programs, or in the picture magazines that blossomed in the thirties. Their careers were a varied lot, but most of these women and men came to documentary photography in the belief that it was the sole medium through which they could satisfactorily express themselves and examine Depression America.

The painters-turned-photographers believed they could more directly confront problems of the day on film than on canvas. Russell Lee was one of these, a chemist who had first turned to art when his job in a chemical plant proved too boring. But when he found that even painting could not capture what he envisioned, and when he realized "that there was a lot more in this world" than he was able to put on any canvas, Lee began to photograph country fairs, Depression-induced farm auctions, and bootleg coal miners. In 1936, the RA's photo section clinched his commitment to documentary photography by hiring him to continue making precisely the same sort of pictures. John Collier, Jr., son of Indian Commissioner John Collier, was another documentary photographer. He had studied painting under Maynard Dixon (Lange's first husband) and worked as a muralist before he came to feel that painting could not adequately convey his messages. Accordingly, Collier shifted to photography, "a medium that was more articulate" and seemingly capable of "understanding without getting involved in a decadent level of fine art." The RA-FSA photo section eventually hired Collier after reviewing his 1938 portfolio on Spanish-American sheep herders.[19] Yet another photographer, Jack Delano, had studied illustration as a young man in Philadelphia. But with the Depression he switched to photography and, like Lee, produced a study of Pennsylvania's bootleg coal miners. Believing that he had single-handedly invented documentary photography, Delano was surprised to learn of the existence of the RA-FSA project and promptly used his pictures of coal miners to win himself a place on the project. Among these converts to photography, Ben Shahn had been by far the best painter. Shahn began taking photos after receiving some rudimentary instruction from his studiomate, photographer Walker Evans, and intended to use the prints merely as "sketches" to aid him in his painting. But when he landed a temporary post with the RA, Shahn became so excited over the camera's capabilities that he decided to abandon painting forever.[20]

Besides these former painters, there were other photographers who had their roots in journalism or commercial photography. During the Depression, though, their assignments increasingly seemed too narrow, and they turned to the less constrained field of documentary photography. Carl Mydans, for example, completed journalism school and took a job writing for a New York banking magazine. Mydans's avocation was photography, however, and he became more interested in the documentary pictures he made during his lunch breaks than in the commercial articles he wrote during working hours. He moved to a new post at the RA, then into the photography section, and eventually on to *Life* magazine. Like Mydans and many of the others, Marion Post Wolcott was drawn into photography even though she had planned upon a quite different kind of career. She majored in education and child psychology at college, and afterwards went to work as a teacher. But she acquired an interest in cameras and became the photographer for the women's section of a Philadelphia newspaper. At first the work was fascinating, yet over time her fashion assignments, like Bourke-White's advertising contracts and Mydans's banking articles, seemed tragically incongruous with the poverty of the 1930s. Coming to prefer the documentary approach, Post Wolcott marshaled her introductions and won herself a position in the FSA.[21] Similarly, Robert Disraeli and Eliot Elisofan became dissatisfied with their work as commercial photographers and moved into documentary photography with its more diversified range of subjects. Eventually both men worked for picture magazines like *Life*.[22]

The Depression was instrumental in bringing Walker Evans and Berenice Abbott back from Europe and home to the United States. These expatriates were already well set in their careers when the Crash hit, and when they returned to America, both continued to expand the visions they acquired overseas. In his youth Evans had hoped to be a writer, and, as did many of his like-minded contemporaries, he left America for the seemingly more inspiring atmosphere of Paris. But there he began making photographs, and by the early thirties the camera had completely lured him away from the pen. "Somewhat guiltily" he neglected his writing and "became very engaged with all the things that were to be had out of the camera." He rejected the abstract, emotional emphasis of Alfred Stieglitz and in the Depression became the most lyrical of documentary photographers, collaborating with James Agee in the creation of *Let Us Now Praise Famous Men* (1940) and working for a time in RA-FSA. As with Evans, photography also enticed Abbott away from her earlier calling. In the early 1920s she had sailed to Europe in order to study sculpture. But her plans changed. Rather than sculpting, she worked with Man Ray, a practitioner of abstract, lensless photography, and over time became a popular Parisian portrait photographer herself. Toward the end of the decade, she met Eugene Atget, an aged French documentary photographer who roamed Paris taking pictures of its streets and street people. Coming to prefer Atget's "relentless fidelity to fact" over Ray's abstractions and her own portraiture, Abbott returned to America in 1929 and decided that she would adopt Atget's style and undertake a project similar to his lifework. Laboring first on her own, and later through the

Federal Art Project, Abbott photographed the atmosphere and architecture of Depression New York, and eventually turned her portfolio into a
book, *Changing New York* (1939).[23]

Simultaneously and independently, such people came to documentary
photography, weaving a new genre out of the disparate threads that, unbe-
known to them, had existed for over half a century in the works of Atget,
Hine, Riis, and Brady. Their fascination was part of a broader phenomenon at work in American culture of the 1930s. With the Depression,
photography moved closer to the center of American intellectual concerns
than it had ever been before, and it became a common creative outlet and
explanatory metaphor for some of the country's more talented minds.
Technical innovations doubtlessly played some part in this increased activity, for as Carl Mydans noted, faster films and smaller cameras greatly
expanded photographic possibilities, freeing photographers to work in remote, poorly lit places. But during the thirties, photography's magic attracted people not necessarily drawn to the documentary motif; Ansel
Adams was a professional pianist when he turned to making his eloquent
landscapes in the Depression, and Eliot Porter threw over a successful
medical career to commence his vibrant nature photography. Photography's peculiarly gripping appeal extended even to others who did not
become professional photographers in their own right, but who still found
the camera or its products compelling. When novelist John Dos Passos
composed the *U.S.A.* trilogy, he chose not to have a narrator's *voice*, and
instead introduced an all-seeing narrator's *presence* that he called "the
camera eye." Similarly, Archibald MacLeish began work upon a poem in
which he hoped to use photographs as illustrations accompanying his verbal descriptions; the documentary photographs proved so much more insistent than his words, however, that MacLeish considered the final
manuscript, *Land of the Free* (1938), to be "a book of photographs illustrated by a poem." Photography's attraction also extended into mass
culture, where magazines such as *Life* and *Look* not only emerged, but
managed to flourish with the Depression. A contemporary political scientist, James McCamy, examined the magazines' success and concluded that
they were able to capitalize upon a deep-seated "picture hunger" that
existed among Depression Americans. Judging from Russell Lee's experiences, that hunger was indeed deep. In a remote Texas farm town, Lee
found a one-horse farmer who not only allowed himself to be photographed, but upon learning about Lee's project to describe the Depres-

sion through photographs, dug into his pocket and contributed a hard-won nickel to the cause.[24]

Photography, and especially documentary photography, thus exerted a strong appeal upon the American mind of the 1930s. Perhaps it was that still photography, capturing reality in an infinite set of discrete images, managed to echo the endless fragmentation that seemed to characterize Depression America. More probably, though, the camera's attraction lay in its ability to capture experience immediately and directly, providing images with a beguiling air of authenticity. Verisimilitude in general and photography in particular have proven alluring to Western minds during times of disruption. Photography's earliest years in Europe, for example, were contemporaneous with the tumult following the unsuccessful revolutions of 1848, a period when artists such as Gustave Courbet also embraced realism in their paintings. Later, in the similarly troubled times of the 1930s, American intellectuals like Nathan Asch exhibited a preference for raw data such as the travel report, and, to many, photography seemed likewise able to present facts without interpretation. Documentary photographers themselves knew of this attraction, but unlike other Depression intellectuals, they were less inclined to see the camera as an instrument of blind truth and more often considered it an extension of the photographer's own ordering and arranging eye.[25]

Many of these documentary photographers worked at some time for the federal government's Resettlement Administration or its successor. Created under executive order in 1935, the RA was one of the more reform-inclined and class-conscious of the New Deal agencies, aiming its programs at the nation's poorest farm families. The Department of Agriculture absorbed the RA in 1937, giving it a new name in the process, Farm Security Administration. Rexford G. Tugwell, a Columbia University economist, was RA's first administrator, and in 1935 he hired his graduate assistant, Roy Stryker, to head the agency's Historical Section.[26] Under Stryker's administration the Historical Section became a purely photographic unit and a work place for Lange, Lee, and others. But for all they owed him, the photographers who worked for Stryker did not go forth to capture *his* vision of Depression America. An an administrator, Stryker was loyal, protective, and stimulating, and he proved to be an effective photo editor over the years, too.[27] His main concerns, however, were with prerogative and power, the bureaucrat's desire to expand his dominion within the larger agency and protect his turf from intrusions.

The smooth workings of the outfit were more his concern than the quality of the Section's output, and he once fired Lange, despite his recognition of her talent, because she was uncooperative.[28]

When he began his job, Stryker had no firm idea what sort of pictures the Historical Section should make. His earliest notion was to record *all* the RA's activities, and he set out, in Shahn's words, "to photograph even the very typewritten memoranda that came through." Shahn and Evans were already working for the government when Tugwell formed the Historical Section, and when transferred into it, they exercised the greatest influence over its photography. Evans' pristine and shimmering photographs set the esthetic and technical standards that the rest of the photographers sought to meet, while the content of agency photographs generally followed Shahn's political inclinations. In an organization that had no original direction, which was as Stryker characterized it, "like Topsy—it grew," Evans and Shahn provided the most significant models for the other photographers' approaches, styles, and topics. Responding in 1962 to an inquiry about the Historical Section, Stryker emphasized his lack of preconceived direction, underscored the photographers' role in determining the Section's growth, and stressed that prevailing descriptions of the Section talked "too damn much about Stryker."[29]

The RA-FSA photographers as a matter of course made many pictures that were direct assignments, records of agency projects, publicity shots, and the like. But seldom did such routine duties limit the type or number of photographs they could take. Shahn, Post Wolcott, and Collier all felt that they had sufficient liberty to shoot whatever they wished. Even Lange, whom Stryker fired, described the organization as having "an atmosphere of a very special kind of freedom," calling it a place "where you found your own way, without criticism from anyone." Though Stryker occasionally disciplined people, he did so more for violations of routine than because of the pictures they made. The Historical Section thus granted its photographers remarkable independence, and a number of years later, Carl Mydans likened his own sense of freedom "to the feeling one would have if one was on holiday somewhere traveling around with cameras and photographing whatever one thought interesting."[30]

Of course, the continuation of that freedom depended upon the continued existence of the Historical Section. During the early years when RA-FSA wanted photographs of despair and injustice to demonstrate the need for its programs, the photographers' work contributed to the agen-

cy's goals and seemed to require little justification. But by the early forties, as the Depression appeared less pressing to Washington and the
threat of war became more widely sensed, Russell Lee and John Collier
felt compelled to explain that their interests corresponded with the government's, or, more accurately, that allowing photographers to continue
with the same degree of independence would serve the government's
interests. They argued that photographs of the country's diverse sections
would increase Americans' understanding of each other, promote unity,
and so insure a solid front against potential enemies. Likewise, ties with
the European allies would become stronger if they saw photographs depicting America's European heritage.[31]

In this way, many documentary photographers found a hospitable working environment within the RA-FSA. Roy Stryker was the Historical Section's director, and he did the hiring and firing. But it was the photographers who shaped the techniques and content of its photography,
and under their careful molding, the Historical Section became the most
significant organization committed to documentary photography in Depression America.

The Melioristic Impulse

Several impulses led photographers to produce documentary works.
The most common and most obvious of these motives was a desire
to criticize the Depression's suffering and provide some comfort for
those who suffered. Photographers could be quite explicit in their
notions of what was wrong with the United States, and with their
pictures they pointed to a host of American social ills, afflictions that
ranged from racism to poor soil management. In their personal politics,
they endorsed an equally specific set of liberal solutions to the country's
problems, programs such as Social Security, migrant camps, and community planning.

For all this, there was a certain ambiguity to the work they produced.
Their early images were more often than not pictures of miserable people
in need of some form of help, without suggesting what that help should
be. A number of factors help explain this characteristic vagueness. For
one thing, documentary photographers were largely middle-class people
who became distressed when the Depression presented them with unac-

customed sights of extensive human misery. Although upset over these scenes, their immediate mission was not so much to repair the broken nation as it was to share their distress and shock other comfortable Americans into realizing that a crisis did indeed exist. Additionally, documentary photographers chose to concentrate on "people, only people," a focus that contributed to the vagueness of their social messages. The appearance of human suffering is remarkably similar from one face to another. Surroundings can *help* distinguish a destitute coal miner from a destitute factory worker, but there is no inherent difference between their looks of pain. Finally, in comparison to verbal expression, photography simply falls short of denotative power. It can convey irony, praise, or damnation superbly, but almost always requires words to offer more analysis. The photographer may be able to show a miserable tenant farmer, yet it is difficult for the picture-maker to show just what he favors as remedies for the tenant's misery: direct subsidies, educational programs, relocation, or any of a number of other possibilities. Although documentary photographers wanted to help suffering people by advertising their pain, seldom did the photographers offer specific ways to end the pain. Thus their efforts were imbued with an indeterminant meliorism, a feeling that if suffering could just be exposed, then surely it would be eased *somehow*. John Collier shared this sentiment with the others and perhaps voiced it best when he claimed that each documentary photograph "would do something for somebody someday."[32]

To make their case that Americans needed help, documentary photographers sought out the most distressed areas of the country. Such places seemed likely to have the misery they hoped to record, and they sought out those locales with a certain perverse tenacity, for, while they hated suffering, they also needed it to make their points. Jack Delano once wrote back from the field saying that in order to get the best pictures for a project, he was searching out the worst areas around Ithaca, New York. When Arthur Rothstein learned that landowners near Herrin, Illinois, were forcing tenant farmers out of their homes, he quickly set out to photograph the displaced families who had set up their makeshift camps along the roadsides. In late 1936 and early 1937, Russell Lee found plenty of material to photograph in Iowa and Illinois: distressed economic conditions, undernourished children and livestock, and a large number of "miserable dwellings." He continued to search for terrible conditions throughout 1937, ranging as far west as Montana. While similarly exploring the conditions of migratory field workers at truck farms near Belle Glade, Florida, Marion Post Wolcott joyfully reported that "there's good material for me here, conditions are awful at all times."[33]

In order to show the maximum amount of suffering in photographs, Post Wolcott admitted, "You wanted to slant them—if you would call it slanting."[34] She and other documentary photographers needed misery to make their pleas for assistance, and they not only sought it out, they also strove to make it as obvious as possible in their photographs. One way of achieving this was to show people with particularly dilapidated houses, as Lange did in "Old Age," a picture of a drooping elderly man sitting on his equally sagging front porch. Post Wolcott's photo of packing workers' housing (Figure 10) shows similarly miserable conditions. This family has few amenities, its child is shoeless, and the roof is simply a tattered piece of canvas. Yet there are signs that these people have not succumbed to their misery, for their prominently displayed broom and washboard testify that they battle against the squalor rather than willingly accept it. Their incongruous tricycle even suggests that they may still engage in play. Post Wolcott thus managed to slant her photograph, and she did so in two ways. First, from among the dwellings available at this migrant camp, she selected an especially dilapidated one (*not* the neat, gaily striped tent in the background), and she included the boy lest any viewer doubt that people actually lived in such a place. Secondly, she contrived the photo so that the viewer would see not just filth, but cleaning implements that indicate that this filth is unacceptable to those forced to live in it.

Photographers could concentrate upon housing as Wolcott did with this picture. Yet the close portrait of some depressed-looking person was an even more effective way to convey woe. Lange used this method with particular effectiveness in any number of pictures, including one portrait of a migrant coal miner's tubercular daughter, who with her downcast eyes, bowed head, and sunken cheeks exhibited virtually every classic sign of despair save tears. Mydans's portrait of a young girl (Figure 11) works in much the same way. He managed to capture this child while she was wearing not only a dirty dress, but also a particularly heartrending look, an expression that suggests that her circumstances have robbed her of childhood's lightheartedness. Mydans enhanced the impact of this portrait by catching the girl as she stared directly into the camera; in a photograph, as in actual life, eye-to-eye contact virtually compels the viewer to pause and register the person facing him rather than move along to the next object within his field of vision. Mydans thus caught a distressed-looking person at just the right instant. He was not quite so successful, though, with yet another technique he used in the photo. In closely framed photographs such as this one, the photographer tries to empty his composition of extraneous figures and therefore force the viewer to concentrate upon the central image. But Mydans failed to accomplish this with Figure 11, for peeking into the upper left corner of the photograph is a second child, a boy who clutters the composition with his presence and seems more curious than wretched.

Lange's "Migrant Mother" (Figure 4) is a better composition. Although the woman in this photo does not stare directly into the camera, Lange's close framing combines with the woman's puzzled and tentative expression to produce a sympathy-evoking image that is a masterpiece of composition and an outstanding example of a face captured at just the right instant. This was the last in a series of five exposures that Lange made, and the one that she favored for exhibition or publication. "Migrant Mother" is the most effective not only because it is more closely framed than the other four, but also because it has a more riveting blend of images. In one of the other pictures, the woman is nursing, a symbol Lange employed successfully elsewhere; but here the mother and child have not composed themselves into a graceful arrangement, and the woman's brow is not so worried-looking as in "Migrant Mother." In two of the other frames, she is as troubled as she appears in "Migrant Mother," but in these pictures the children gaze contentedly at the world rather than hiding from it behind their mother. The first photo that Lange made is the least effective of the five, for although it displays the ragged tent better than the others, the mother appears much less vulnerable and isolated; several of her seven children surround her, and the oldest daughter looks mature enough to be of help around the camp. Beginning with this first photograph, made from a distance of about twenty yards, Lange moved closer and closer until she was practically atop the family and finally took the "Migrant Mother" frame. Unlike the single frame that might be made without the subject's cooperation or even knowledge, a series of photos such as this is more dependent upon the subject's participation. Lange's "Migrant Mother" pictures reveal a good deal about the relationship between the photographer and the migrant, for both women participated in the making of the image. No mere passive object, the mother actively shifted her body, moved her head one way and then the other, and arranged the children around her. Photographers may have *taken* many candid photographs, but as series such as this one indicate, their Depression images were also in large part *given* by subjects like this stranded woman.

In addition to the close portrait, there was still another technique for playing upon the viewer's emotions. In these pictures, photographers selected some occasion that the viewer would normally expect to be a joyous celebration and showed instead how Depression circumstances made the event a joyless one. Lee's Christmas dinner (Figure 12) is one such photograph. Here the main course is not turkey and dressing but potatoes and cabbage; the children come to supper not in new clothes but in rags; and where one might hope to find new Christmas toys, there are no presents in sight. Lee said that the conditions in this house "really shook and angered me," and he managed to convey a hefty portion of his anger with this picture of kids on Christmas Day.[35] Lee's photo needs its caption to work, for without knowing what day it is, the viewer cannot grasp the incongruity that was Lee's emphasis. In contrast, a picture such as Mydans's baby girl or Post Wolcott's lean-to house is less dependent upon words to convey the photographer's particular plea for help. Yet there is a common thread connecting these pictures, for each employs children or women as its focal point. Indeed, in their images of Depression suffering, Lee and the others repeatedly concentrated upon women or children, and if possible, upon women and children together. In accounting for the preponderance of such images, one might plausibly argue that women and children suffered more than men during the Depression (or at least that men felt more compelled to mask their suffering). Accordingly, the odds were good that photographers looking for despair would happen to find it upon the faces of women and children. But given how selective documentary photographers could be—and how readily they subscribed to the belief that a good photograph is an arranged one—it seems likely that they chose women and children quite purposefully. The despairing portraits of women and children occur so frequently as to suggest that Lee and the others believed women and children occupied a special place in American hearts. If only the photographers could demonstrate that the Depression hurt people who seemed so *unworthy* of suffering, then perhaps Americans would act to ease that suffering.

Sometimes the photographers' subjects insisted upon looking contented when the photographers wanted despair. Post Wolcott, for example, was disappointed to find that Florida packinghouse workers were underemployed when she visited the state; since they were not working, "they don't look tired." Collier likewise complained that only rarely did the workmen in an industrial plant "look like the symbolic workman is supposed to look like. . . . None of that grim stuff, many are kids or nice looking old men with white hair." But the photographers seldom rested until they had their pathos. Ben Shahn worked with typical perseverance. He stopped at a Resettlement Administration project housing people who had been moved in from an impoverished area. But for Shahn, the project's "neat little rows of houses" were simply "impossible to photograph," for his subject was poverty rather than plenty. Shahn asked the clients about the houses they had abandoned and went *there* to get the pictures he wanted. [36] As a good documentary photographer, Shahn did not settle for the scene at hand, but sought out one matching his own vision.

Documentary photographers could at times go beyond their generalized emotional appeals and deliver specific condemnations of Depression conditions. Like novelist John Steinbeck, both Lange and Lee were angered over the rapid pace of agricultural mechanization, a process that replaced farm families with machines so quickly that it drove many farmers to become migrant laborers. To make his complaint about the situation, Lee photographed an abandoned and shuttered farmhouse on the North Dakota plains, suggesting that it was a home, and not just a house that had been lost to mechanization. Lange studied the problem under the tutelage of her economist husband and had a fairly thorough understanding of it. Her photographic treatment (Figure 13), with its strong emphasis upon line and texture, looks something like an exercise in modernist esthetics, but it was the social problem of mechanization-induced displacement that most concerned her. Utilizing a low angle of view to achieve a dramatic composition, she emphasized the long, perfectly plowed furrows that seem to lead up to the very doorstep of an abandoned Texas farmhouse. The building stands small and isolated in the machine-worked landscape, looking as though an earth-scouring behemoth had chased the occupants from their home. It was photographs such as these that inspired documentary movie maker Pare Lorentz, and that led him to hire Lange as a consultant when he made *The Plow That Broke the Plains* (1937), a film about the Dust Bowl drought. Of course, such conditions were in part products of the weather. With droughts and floods, the weather seemed to have turned against people in the thirties, and the

photographers showed the human consequences of such climatic disas-
ters. Yet they repeatedly emphasized that the agonies of drought, flood,
and soil depletion were not solely the products of whimsical nature.
Through poor land use, humans had contributed to each of these problems, and Post Wolcott in North Carolina and Rothstein in Oklahoma both
illustrated the process of unchecked soil erosion. Rothstein, for example,
could have made his Oklahoma photograph (Figure 14) a close-up of erod-
ed soil by itself. But he chose instead to include a farm boy in the picture,
suggesting that humans were intimately tied to erosion, as both its cause
and as its victims.[37] The gullied hillside is a product of human activity,
just as the house is, and yet humans must depend upon the soil just as the
lad leans upon the building.

If the photographers complained about soil erosion, there was also a
more overtly political dimension to their criticisms of Depression America. Most of the photographers were liberals, and as they surveyed the
country they condemned many long-standing social inequalities that only
seemed to have exacerbated the suffering of the thirties. Racism was the
most common of their political subjects, and many of them composed
photographs that were harsh criticisms of the country's racial prejudices.
Lee photographed segregated drinking and toilet facilities at an Oklahoma City streetcar terminal, and near Los Angeles, Lange made a picture of the Ford Motor Company's demeaning stereotype of a black woman in a billboard advertisement. Post Wolcott visited a tavern in Birney,
Montana, and captured the blatant contradiction between two signs behind the bar. One proclaimed that America was a place of "justice for all,"
and the other said there would be "positively no beer sold to Indians."[38]
Rothstein's "Plantation Owner's Daughter Checks Weight of Cotton"
(1936; Figure 15) is one of the more intricate of the racial pictures. In this
cotton field tableau, Rothstein showed that Texas race relations had
changed very little from antebellum plantations—black workers still picked the cotton while white owners judged the worth of their toil, and white
children still had authority over black adults. The scene also testifies to
the inequity of work on a southern cotton plantation, for while the blacks
have worked their clothing to tatters, the white girl's dress remains clean
and unmussed.

Racism was not the only thing about American society that upset the
photographers, and some of them went on to lambaste the country's un-
equal distribution of wealth. Lange had a well-developed sense of social

justice, which helped her see the irony she conveyed in her photograph of a billboard extolling the virtues of a train ride that the hitchhikers obviously could not afford (Figure 16). Lange's point is so obvious that it's virtually transparent, and one grasps her intention almost immediately upon seeing the photograph. But it took a certain heightened awareness to interpret the scene as worth photographing, for both hitchhikers and the Southern Pacific's advertisements were commonplace in the visual landscape of thirties America. Even Bourke-White, who with her business background was not among the most progressive of the photographers, saw the inconsistencies. She captured a line of flood refugees queued up for relief in front of another billboard, this one proclaiming that America possessed the "world's highest standard of living." Post Wolcott belittled those who benefited from such economic inequality with her unsympathetic portrait of R. B. Whitley, the potbellied, cigar-smoking owner of the general store (and therefore one of the wealthier citizens) in tiny Clayton, North Carolina. Shahn had the most highly developed political sensibility of the documentary photographers, and his social commentary had the greatest bite to it. His portrait of a policeman "On Duty During Strike" in Morgantown, West Virginia, is a product of that sensibility. The officer's prominently displayed pistol suggests that those in power in Morgantown use the force of arms to maintain their positions when threatened with a strike, and the deputy's ample girth hints that they control the officer's loyalty primarily by making sure he is well fed.

These indictments of American class structure and racism were often in close correspondence with Communist analyses of the United States. Given the documentary photographers' left-of-center political orientation, and with the Communist Party's increased activity during the decade (especially its courtship of fellow travelers during the Popular Front period of the later 1930s), the two groups naturally crossed paths throughout the Depression. Photographs could provide the Communists with potent ammunition against capitalism, and the Party could offer photographers an ideological rigor that they frequently lacked. As good observers, the photographers certainly took note of Communist activities. When working in the upper Midwest, Lee followed with considerable attention the rifts between Stalinists and Trotskyites in the Minneapolis-area farm movement. Shahn was a member of an organization called the Artists' Union, and he willingly worked alongside other members whom he knew to be Communists. Lange was openly recruited to attend Party-sponsored functions in San Francisco, and she believed that those invitations came from folks who had only the best intentions. When she looked back upon the Depression, she thought that joining with the Communists might well have been "the right thing to do in those days." After all, the times were troubled, the Communists had plans for attending to those troubles, and there was "very much to be said for participating in groups of people who were ready to take action."

Occasionally they went so far as to join Party-sponsored organizations such as the Photo League. Deriving its inspiration from Russian film makers, and at its inception a cultural wing of the Workers' International Relief, the Photo League published its photographs in the *New Masses* and punctuated its meetings with entertainment by Pete Seeger and Woody Guthrie. Abbott, Lange, Rothstein, Elisofan, Delano, and Shahn were League members, and Bourke-White one of its lecturers. Yet despite its early political preoccupations, by the time Lange and the others joined the League, its discussions tended to center more upon photographic technique than upon ideology. Willing to work with Party members, documentary photographers charted their own courses if the Communists became too insistent. Collier, for example, realized that left-wing messages could be seen in his photographs, but insisted that he had composed his pictures independent of "all this horsey nonsense about Marxist principles." Shahn worked alongside Communists in the Artists Union, yet he quickly resigned from its editorial board when the Communists suggested that he accept Party direction of his work. Lange also kept her distance from the Party, but for more personal reasons. Although she was invited to Communist functions, she chose to stay home in deference to her conservative first husband, Maynard Dixon, who "was a Californian to the extent that he believed in lynch laws," and objected to any participation in Party affairs. If such sentiments led Lange and Shahn to be independent of the Party, geography doubtlessly accounted for some of their colleagues' independence. Lange worked out of San Francisco and Shahn out of New York, cities where the Communists were strong. But the other documentary photographers came from places that were not centers of thirties radicalism and so felt less strongly the pull of the Party's influence.[39]

Reformers but hardly revolutionaries, documentary photographers were interested in evoking sympathy or rendering social criticism. Walker Evans shared most documentary impulses with these other photographers, but he possessed few of their reformist inclinations. A Sorbonne-trained product of Phillips Academy and Williams College, Evans took issue more with America's Babbittry than its social structure; he began his career certain that he "was damn well going to be an artist and . . . wasn't going to be a business man." The documentary photographer most concerned with esthetic issues of composition and light, he portrayed the same sort of people the other photographers did. But Evans approached his subjects more in an appreciation of the order they managed to bring to their lives, than in any effort to help them better their lives. Where the others concentrated on people, Evans was more inclined to photograph people's possessions (Figure 17) and more often made pictures of things than of humans. When he did make pictures of people, he often allowed them to arrange and preen themselves before he snapped his shutter, and the resulting stiffly posed compositions more closely resemble traditional family portraits than do the sympathy-evoking photos Lange and the others produced. Evans believed his work was art, and "since art is really useless," it could serve no social purpose. He shared this belief with writer James Agee, and accompanied Agee on his 1936 trip to Alabama. Evans's purpose was not to collect evidence for social reform, but instead to satisfy his own quite personal curiosity about how southern tenant farmers were surviving the Depression. Throughout the thirties Evans saw his mission as more esthetic than political, and he seldom became excited over those distressed conditions that so aroused other documentary photographers. When, for example, Evans was faced with all the photographic material thrown up in a catastrophic flood, a flood that inspired some of Russell Lee's work, Evans scarcely responded. His traveling companion, the assistant chief of RA-FSA's photo section, had to prod Evans to go out and photograph and "had a job annoying Walker out of his lassitude."[40]

If Evans was ambivalent about social criticism, there were others within the photography world who outright rejected it. The Group f/64 photographers saw the political possibilities within documentary photography, and they were therefore inclined to dismiss documentary work. Ansel Adams, like Edward Weston (Figure 9), was an active cameraman in the 1930s and a member of Group f/64. Adams shared little of the documentarians' interest in portraying suffering or in criticizing social evils. In place of their emphasis on the everyday and the human, Adams stressed the beauty of nature, producing magnificent prints of settings such as

Yosemite's towering mountains. He understood the Depression's devastation upon the land and felt compelled to "grant that the times are portentous." But when it came to photographing May Day celebrations, evictions, underpaid workers, or other documentary fare, Adams exclaimed, "I'll be damned if I see the real *rightness* of being *expected* to mix political economy with emotion *for a purpose.*" He called himself a purist and admitted that the stance made him appear cold in contrast to the warmth of the documentary photographers.[41] Weston agreed and assured Adams that "there is just as much 'social significance in a rock' as in 'a line of unemployed.'" Ironically, from among all the documentary photographers, Adams chose to rail against Walker Evans, the one closest to his own sympathies. Writing to Weston, Adams complained that Evans's picture book, *American Photographs* (1936), was left-wing, gave him a hernia, and had its few beautiful photographs "lost in the shuffle of social significance."[42]

Arranging the Depression's Appearance

nsel Adams thought that documentary photographers were mostly interested in making dismal pictures to improve Americans' welfare. Certainly the melioristic impulse was a key element in their photography, but their eloquence with dejected faces and worn-out hills kept Adams and others from seeing another of their motives.[43] Documentary photographers wanted to comprehend Depression America as well as improve it, to exercise a personal as well as a political control over their environment. To accomplish this, documentary photographers believed, they must confront the Depression; only by grappling with its grim features could they retain personal equilibrium in a topsy-turvy world.

San Francisco had been a terribly muddled place for Lange, and to calm her own confusion, she abandoned studio photography and ventured into the streets. Lange pursued this type of work for the rest of her career, and to remind herself of her commitment, she kept on her door Francis Bacon's admonition that "the contemplation of things as they are . . . is in itself a nobler thing than a whole harvest of invention." Other photographers echoed Lange's concern for things as they are, and they came to share Bourke-White's abiding concern with the Depression's "reality."

The crisis had brought a halt to the industrial scenes that fascinated Bourke-White, and in her drive "to get close to the realities of life," she first photographed the Dust Bowl and then the impoverished South. Likewise, Theo Jung rejected romantic pictorialism such as F. Holland Day's portrait of Christ (Figure 8), for it seemed to him that such photography was "just a series of clichés." Jung's preference was for what he called "real today" things and people, and he set about photographing the poverty and unemployment that seemed the most "real" aspects of the moment. Such pictures seemed able to meet an important need in Depression America. Edwin Locke, assistant chief of the Historical Section, believed that documentary photography was "part of the sovereign world of fact," and therefore perfectly suited to the country's immediate need for "hardheaded" thinking. Lange preferred this hardheadedness throughout her career, and in later years, she continued to demand that photographers "deal with what *is*" and insisted that they "retire from what *might be*."[44]

Berenice Abbott most fully articulated this desire to confront and understand the contemporary world. Such comprehension was a psychological necessity for Abbott, and she insisted that "daily experience must be translated into order and meaning." Her Depression photography was a decade-long effort to execute such a personal translation. This was no easy task, though, for it seemed that "the bizarre happenings of everyday existence" rolled by with such rapidity and novelty during the 1930s that each instant had about it an air of "fantastic unfamiliarity." Photography, with its split-second images, was ideally suited for arresting those moments, far superior to the older medium of painting; while the painter required considerable familiarity with his subject, the photographer needed only a camera to stalk even the most unfamiliar subject and "relentlessly capture" it. Abbott knew a great deal more about the history of photography than did most of the other documentary photographers, and one predecessor whom she singled out for special praise was Mathew Brady. With his pictures of Civil War battlefields, Brady seemed praiseworthy because he had met the distressing challenge of *his* day and dealt with its gore photographically: "It was reality he photographed, the objective world, a world which in this case happened to be a world of war and death."[45] Abbott's major project, which she worked on throughout the 1930s, was to document New York City in its Depression metamorphoses. Like Brady's fields of corpses, the crisis-ridden city seemed to Abbott a "dreadful reality," one she must photograph so as to extract for herself a sense of "order and meaning."[46]

Abbott wanted to "capture" the actual world "relentlessly," and the other documentary photographers likewise stalked "reality." They employed an array of techniques for catching it, and their compositions were the carefully crafted cages in which they retained and exhibited those aspects of the thirties that seemed most "real" to them. Eventually they subdued their prey, wrestling with the decade's "reality" in two main ways. Sometimes they staged the scenes before their cameras, and at other times they tried to sneak up on their subjects.

Though there is nothing more inherently "real" in a candid photograph than in one where the subject knows of the camera's presence, the candid shot had considerable appeal for some documentary photographers in their quest for "reality." These aficionados of spontaneity shared Abbott's belief that "before we can photograph people as they truly are, we must be able to snap them off guard."[47] To do just that, Shahn, Jung, and even Evans employed a device known as the right-angle viewfinder. This attachment allows the photographer to stand at right angles to his subject, giving the impression that he is facing away from the subject and making a picture of something else. In Shahn's Circleville, Ohio, street scene (Figure 18), the window reflection clearly shows Shahn making such a picture while his subjects look on with interest and even amusement, but obviously without any self-conscious regard for their own appearances. Had these men known Shahn was making *their* picture, it is likely that they would have assumed different poses, postures that to Shahn seemed less "real" than the ones he captured here. On one occasion, a Kentucky sheriff hauled Shahn into court for making pictures in a recently robbed post office. Shahn showed the judge his credentials, and while the justice was lecturing him on taking photos in security-sensitive places, Shahn succumbed to the lure of the candid and photographed the judge through the special viewfinder. Walker Evans was similarly surreptitious in his series on anonymous subway riders. In 1938 and again in 1941, he rode for hundreds of hours with the lens of a small camera peering out from between the buttons of his overcoat, making pictures of the riders who happened to sit across the aisle from him. These photographs are a major departure from the main body of Evans's oeuvre, and so bespeak the intense appeal of candid photography during the thirties. Evans normally made his pictures with great care and attention to detail, but in these subway portraits, he left to chance such essential elements as focus, lighting, and even subject.[48]

All candid pictures violate the subject's privacy to some degree, and Bourke-White conducted the most startling invasion of privacy. To capture the frenzied climax of a Holiness Church service in the South, she and Caldwell circumvented the church's locked doors by jumping through its open windows. The congregation wanted no pictures made of its services. But Bourke-White took advantage of the worshipers' preoccupying ecstasy and made picture after picture as Caldwell kept her supplied with fresh flashbulbs from the stock in his pockets. When the congregation's excitement began to subside, and it appeared that the group's attention would turn upon the two intruders, Bourke-White and Caldwell sensed that they would not be welcome. They hopped back through the same windows and hurriedly left town.[49]

Despite the differences in their styles, Bourke-White and Shahn both used some form of the candid approach in their pursuit of "reality." But for all their wiles, these candid photographers usually accepted the scene as they found it. Other photographers, such as Arthur Rothstein, did not rely upon the capriciousness of circumstance to provide the scenes they wished to photograph. Believing it was the photographer's eye that determined what was "real," they thought it not only permissible for, but almost incumbent upon, him to sift through the infinite possibilities and manipulate the setting to achieve the particular image he desired. Lange felt that a good documentary photograph should overcome the encumbrances of what she called "local detail" so that it most clearly presented the photographer's message. Applying her principle, she retouched "Migrant Mother" (Figure 4), removing from the negative a bit of local detail, the migrant mother's thumb, that had strayed into the foreground and detracted from Lange's composition. That thumb may have been part of the literal view the camera had seen, but it only cluttered the vision that was in her mind's eye, and she thought it legitimate to remove the thumb. In like manner, Jack Delano argued that a documentary photograph should *not* be "nature in the raw"; the photographer must refine his composition when making a picture, eliminating all extraneous images so that the final product does not merely reflect but is "an expression of the essence" of the photographer's vision. In his game with John Collier, John Vachon had similarly defined a "good photograph" as "a false or exaggerated composition" of what the picture-maker deemed to be "a true or

typical situation." Russell Lee agreed with these principles. After reading
The Grapes of Wrath, Lee decided that Steinbeck had described some
pretty typical situations and left for Oklahoma "to pick up . . . the shots
that are so graphically told." Those scenes were not quite as typical as Lee
thought, however, for it took him over a month of searching before he
finally found an Oklahoma family that resembled Steinbeck's characters.
Throughout his search, Lee was sustained by the belief that he should
photograph Oklahoma not as it was, but as he and Steinbeck thought it
should be.[50]

To achieve compositions like Vachon's "good photograph," the photographers frequently posed their subjects. Eliot Elisofan, for example,
campaigned for more city playgrounds and wanted a picture of young boys
who, without other recreational options, resorted to hitching rides on the
backs of streetcars. He had often witnessed these scenes, but each time
he saw some boys riding, he was without his camera, and when he did
have it, there were never any boys around. Elisofan finally offered to pay
two youngsters to pose as though they were hitching rides, and the boys
accepted after Elisofan promised that their pictures would not appear in
the papers where their parents might see them poised dangerously on
some streetcar. Vachon was likewise willing to stage photographs for a
story on the life of a corn farmer and wrote from the field that he had
taken "some faked shots of getting the planter ready and planting with
horses." Jack Delano posed his subjects with even more care than did
Elisofan or Vachon. One of Delano's favorites from among his Depression
photographs was "Interior of Negro Rural Home" (1941; Figure 19),
which he believed was "as documentary and as direct as everything else
we were doing."[51] All of the people in this picture are carefully placed,
and the entire scene painstakingly framed. The girl stands in the doorway
of a long hall, while her grandfather is seated in the middle distance, and
what appear to be her mother and grandmother are in the background.
Through this use of space and generations, Delano managed to convey a
sense of time that is very difficult to achieve in still photographs: from
background to foreground, this picture sweeps from the past into the
present and then looks out upon the future. There is a note of protest
here, too, for in Delano's "reality," the girl's ancestors have lived for generations in the poverty of that weathered Georgia farmhouse. Beyond this
the photograph becomes more ambiguous, however, for the girl's con-

tinued stare out of the doorway may suggest that she sees a brighter to-morrow beyond the house, or it may say that she is looking towards a future that is no better than the present.

Delano respected Walker Evans's strict compositions, and "Interior of Negro Rural Home" was a conscious imitation of Evans's work. Like Delano, Evans manipulated his subjects and arranged scenes to fit both his artistic tastes and interpretive intent. In a 1935 interior of a West Virginia miner's home, for example, Evans moved several pieces of furniture to achieve a good composition. The next year in Vicksburg, Mississippi, he carefully posed men outside a barber shop in order to suggest messages about the social role of sidewalk interchange in a Southern town. There were several of these Vicksburg photos, and when examined indi-vidually—as Evans intended—each seems straightforward and unar-ranged. But when viewed together, the Vicksburg pictures reveal Evans's careful construction of his images, and the high degree to which his sub-jects cooperated with him in achieving those images. This passion for de-sign and order emerges even more clearly in his interior photographs. When Evans went with James Agee to rural Alabama in the summer of 1936, he photographed inside tenant farmers' houses and produced a number of cool, crisp pictures such as Figure 17, "Washroom and Kitchen of a Cabin." These tenant cabins fascinated Agee, too, and Agee made detailed inventories of their contents, word pictures that correspond in large part to Evans's photographs. But when Evans's images depart from Agee's words, we can see how willingly Evans arranged things in order to achieve the images he wanted. To get a satisfactory set of visual lines, he removed a union suit from its nail in one room and, in other rooms, moved furniture for more pleasing arrangements. He was similarly active in the kitchen of Figure 17. This room was normally cluttered and not all that clean; Agee noted that the table, which smelled of mold, was usually covered with utensils and condiments. Yet of all the objects Agee listed, only one remains on the table, a lamp that hints of light and order rather than the confusion Agee mentioned. Apparently Evans also added the butter churn to the room, an object that works nicely to keep the eye moving from the washbasin in the foreground, to the lamp in the middle distance, and on to the background. Thus, although "Washroom and Kitchen of a Cabin" initially seems a casual and straightforward picture, it is actually a carefully contrived composition.[52]

Of the documentary photographers who staged their photographs, Arthur Rothstein was the most articulate apologist for the practice. Rothstein had come to documentary photography more by chance than design. As an undergraduate at Columbia, he had been an active member of the campus camera club, where he met Abbott and Bourke-White. Rothstein's plan was to go on to medical school, but when the Depression ruled that out, he accepted a job that Roy Stryker, his former teacher, offered him in the Historical Section.[53] Rothstein's phrase for staging pictures was "direction in photography," and the direction he brought to his photographs eventually earned him a good deal of criticism. Writing in 1942, Rothstein argued that as long as "the results are a faithful reproduction of what the photographer believes he sees, whatever takes place in the making of the picture is justified." "Reality" was thus synonymous with the photographer's vision, and the photographer could justifiably control the subjects and arrange the scene so that they corresponded to his conception. When Rothstein visited Arkansas in 1938, he wanted to photograph impoverished rural people, and the anxiety that he assumed would accompany their poverty. But each time he approached people with his camera, they did not look fearful; instead they smiled and posed stiffly. To overcome this obstacle in his pursuit of "reality," Rothstein enlisted an assistant to engage the subjects in conversation. He retreated into the background, lurked there until the subjects expressed fear or concern during the conversation, and then snapped their pictures. By using this trick, Rothstein got the results he wanted in his photograph of an Arkansas sharecropper's anxious wife (Figure 20).[54] Here Rothstein selected images that were standard ones for the Depression's social artists and writers. As supposedly the "weakest" members of society, women and children became virtual icons, for they served as convenient representatives of the many defenseless innocents who had fallen victim to the Depression. There was an additional, more subtle, dimension, too. Children could do double duty as both victims *and* as symbols of the future, while pregnant women, especially if distressed-looking, were a bonanza of symbols—vulnerable, beleaguered, and yet the literal bearers of the future. In "Sharecropper's Wife and Child," Rothstein managed a potpourri of images: poverty, childhood, pregnancy, and even anxiety.

Rothstein advocated a remarkably active photographer's role and passed along examples of good technique. In one example, a photographer named Peter Sekear had been working on a project in which he wished to show that city children lacked adequate playground space. Sekear found just the scene he wanted, a group of boys fighting in a gutter in Youngstown, Ohio. When the boys saw him, though, they lost interest in their fight and came over to examine him and his equipment. To re-create the scene, Sekear pulled some change from his pocket, threw the coins into the gutter and contentedly snapped away as the boys went back to squabbling. Rothstein's suggestion was remarkable: in pursuit of a scene corresponding to his own vision, the photographer could legit-imately provoke a fight. Another of Rothstein's examples came from his own work. His picture "Farmer and Sons Walking in the Face of a Dust Storm" (1936; Figure 21) is one of the more famous Depression pho-tographs, perhaps the single image most frequently associated with the words "Dust Bowl." Rothstein had hoped to show the efforts Americans exerted as they struggled against the drought, and he eventually located a suitable locale for his photograph, parched Cimarron County in the Oklahoma panhandle—the very heart of the Dust Bowl. Rothstein se-lected a set of willing subjects and then photographed them at just the right place on their well-drifted farm. The photo implies that these three Oklahomans are seeking shelter in their *house.* But Rothstein had chosen to photograph them as they walked toward their *shed,* a building that was more evocative of dust and poverty than were other buildings on the farm. If the people had not assumed just these stances, Rothstein indicated that it would have been appropriate to pose them in the desired attitudes. To give the impression that these people were struggling, it would have been acceptable to ask the little boy to drop back and put his hand over his eyes, and the farmer could have been asked to lean forward as he walked.[55]

An aura somewhat akin to biblical literalism surrounds still pho-tographs, and people are frequently upset when they discover the pho-tographer has been this active in composing a scene. Rothstein felt the brunt of such hostility after he had taken some pictures in North Dakota. Near Fargo he found a parched alkali flat complete with a cow skull—just the scene, he thought, to convey his vision of a severe drought. Rothstein took five different photos, some with the skull on sun-cracked soil, and others after he moved it to a grassy rise. He quietly filed the photos with FSA and, for a while, nothing came of them. They surfaced, however, when President Roosevelt came to North Dakota to investigate drought conditions and announce the measures his Democratic administration would take to help ease the dry spell's impact. A local Republican booster and newspaper editor took exception to both FDR's programs and the insinuation that his state was a desert. His paper carried Rothstein's pictures, proclaimed them fakes, and implied that the government photographer had used the skull as a prop that he lugged around the country with him. The story made good copy and a nationwide furor developed, for most people viewed photographs with more literal expectations of "reality" than Rothstein had.[56]

Thus documentary photographers were hardly passive image makers. With an impressive kit bag of techniques, Rothstein and the others could stage their subjects, catch them in candid moments, and provoke their emotions. The goal was to keep luck and accident to a minimum in the making of any given photograph. In at least one important way, however, chance did play a large role in their work. During most of the thirties, the only available film was black-and-white stock. But as luck would have it, this nicely fit the photographers' needs. Black-and-white photographs are often stark, and manage to convey quite nicely the somber, even gloomy, atmosphere that documentary photographers needed. Furthermore, black-and-white photography is more capable of abstraction than is color photography, for it is farther removed from the objective world's complex variety of hues. For the bulk of their thirties work, documentary photographers were fortunate enough to have a palette restricted to white, black, and shades of gray. Toward the decade's end they made a few experimental color pictures that are much weaker than their earlier works. Though depicting virtually the same people and places, the color pictures are neither glum nor heroic, but seem instead merely ordinary and familiar.[57]

These women and men came to documentary photography in hopes of confronting the pressing problems of the 1930s. Employing techniques such as Shahn's candid approach or Rothstein's staging, they grappled with the vistas they encountered and wrestled them into shapes according to their own visions. Not too surprisingly, the images they produced tended to correspond with their reformist notions; Delano's Georgia cabin complained that black families endured poor housing, and Rothstein's dusty pictures appealed for drought relief. The documentary photographers set out to find "reality," and a good portion of the "reality" that they captured managed to validate their own political positions.

Preservationists with Cameras

empus fugit. To documentary photographers this seemed one undeniable lesson in the Depression's "reality." All about them were things that had once appeared quite enduring, like Bourke-White's smoke-belching factories, but which now proved to be quite ephemeral. The flow of events appeared to have quickened during the economic crisis, sweeping before it a host of institutions and customs as one catastrophe followed close upon another. The past seemed to be receding at a constantly accelerating rate, and for all its gravity, the present acquired an ever more transitory appearance. This perception of a quickening pace of change was another component of the decade's documentary photography. Not only did photographers wish to comprehend the Depression and protest its hardships, they also wanted to preserve and record those aspects of life that appeared to be passing with it. They made pictures of those things they hoped would pass and those they hoped might endure, remembrances of both the decade's immediate pains and its inherited legacies. Documentary photographers thus had a preservationist impulse among their picture-taking motives, a desire to save for the future some of the past's fading vestiges and the present's fleeting moments.

By its nature the still photograph is a recording document. In that instant when the photographer opens his shutter, a brief reflection of the everchanging world becomes imprinted on a light-sensitive surface. But the making of a photograph is not an attempt to stop the flow of time or to achieve some dormant state in which all action ceases. The very act of preserving things, be they peaches or perspectives, contains an inherent admission of time's inexorable flow. Preserving merely lessens the effects of time's passage so that an aspect of the past remains readily at hand for future use or contemplation. The ubiquitous American photograph of festive occasions like weddings or vacations does not make those events last forever, nor is it intended to do so. It simply helps one remember the event.

When documentary photographers of the 1930s recorded aspects of the day and glimmers of the past, they were not trying to stop the process of change nor to return to the past. Instead, they wanted to insure that both past and present would remain familiar. Among the photographers, Berenice Abbott pursued this work with the greatest intensity. She described her photographs of New York's architecture and street scenes as the products of a "fantastic passion," a fervor she inherited from Eugene Atget. Existing only on milk, bread, and sugar, Atget had lived in extreme poverty to satisfy his own obsession to photograph Paris. But, as Abbott told his story, Atget's pictures were worth any amount of hardship, for they showed later generations aspects of the city that no longer existed. Converted to his cause, Abbott returned from Paris to become the Atget of New York and gave herself over to "capturing the vanishing instant." The revealing title of her collection was *Changing New York* (1939), and while she presented photographs of things slated for replacement, such as old buildings or the city's pushcart vendors, her pictures and the accompanying text accepted their passing without remorse. Abbott's goal was to achieve a continuity between the past and future, not to halt or lament the vanishing of any particular instant. This was important business, and she stressed that her photos required all the detail and precision that documentary methods allowed, for the city "must be photographed as through a microscope if photographs of the *now* are to have any value for the future."58

Others shared Abbott's interest in preservation, if not quite her passionate commitment to it. Russell Lee felt it was incumbent upon photographers to capture the present for future generations. When traveling in the Plains during the summer of 1937, Lee discovered that since 1876 the Northern Pacific Railroad had kept a photographer in the region and had provided him with an exceptionally well-equipped photographic rail car. Although the photographer had been technically competent, Lee complained that he had "missed most of the really vital shots." The company cameraman made countless negatives of ceremonies, but failed to record those passing vistas that seemed so important to documentary photographers: "There wasn't a single picture, for example, of the original prairie grass." Likewise, Walker Evans saw a part of his quest as the recording of things that he said were "passing out of history." With this phrase, Evans demonstrated a subtle understanding of the matter; the unregistered idea or event *is* lost—though part of the past, unless it is recorded in some way, it will pass out of that recollection of the past that we call history. Evans stressed that his interest in the past was not a mawkish one. As he perceived it, "to be nostalgic is to be sentimental," and his intention was to be objective and dry-eyed. He hoped his work would resemble Marcel Proust's *Remembrance of Things Past;* and while it might just be possible to "read Proust as 'nostalgic' . . . that's not what Proust had in mind at all." Similarly, John Vachon argued that the right-minded photographer would be a preservationist and strive "to freeze instantly the reality before him" so that others could later experience it. Lee shared this belief. Since it was not a common sight in the 1930s to see someone wandering about taking pictures, Lee habitually explained to bystanders that he was making a history of the present.[59] Like people who make time capsules, these photographers had the urge to squirrel away some aspect of the present for safekeeping.

Not all of them viewed the demise of the past with equanimity, however. Lange's tractored-out farm (Figure 13) goes beyond depicting the passage of small farms on the plains and laments the coming of mechanization. John Collier likewise complained that the industrialization of a New England town was more than the passing of a formerly close-knit community, it was an "American Tragedy." Of all the photographers, Lange achieved the best integration of complaint, pathos, and preservation in her work. In Texas, she found an elderly black man and captioned his portrait "Born a Slave" (1936). In making this picture, she did more than give subsequent generations a remembrance of slavery. She also employed the man's plaintive expression and obvious poverty in an effort to get her white contemporaries to redress the sins of their ancestors by coming to the man's aid. Her most vivid combination of protest and preservation, though, is a picture of an oxcart traveling in front of a Ford dealership (Figure 22). In this one scene she managed to show a passing form of transportation and its replacement, while simultaneously complaining about the economic inequalities of a land where one could find such a rickety cart alongside a sign touting the glories of a V-8. Advancing technology sometimes "raises standards of living," but it also "creates unemployment," and it is up to documentary photography, Lange proclaimed, to capture "the evidence of these trends—the simultaneous existence of past, present, and portent of the future." Like Lange, Robert Disraeli believed that the thirties were a time of struggle for racial and economic justice, but while Lange still tried to recruit people for the struggle, Disraeli believed the fight was mostly won. To him, the battle had been courageous and gallant, and he wanted to make sure that his descendants appreciated all its glory. Putting aside what little humility he might have possessed, Disraeli declared that documentary photographs would give future Americans the opportunity to worship his own generation. He was sure that succeeding ages would study documentary photographs and then exclaim "those are the faces of our ancestors who overcame their difficulties with heroic determination and forced themselves upward into the sun and into the golden air."[60]

By the late thirties and early forties, the photographers' urge to record had grown beyond a desire to preserve the most important circumstances of the day. Many came to feel that *every* aspect of American life was a fit subject for their cameras. Elisofan put it most bluntly when he urged his fellow photographers "to go out and record life." Shahn and Lee both came to believe that the Historical Section should not merely concentrate on the country's most destitute people and argued that their pictures should also portray what Lee called "the daily lives of the common people," the circumstances of clerks or factory hands who had managed to avoid unemployment. Likewise, when Post Wolcott began working for the section in 1938, one of her first major objectives was to photograph the unimpoverished side of American life. This phase of the preservationist impulse, as Edwin Locke perceptively labeled it, was an effort to compile a sort of "photographic Doomsday book." Just as the original Doomsday Book aimed to survey all of medieval England, so the documentary photographers sought to make a visual catalog of thirties America.[61]

John Collier came to think of himself as an anthropologist with a camera, echoing a broader Depression fascination with anthropology that emerged in the works of people like Stuart Chase and Ruth Benedict. Documentary photographers like Collier set out to capture Americans' traditions and communities, not in order to praise or glorify them as a nationalist might, but to classify and categorize them as a social scientist would. Collier himself concentrated on the traditions of ethnic groups within the United States, studying Amish farmers in Pennsylvania, Portuguese fishermen in Rhode Island, and Acadian farmers in Maine. Russell Lee was interested in the levels of violence in mining communities and planned to visit a particular town on a payday that promised "fights, drunks in the gutters and everything else you might associate with a mining town." For his part, Jack Delano believed that an important part of his task was recording indigenous North American traditions, and when he found himself in Ledyard, Connecticut, on Thanksgiving Day of 1940, he set about photographing a local family's ritual feast.[62] Typical of the anthropological photographs was Post Wolcott's picture of the rail depot in

Newport, Tennessee (Figure 23). It documented a custom one could find repeated in innumerable small communities across the country—as was their habit, the townsmen gathered at the station to exchange gossip and to wait, often with no particular reason, for the train's arrival. Rather than anything particularly newsworthy, the photo records a mundane scene, and the townspeople strike appropriately nonchalant poses: some sit on car bumpers, others lean on buildings or poles, and still others have their hands in their pockets.

In making their chronicles of the thirties, the photographers not only could control subsequent images of the decade, they also could gain a sense of control over time. Rather than lying prone before the flow of time, the photographer approaches the present with a selective vision, framing and arranging his subject, all the while choosing from the many possible points of view just which aspect will represent the moment. Events do not merely transpire for the photographer, they are a passing parade from which he selects according to his own vision, bringing an image of the present into conformity with *his* notion of the way things are. By practicing his trade, the photographer is no longer so embroiled in the transactions of the present, but instead stands sufficiently removed from the action to maintain his focus. In this way, bringing Abbott's "order and meaning" to experience went beyond just making spatial arrangements of the sort Rothstein or Delano produced. It also entailed the location of a comprehensible pattern within the flow of time.

Measuring Americans' Strength

An abiding curiosity was a final facet to documentary photography. Besides striving to ease suffering, capture "reality," and preserve the past or present, by the later thirties photographers also wanted to know how Americans were weathering the Depression. Jack Delano neatly summarized this aspect of documentary photography when he recollected that he and his compatriots were "feeling the pulse of the nation through its people."[63] Whereas a photographer like Edward Weston had a very low estimate of the average American, the documentary diagnosticians felt quite differently. As they set out to take the nation's pulse by photographing its citizens, they began with the assumption that the common person was a dignified creature. Delano thought that the photographers "all had a respect for human beings" and believed they strove to say "something decent about the dignity of mankind" with their pictures. Similarly, when Russell Lee photographed people, he hoped to convey the image of dignified individuals who had fallen on hard times. Furthermore, a guiding principle for Historical Section photographers was that they should go beyond the superficial aspects of poverty to delve into a subject's character, and that they should never give a ridiculing image of anyone.[64]

Given this initial orientation, it is not surprising that documentary photographers found the nation's pulse quite strong, and its people warm and courageous. Time after time, they produced pictures of people who appeared to be surviving their difficulties in good form, folks who maintained hopeful outlooks despite their circumstances. Yet there was always a tension between the photographers' vision of a stalwart America and their crusading impulse. They were both vexed and relieved to find so many confident faces. Although their discoveries settled many personal uncertainties about the Depression and suggested there was some stability amid its confusion, portraits of people determined and able to make it on their own were hardly good cases for social welfare. Lange better than any of the others managed to achieve a delicate balance between strength and pathos in an individual photograph, which she rendered in pictures like her portrait of the migrant family from Oklahoma (Figure 5). Although the young mother's determination dominates the picture, Lange also made a play for the viewer's sentiments through the less assured child and the family's decidedly impoverished housekeeping. Other documentary photographers, however, were not nearly so successful in integrating their messages and tended to produce distinct sets of images—some that were sympathy-evoking social criticisms, and others that portrayed strong, confident people.

Marion Post Wolcott held that the successful photographer must be able "to see, to sense the essence or guts of a person." Others agreed that a photographer could peer into a person's soul, and they employed their cameras as spiritual metal detectors, devices not for finding copper or iron, but for testing the mettle of the people they photographed. And when they used their cameras in this way, they often found strong, resilient stuff. Post Wolcott discovered that although the Depression had dealt Americans some severe blows, they were not as beaten down or apathetic as she had expected they would be. When she went to Memphis she discovered that there people still had the spirit to jitterbug, and she photographed them dancing to jukebox music. For his part, Jack Delano managed to locate some of the happiest of people working at some of the most tiresome of tasks. Tobacco harvesting is a long and tedious job, but the Connecticut harvesters whom he portrayed were positively jovial even in the middle of their tobacco shed. When Delano went to Georgia, he claimed that the South was "the most tortured, primitive, poverty stricken (economically and socially) wasted area" he had ever seen. But despite those handicaps, he discovered such great potential in the region's people that he believed "the South *must* come out of it even tho it has so many strikes against it." He located just the person to convey this quality, a young woman (Figure 24), who, despite the drudgery of her cotton chopping, can radiate serenity and confidence. Delano here executed an outstanding character study, arranging his composition so that the light gently washes the woman's face and capturing in her hands a pose that suggests her casual command of, rather than servile surrender to, her hoe. Her hat frames her face nicely, and her head, slightly cocked to one side, is more evocative of repose than fatigue. Such people emerged virtually everywhere the photographer looked. Russell Lee's partner during many of his expeditions was Jean Lee, and she reported that they discovered "a tremendous pride and a tremendous courage" among Americans wherever they went. The Lees saw many people "along the ditch-banks, and they didn't have anything." But seldom was there "a person who really felt whipped."[65] Indeed, the migrant workers whom Russell photographed were far from defeated. Though camped along Oklahoma ditch-banks (Figure 25), they still have the spunk to sing and play the guitar. If it were not for Lee's caption, one might easily conclude that this man is on a picnic, enjoying the sunshine and wearing his hat at a jaunty angle.

There were other such people in Klamath County, Oregon. There Lange found a former Nebraska farmer who had been forced to become a migrant farm laborer. Yet even these circumstances failed to dishearten this amazing man or his wife (Figure 26). They live as migrants, but their kitchen utensils are neither stained nor dented. The woman is fashionably dressed, wears jewelry, and perhaps even uses lipstick. The man looks more like a smug Clark Gable than someone who has lost his livelihood, and he carries his dapper pipe with obvious self-confidence. He also seems confident of the nation's course, for he has enrolled in the new

Social Security program and on his arm proudly displays a tattoo of his account number. (Of course these were the days before Americans knew much about the tattoo serial numbers of the Nazi concentration camps, or that Social Security numbers could help strip away individual identity in depersonalized bureaucracies.) Even Walker Evans managed to convey the feeling that Americans had not surrendered to the Depression. Though his pictures were of things, rather than people, they were often human artifacts that could convey messages about people. His washroom and kitchen (Figure 17), for example, show a family's obvious poverty, but the picture also suggests that they have remained neat despite their condition; in placing the washbasin and towel in the foreground of the photograph, Evans showed that although these people are poor, they are still proud enough to stay clean. In others of his pictures, Evans's Americans maintain a buoyant idiosyncrasy, a blithesome incongruity that they display in signs and store fronts such as those of a South Carolina fruit stand which also served as a fish company, art school, stenographer's office, and historical site (Figure 27). Certainly no "mere" Depression could disturb the likes of these people, and Evans carefully framed his picture to wring every possible drop of character from the setting.

Margaret Bourke-White was the sole exception to this general depiction of people as cheerful, dignified combatants against the Depression. She thought that the Dust Bowl had numbed and bewildered Americans, paralyzing them with fear, and she portrayed Southern tenant farmers who were equally full of despair (Figure 7). Unlike other documentary photographers, Bourke-White did not approach her subjects with the assumption that they were noble, and though her people were victims of circumstance, she did not celebrate their ways of coping with their plights. Instead, she pitied the cultural forms their efforts took. When traveling in the South, for example, she saw the enthusiasm of black Christianity as the feeble expression of a people who had no other means of fulfilling themselves. She enjoyed the excitement of black worship well enough, though, for it reminded her of "some tribal ritual." But a similar frenzy in a white church seemed pitiful, a "shoddy little ceremonial. . . the very antithesis of religion," which only demonstrated that the celebrants were deprived of the movies, books, and other accoutrements that Bourke-White thought any civilized people should possess. [66]

For the other photographers, though, Americans were a dignified lot who possessed a character that helped carry them through the trials of the decade. As the thirties passed and the economic crisis slowly eased, the Depression gradually faded from the center of documentary attention. Photographers made fewer and fewer political pictures, and their character studies began to emphasize not so much Americans' abilities to endure hardship as the quirkiness that Evans had portrayed in the combined art school and fish company. Russell Lee shared that growing fascination, and when he found the village of Pie Town on his New Mexico road map in 1941, he decided that any place with such a unique name was worth visiting. What he found there pleased him to no end, and he devoted an entire photo essay to covering the town. Lee's Pie Towners were free-spirited individualists who wrestled their livelihoods from a hostile environment and occasionally helped each other over the rough spots. Rather than suffering, this sort of crusty determination now seemed more important to photograph. Similarly, as Arthur Rothstein continued in his work, he came to believe that "a kind of individualism existed among people, an inability to conform" that he strove to capture in his compositions.

It was John Vachon, however, who met the most impressive array of audacious nonconformists, and he quickly fell under their spell. He eagerly photographed one old man who lived in the town dump and who displayed "a magnificent sense of humor." Somewhere near Big Hole, Montana, Vachon made friends with a sheep rancher who took him deep into the range country, cooked him a meal in the open, and gave him his first horseback ride. (This fellow was hardly the defeated victim that Nathan Asch's sheep herder had been.) Although Vachon felt the rancher was an "individualist type which has probably outlived its usefulness," Vachon still thought this character was the salt of the earth and an irresistible subject. But it was in North Platte, Nebraska, that Vachon found his greatest infatuation. At a local bar he discovered Mildred Irwin, "a big fat blond woman of 45 or so, with a beautiful red smary paint job" (Figure 28). She had been an Omaha prostitute for nearly twenty years and had then retired to North Platte to play honky-tonk piano in the bar and sing "like Sophie Tucker—only very nasty songs." Completely smitten with this woman, Vachon took picture after picture of her, and "made 3 trips back to the hotel for more flash bulbs." By the late 1930s and early 1940s, documentary photographers were increasingly on the lookout for the likes of Mildred Irwin and searched less and less for subjects like Lange's "Migrant Mother."[67] As conditions slowly improved and the crisis receded, it seemed less important to promote social legislation or confront the "realities" of the decade, and documentary photographers gradually turned to savoring the eccentricities of the people they met.

Variety: The Universal Constant

Despite documentary photography's shift from politics to personalities in the late 1930s, there was a certain continuity within the genre. Throughout the decade, the photographers had an abiding concern with order and steadfastness. They composed their crusading pictures in hopes of relieving some of the pain and confusion they beheld, and ended by celebrating an unconquerable human spirit that seemed to live on regardless of the Depression's suffering and turmoil.

Ben Shahn was especially concerned with constancy and order. As a young painter in the late twenties, Shahn conducted an exhausting search for a style and a topic that suited him. Great examples abounded, but existing approaches and subjects seemed so thoroughly developed that they offered the beginning artist no new frontiers. He wished that the present held out some great sustaining theme and regretted that it was not a period "when something big was going on, like the Crucifixion"—an odd topic for the Jewish Shahn to choose. Continuing to search, he remembered the Sacco and Vanzetti case, and came to feel that *there* lay the sort of topic he could use. In the prejudice and political intolerance surrounding the trial and executions of the two Italian anarchists, Shahn discovered a topic that offered unlimited possibilities, for the atrocity seemed so immense that it could inspire innumerable paintings. He could also help bring some balance to the social structure by using his canvases to lobby for the rights of other oppressed people. Then, as the Depression grew worse and its suffering more widespread, Shahn began to think that he really did live in a time when "something big was going on." The Sacco and Vanzetti case seemed merely one manifestation of the many injustices within American society, and Shahn found that the leftist analyses of New York's young artists and intellectuals provided a powerful interpretation of the Depression's maladies. Adopting what he called their "Union Square" point of view, Shahn began composing paintings that would illustrate capitalism's responsibility for the prevailing pandemonium and induce Americans to bring a Marxist order to their society. Working away at his paintings, Shahn sharpened his techniques by apprenticing himself to Diego Rivera, the radical Mexican muralist.[68]

Shahn's goal was to win the sympathies of his viewers, playing upon their emotions to convert them to his campaign for social justice. He believed that few in his audience would disagree with the general proposition that injustice ought to be eradicated. But by itself, that did not seem enough to get people actively involved in the battle, and in order to secure that involvement, Shahn thought it was necessary to lead people to a sense of *personal* empathy with society's victims. "One has sympathy with a hurt person," Shahn reasoned, "not because he is a generality but precisely because he is not."[69] Documentary photography proved quite able to present all the woe involved in particular cases of injustice, and so Shahn left painting and adopted photography as the best way to win his audiences' sympathies. Like the traveling reporters who wanted case histories rather than statistics, Shahn came to prefer focusing upon individual lives rather than large social forces.

As he traveled for RA-FSA, Shahn felt his earlier political generalizations begin to falter in the presence of the particulars he encountered. When he prepared to visit a mine strike in West Virginia, Shahn decided that the easiest way to break the ice with pickets would be to prove that he, too, was a good union man. Thinking that strikers would naturally smoke union-made cigarettes, Shahn armed himself with a pack of unpopular, but union, cigarettes. At the struck mine, he offered one to a picket. But the striker did not behave as Shahn believed a good union man logically would. With a curt "the hell with that," the picket shunned the offered smoke and pulled out his own non-union, but popular, cigarettes. Shahn found this "shocking" and remembered thinking, "My God! They're not consistent." The more he traveled about the country, the more Shahn encountered other people who acted neither consistently nor in accord with the radical preconceptions he had taken into the field. He had expected to find Depression-besieged Americans uniformly eager for social reform or revolution. Instead, he came across "people of all kinds of belief and temperament, which they maintained with a transcendent indifference to their lot in life."[70] Encountering such diversity and indifference, Shahn slowly changed his sense of artistic purpose. He came to care less about evoking pathos or composing social critiques, and more to believe that "in art it was the individual peculiarities that were interesting." Shahn began photographing the disparate people he encountered and found himself especially drawn to individuals who seemed wonderfully inconsistent within their own lives: a man who painted his barn with scenes of both war and plenty and entitled it "Uncle Sam Did It All"; southern storytellers who could spin marvelous tales and be obnoxiously bigoted; or a man who talked one of his two partners into simultaneously playing the harmonica and guitar so they could have a three-man quartet. As Pie Town attracted Russell Lee, so Shahn became fascinated with unique-sounding places like Pity Me, Tail Holt, and Bird-in-Hand. The crazy quilt of American oddities enthralled Shahn, and though he continued to produce protest images up through the Vietnam era, by the late thirties, the celebration of American eccentricities seemed more important to him than producing social criticism. As Bernarda Shahn, his colleague and wife put it, "Ideologically Ben was at the time considerably more under the influence of Walt Whitman than of Rivera."[71]

Shahn had begun the decade in search of an enduring theme and in hopes of bringing a more just organization to American society. By abandoning political criticism to extol his eccentrics, had he come around to singing the glories of chaos? No—at least not in his own mind. He believed that in these diverse Americans one could discern a certain kind of order. All those constantly various people illustrated nature's supreme constant, *variety*. In Shahn's words, "The universal is that unique thing which affirms the unique character of all things."[72]

Documentary photography arose out of a desire for order and constancy that Shahn and the others shared. Confronted with the terrible chaos of the Depression, people like Dorothea Lange and Margaret Bourke-White found that the demands of the decade rendered their earlier work impotent, and they turned instead to documentary photography as the only satisfactory way to confront the pandemonium about them. Thousands of times they photographed the suffering they beheld, selecting settings and subjects that they hoped would encourage other Americans to support legislation to reduce the Depression's misery and bring stability to its wrecked lives. Steeling themselves, they took up their cameras and set out to capture what Berenice Abbott called the "dreadful reality" of the 1930s, and they approached it with photographic devices and techniques that allowed them to mold the shape of their pictures to fit their own notion of what the era's "reality" was. Not content with simply arranging people or objects to suit their visions, they also sought to bring shape to the flow of time by preserving portions of the past and present that seemed unlikely to survive the ever-quickening tempo of the thirties. These photographers also wished to know how Americans were holding up during the crisis, and what they found proved quite comforting, for their Americans met adversity with unswerving dignity and courage. That indomitable spirit was a constant that one could rely upon, a bedrock beneath the decade's troubled surface, and as the crisis passed, the photographers tended to turn away from their earlier political works and explore the individual peculiarities of the Depression's survivors. At first seeking pattern and order amidst the Depression's chaos, the photographers believed they had found it by the time the crisis faded.

1. Dorothea Lange, "Mrs. Kahn and Child," San Francisco, 1928. (Dorothea Lange Collection, © 1982 Oakland Museum, City of Oakland.)

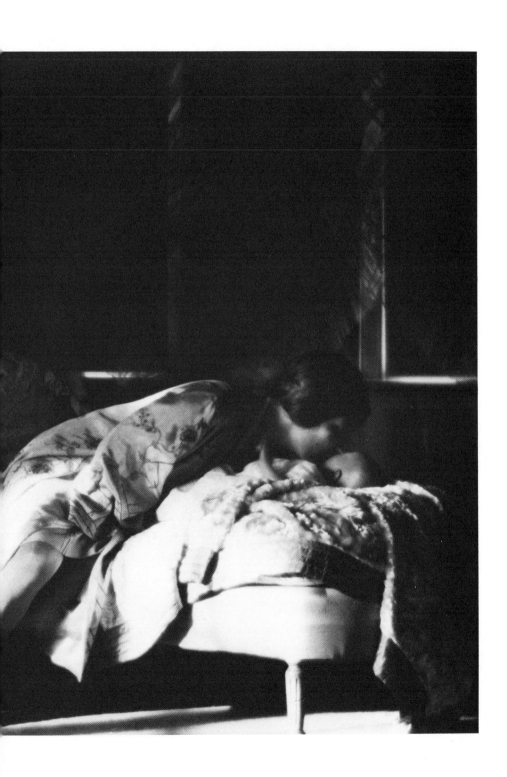

2. Dorothea Lange, "Man Beside Wheelbarrow," San Francisco, 1934.
(Dorothea Lange Collection, © 1982 Oakland Museum, City of Oakland.)

3. Dorothea Lange, "White Angel Breadline," San Francisco, 1933. (Dorothea Lange Collection, © 1982 Oakland Museum, City of Oakland.)

4. Dorothea Lange, "Migrant Mother," Nipomo, California, 1936. (Library of Congress.)

5. Dorothea Lange, "Drought Refugees from Oklahoma Camping by Road,"
Blythe, California, 1936. (Library of Congress.)

6. Margaret Bourke-White, "Otis Steel Company," Cleveland, Ohio, c. 1928. (Estate of Margaret Bourke-White, George Arents Research Library, Syracuse University.)

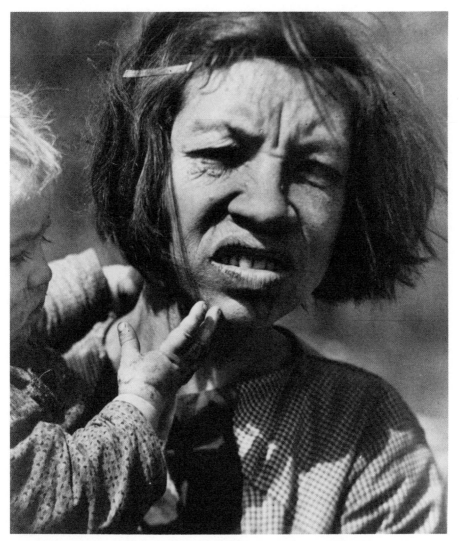

7. Margaret Bourke-White, "Snuff Is an Almighty Help When Your Teeth Ache," McDaniel, Georgia, 1936. (Estate of Margaret Bourke-White, George Arents Research Library, Syracuse University.)

8. F. Holland Day, "Father Forgive Them: They Know Not What They Do,"
1898. (Library of Congress.)

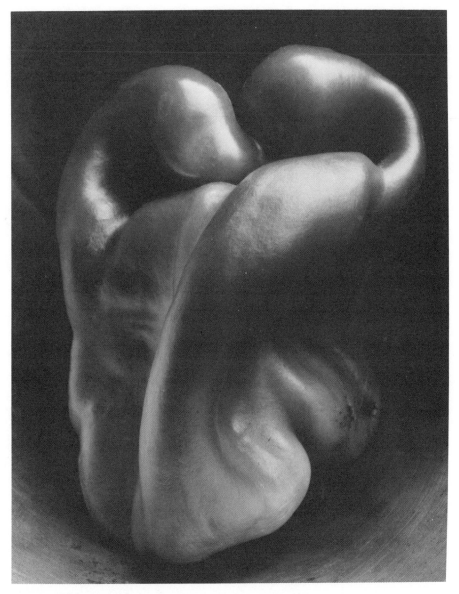

9. Edward Weston, "Pepper No. 30," 1930. (© 1981 Arizona Board of Regents. Center for Creative Photography.)

10. Marion Post Wolcott, "Migrant Packinghouse Workers' Living Quarters," near Canal Point, Florida, 1939. (Library of Congress.)

11. Carl Mydans, "The Baby Girl of a Family Living in the Area," near
Lexington, Tennessee, 1936. (Library of Congress.)

12. Russell Lee, "Christmas Dinner in the Home of Earl Pauley. Dinner Consisted of Potatoes, Cabbage, and Pies," Smithfield, Iowa, 1936. (Library of Congress.)

13. Dorothea Lange, "Abandoned Farm House on Large Mechanized Cotton Farm," Texas, 1938. (Library of Congress.)

14. Arthur Rothstein, "Oklahoma," undated. (Library of Congress.)

15. Arthur Rothstein, "Plantation Owner's Daughter Checks Weight of Cotton," Kaufman County, Texas, 1936. (Library of Congress.)

16. Dorothea Lange, "Near Los Angeles, California," 1939.
(Library of Congress.)

17. Walker Evans, "Washroom and Kitchen of a Cabin," Hale County, Alabama, 1936. (Library of Congress.)

18. Ben Shahn, "Street Scene," Circleville, Ohio, 1938. (Library of Congress.)

19. Jack Delano, "Interior of Negro Rural Home," Greene County, Georgia, 1941. (Library of Congress.)

20. Arthur Rothstein, "Sharecropper's Wife and Child," Arkansas, 1938.
(Library of Congress.)

21. Arthur Rothstein, "Farmer and Sons Walking in the Face of a Dust Storm," Cimarron County, Oklahoma, 1936. (Library of Congress.)

22. Dorothea Lange, "Eden, Alabama," 1936. (Library of Congress.)

23. Marion Post Wolcott, "Men Standing in Front of the Railway Station," Newport, Tennessee, 1939. (Library of Congress.)

24. Jack Delano, "A Moment Off from Cotton Chopping," Greene County, Georgia, 1939. (Library of Congress.)

25. Russell Lee, "Roadside Camp of Migrant Workers," Lincoln County, Oklahoma, 1939. (Library of Congress.)

26. Dorothea Lange,
"Former Nebraska
Farmer, Now a Migrant
Farm Worker," Klamath
County, Oregon, 1939.
(Library of Congress.)

27. Walker Evans, "Storefront and Signs," Beaufort, South Carolina, 1936. (Library of Congress.)

28. John Vachon, "Mildred Irwin, Entertainer in Saloon at North Platte, Nebraska. She Entertained for Twenty Years in Omaha before Coming to North Platte," 1938. (Library of Congress.)

Arthur Rothstein, "Entering Utopia, Ohio," February 1940. (Library of Congress.)

FOUR

Fate Refurbished:
The Depression's Social
Novelists

R ichard Wright spun tales of doom and then leavened them with a measure of hope. "Long Black Song" is one such tale, the story of Silas, a black farmer in the South. After a lifetime of effort, Silas has attained the rare security of owning his own farm. One day he sells his harvest in town, nets a nice profit, and leaves for home happy—the money will allow him to expand his farm and gain more autonomy from the larger white society. But his joy evaporates when Silas returns to learn that a white traveling salesman has seduced his wife, Sarah. In his fury, Silas murders the salesman. But he then chooses not to flee, for Silas realizes that his cherished independence was only an empty dream; a white man could take his wife easily and now other whites will most certainly kill him and seize his farm. Trapped in a world he once thought he controlled, he cries out "there ain nothing Ah kin do." So Silas makes a futile last stand, shoots it out with the approaching lynch mob, and kills a few of the whites before they inevitably murder him.

But Wright chose not to end his tale there. Instead, he turned to Sarah and created for her the vision of a world where lynching could not occur. She sees a future where blacks and whites are not inherently separated from each other, but where they are "all a part of that which made life good . . . linked, like the spokes of a spinning wheel." Just as surely as bigotry had killed Silas, so this brotherhood would yield a world of peace. Wright thus created an alternative to the hatred he had depicted, and ended his story with a message of Sarah's hopeful vision rather than of Silas' miserable helplessness.[1]

Other novelists of the 1930s followed Richard Wright's example. Writing at a time when American capitalism was ill and on the verge of collapse, they composed a body of fiction detailing its symptoms—high unemployment, mass migration, and widespread poverty. Americans appeared to have no more control over their lives than Silas had over his, and they seemed as surely trapped in the faltering economy as he was ensnared in Southern racism. Like Richard Wright, the Depression's other social novelists brought this perception to their work, and depicted humans as the slaves of forces they could never govern. These writers no more approved of American capitalism than Wright endorsed racism, and they strove to condemn it by portraying the plights of its victims as vividly as Wright lambasted racism with his heartrending tales of lynchings. The writers did not stop with protest, however. Having created characters modeled upon real life, they were unwilling to say that either their protagonists or actual people were everlastingly stuck in an unjust world. Social novelists did as Richard Wright had done when he turned from Silas' predicament to Sarah's dream. They took the malevolent fate of their stories and softened it, giving their characters some hope of escape from a world of pain and injustice.

The Social Novel

Social novels of the 1930s composed a distinct genre. Their actors were unheroic, often ignoble, and usually "little" people who came to difficulty because of social or economic circumstances beyond their control. These were books about American society told through its victims; the psychological explorations in these stories dealt almost exclusively with the characters' open discomfort and seldom plumbed their innermost spirits. Vivid portraits of miserable people, these novels complained mightily about the conditions they depicted, and they most often pointed to American capitalism as the responsible culprit. Such books were virtually rooted in the thirties, for they took not only their inspiration but also much of their actual content from events of the day.[2] Yet rather than merely evoking the present epoch, social novels of the Depression portrayed immediate tragedies like hunger and unemployment as the cumulative products of centuries of capitalism.

The social novel was an appealing form to many writers of the 1930s, and most of what they wrote is well forgotten. But there were several novelists like Richard Wright who managed to create serviceable and occasionally outstanding works of social fiction. Attaining the respect of their peers and critics, these authors formed a loose network of associations among themselves and created a sizable body of writing in addition to their novels. John Dos Passos, James T. Farrell, and Josephine Herbst favored trilogies and produced some of the decade's best social novels. John Steinbeck and Erskine Caldwell enjoyed both popular and critical acclaim while writing about down-and-out Americans; Steinbeck's migrant stories tended to be more optimistic than, if not technically superior to, Caldwell's Southern grotesque tales. Although Nelson Algren's skills did not flower until later, he sharpened them by producing harshly realistic novels during the 1930s. Less talented authors like Robert Cantwell, Jack Conroy, Edward Dahlberg, Tom Kromer, and Edward Newhouse also wrote social novels during the thirties, and then went on to labor in other fields. Besides their shared genre, these authors were united by other, more biographical characteristics. They came mostly from working-class or modest middle-class families and managed to spend some time in college. (Richard Wright, the lone black in the group, was the only one without some college experience.) They were a politically active lot, participating in debates, contributing to Marxist magazines, and joining organizations like the John Reed Club or the American Writers' Congress. Their political positions fluctuated during the decade, but most maintained liberal or even radical sympathies.

Critic Alfred Kazin knew many of these authors, and he called them "writers who came up in the Thirties." His designation is appropriate, for of this group, only Dos Passos and Herbst had established any literary reputation before the Crash. The others came of age during the Depression. These were hard times for beginners in any field, and the literary marketplace offered few bright spots to young novelists. Many hawked their works to journals or magazines, and frequently sections of forthcoming novels appeared in publications such as the *New Masses*. If the publishing industry provided only weak support for these authors, the federal government was no more sustaining. Unlike the Depression's documentary photographers or its social realist painters, social novelists did not receive extensive New Deal support to carry on their work. Only three, Wright, Algren, and Conroy, were in the Works Progress Administration (WPA) Writers' Project. Two others who found jobs in New Deal agencies hardly had time to exercise their talents as novelists—Kromer spent fifteen months in a Civil Conservation Corps camp, and Steinbeck conducted a WPA census of dogs on California's Monterey peninsula. Though there were exceptions like Dos Passos, who managed to live and travel comfortably, most of these young artists were like Steinbeck and Farrell and struggled to get by during the 1930s. Possessing an impressive dedication, they kept creating in spite of their straits.[3]

The hard times helped bring a special toughness and social orientation to the works of these authors. But for all the difficulties of the crisis, the Depression was not a gigantic shock treatment summoning writers back from a netherworld of apathy and into a new one of literary activism.[4] While some *painters* saw the Depression in this way, few social novelists chose to describe it as such a personally wrenching experience. Wright, Steinbeck, and the others did, however, recognize a certain crisis-inspired shift in American literature, and they viewed themselves as part of that realignment. In comparison with novels appearing in the years immediately following World War I, Depression fiction was more concerned with economic forces and social action than with the individual psyche, with the collectivity as opposed to the individual, and with the poor rather than with the middle or upper classes. Alienation was a large concern for both periods, but thirties writers dwelt more upon its physical rather than psychological aspects. Yet there were important continuities between the Depression's social novels and the fiction of preceding years. Social novelists operated within the conventions of realism and naturalism that had existed in American literature since the late nineteenth century. They continued to write as the naturalists had, about "forces" working upon people, and they further employed realist devices such as the reproduction of actual speech rhythms, detailed rendering of settings, and close physical descriptions.[5] Like countless predecessors, they were critics of American culture, though their criticisms were more within the tradition of Upton Sinclair and Jack London than that of Henry James or Sinclair Lewis. From the likes of Sinclair and London, they inherited a leftist vision that seemed especially appropriate in the Depression environment of bank failures and farm foreclosures. With this array of techniques, themes, and political perspectives, the social novelists were well within an American literary heritage and often aware of their lineage.

"Social novelists" is something of an arbitrary label for writers such as Steinbeck and Wright. Unlike the Depression's documentary photographers, social novelists never reached an agreed-upon name for their genre. But "social novelists" is useful in distinguishing them from proletarian novelists of the thirties, for despite some similarities, the two groups were involved in different enterprises.[6] The term "proletarian literature" had considerable currency in literary circles of the thirties, but there was never any common denotation to the term; anything from a story by a working-class author to a piece with a generally leftist perspective might be called "proletarian." Some of the few people to speak of "proletarian literature" with any uniformity were Marxist critics like Michael Gold and Granville Hicks of the *New Masses*. They used it as a normative term, indicating the degree to which fiction illustrated the Communist Party line of the moment and how well the plot nourished a reader's radical inclinations. Books that passed this test were usually formula pieces in which the protagonist perceives that the revolution holds his personal salvation, undergoes a stirring conversion to Communism, and becomes a radical activist.[7] *This* certainly was proletarian literature, and social novelists like Wright and Steinbeck would have little to do with it. They resisted incorporating the Party's positions into their fiction and preferred to create their own messages rather than illuminate political dogma. Moreover, while social novelists produced a number of undistinguished novels, their works were on the whole superior to the wooden pieces that unquestionably deserve the proletarian label, books like Clara Weatherwax's *Marching! Marching!*, a lifeless tale that won the *New Masses* prize for best proletarian novel of 1935.

Distinct from their proletarian contemporaries, social novelists also stood apart from other writers who were more concerned with romanticizing the past or probing the individual psyche. Historical romances such as Hervey Allen's picaresque tale of the Napoleonic era, *Anthony Adverse* (1933), and Margaret Mitchell's epic of the Civil War South, *Gone with the Wind* (1936), sold well during the Depression. More than just escapes from the present, such novels provided a meaningful message for the Depression reader, for they showed that individuals could—like Scarlett O'Hara—survive in spite of their chaotic environments. Social novelists likewise stressed survival and perseverance, but they were less inclined to set their novels in a remote past and filled their novels with trials and tragedies that closely mirrored the inglorious *present*. The triumvirate of Ernest Hemingway, Thomas Wolfe, and William Faulkner produced some of the most profound and innovative novels of the decade, works that are largely superior to, and quite distinct from, the social realists' efforts. The Depression ranks as Hemingway's social epoch, and his thirties novels are filled with uncharacteristic political concerns. He set *For Whom the Bell Tolls* (1940) among antifascist fighters of the Spanish Civil War, and in *To Have and Have Not* (1937), one of his characters even abandoned that famous Hemingway individualism to utter the dying words, "a man alone ain't got no bloody fucking chance."[8] But Hemingway's characters had few of the communitarian sympathies that marked the social novelists' protagonists, and his stories were essentially about lonely men engaged in tests of individual courage. Thomas Wolfe's work similarly exhibited an increasing degree of social concern during the decade, but compared to the fiction of a Wright or a Steinbeck, Wolfe's books have little emphasis upon displaced people or social themes. Instead, his prodigious auto-biographical novels look inward to explore the depths of his characters' personalities. Faulkner was probably closer than Wolfe to the social novel-ists, for he certainly shared with them an interest in marginal people, violence, and grimness. But unlike social novelists, Faulkner restricted himself to peculiarly Southern themes, had a haunting sense of an ever-present past, and shared with Hemingway and Wolfe an abiding concern for psychology.[9]

Neither proletarian nor individualistic, the social novelists were united in a common approach that resembled literary naturalism. Naturalism had arrived in the United States at the end of the nineteenth century, when Americans such as Theodore Dreiser and Stephen Crane adopted the style of European naturalists and the theoretical underpinnings of French critic and naturalist Émile Zola. Writing in a naturalist manner, American novelists began describing humans as mere animals in a natural world; people did not act out of free will, but only responded to their environ-ments or instincts. This analysis commanded considerable respect among the Depression's social novelists, for Americans of the 1930s seemed truly at the mercy of uncontrollable forces. Some of the social novelists openly acknowledged naturalism's influence upon their work. One was Edward Dahlberg, whose first novel appeared in the year of the Crash; Dahlberg proclaimed that with this first book he had consciously "begun as a natu-ralist." James T. Farrell had the reputation of being a naturalist, and though his critics used "naturalism" as a label of opprobrium, Farrell ac-cepted it with pride and claimed he "never denied it." Likewise, when an interviewer asked Nelson Algren which authors had influenced his work, Algren proudly pointed to "a tradition, Dreiser, and certainly at the turn of the century, Stephen Crane."[10]

Algren and the others were part of that tradition in another sense. Like their predecessors, they employed naturalism without becoming through-and-through naturalists. As Zola had formulated it, naturalism is deter-ministic, denying both free will and heroism. Dark and gloomy, with little room for lesson-drawing, pure naturalism has never enjoyed much popu-larity among American writers. Novelists have tended to use it for social criticism, as Theodore Dreiser did, or to follow Upton Sinclair and dilute it into social protest. Emerson once said there are no old idealists, and the same might well be said for naturalists. Of the early American naturalists, only Stephen Crane remained very loyal to naturalism, and that was mostly because he died so young that the customary disenchantment had not yet set in. Those of Crane's contemporaries who lived longer invariably tempered naturalism's deterministic gloom. Similarly, the Depression's social novelists, even with their regard for naturalism, never completely embraced it; they refused to surrender to naturalism and cast their characters as the hopeless victims of uncaring fate.[11] Richard Wright's story about Silas and Sarah is a case in point. A true naturalist might well have ended with Silas' death scene, but Wright went on to fashion Sarah's vision of a better future. Like Wright, the others attacked America's present social faults, denied the permanence of those conditions, and forecast some escape from the current mess. Their projected futures often lacked definition, but the social novelists were not stuck in monomaniacal ranting about the contemporary world. They leveled their protests about the present and hoped for brighter days to come. No author better illustrates this than John Steinbeck.

John Steinbeck's Universal Human Family

John Steinbeck's *The Grapes of Wrath* (1939) is the best-known social novel of the 1930s. Though not an especially eloquent or well-crafted book, it possesses an epic sweep and emotional appeal that have helped it dominate subsequent images of the Depression. In its own day, *The Grapes of Wrath* struck many sympathetic chords among both creative Americans and the general public. It inspired paintings, movies, plays, and photographs, and, to Steinbeck's surprise, became a best-seller. Other social novels of the 1930s were woven from much the same material as Steinbeck used, and he drew from a common set of themes that his fellow social novelists also plaited into their work.

Neither the clearest nor most profound of writers, Steinbeck frequently failed to deliver a transparent message in his works. *The Grapes of Wrath* was no exception, and there are numerous possible readings of it that are at odds with Steinbeck's intentions. Some interpretations note the author's concern for dusted-out farmers and see the novel as a piece about

American agriculture, a manifesto proposing Jeffersonian agrarianism as a solution for the Depression's problems.[12] Steinbeck *was* undeniably sympathetic toward the Dust Bowl's victims, although the uprooted farmers were merely his vehicles for a message that had no inherent connection with agrarianism. A more common reading describes *The Grapes of Wrath* as a political novel, a bitter protest against social conditions in the Plains and California, and a leftist call for downtrodden people to wrest justice from an oppressive society.[13] Steinbeck's plot helps evoke this political interpretation, for it has about it an air of social protest and proletarian battle cry. But the analysis only partially conveys Steinbeck's intention. He certainly believed the Joads' suffering was unfair and thought there would come a time when such oppression would end. The means to that end, and Steinbeck's larger message, however, had little to do with political organizing. To ease the Joads' problems, Steinbeck envisioned much the same solution as Richard Wright created for Sarah—a universal community of all people, held together with bonds of love so strong that oppression would be impossible. Yet Steinbeck managed to obscure his meaning. His community was so odd, and his protests so loud, that the political drama virtually overwhelms his larger design. To decipher *The Grapes of Wrath*, we must turn away from the novel itself, take up Steinbeck's Depression experiences, and consider his efforts to give them literary expression.

Steinbeck (1902–1968) was born to a middle-class California family. He attended Stanford University irregularly between 1919 and 1925, left without completing a degree, and then went to New York City where he worked as a newspaper reporter while trying his hand at fiction. Unable to publish the short stories he had produced, he returned to California in the late twenties and began writing novels—books that saw publication but were not commercially successful. Those failures and the general economic woes of the early thirties made for hard times in the Steinbeck household—at one point Steinbeck had to sell his pet mallards to buy writing paper. But he took little note of the social tragedies of the Depression or his own economic straits, for his joy in writing eclipsed all else during the early thirties. As he told a friend in 1930, "Financially we are in a mess, but 'spiritually' we ride the clouds. Nothing matters."[14]

Yet if the early Depression brought no immediate personal turmoil to Steinbeck, its influence certainly emerged in his work. His first two novels had been about people who know precisely what they want and are able to control their lives. But by 1931, as the Depression grew more intense and Steinbeck composed his third novel, he began to write about a different sort of character. Unlike his earlier protagonists, these characters proved unable to direct their lives in the face of uncontrollable events and seemed as much the victims of circumstances as were thirties Americans.[15] At the same time, a personal tragedy struck, and Steinbeck became even more concerned with the theme of unpiloted lives. In the first part of 1933, his mother suffered a stroke that left her paralyzed and eventually took her life. Steinbeck was the closest family member free to handle nursing duties, so her care fell upon him. He did not much mind the unpleasantness of the patient's deliriums and her bedpans, and he accepted it without complaint. The big difficulty for him was "that my work seems to be at a standstill." There were constant interruptions as he tended to his mother's needs, and working at her bedside proved impossible, for the scratching of his pen disturbed her rest. A preoccupied artist more than a dedicated son, Steinbeck became increasingly frustrated with this interference. Since it looked as though his mother might linger for some time, it seemed like there might be a considerable hiatus in his writing. Facing that prospect, Steinbeck became depressed and described himself as in a "blue fog so thick and so endless that I can see no opening in it."[16]

The fog lifted when he stopped complaining about his mother's illness and began contemplating it. An amateur biologist, Steinbeck was interested in the relationship between organic groups and their constituent parts, particularly the manner in which smaller units like cells unite to form larger units like plants or animals. As he observed his mother on her sickbed, he began to regard her as a person who had suffered "a schism of a number of her cells."[17] They had rebelled and she had become ill.

Of all the things made of smaller individual parts, Steinbeck was most interested in the relationship between individual humans and their larger social units. Putting together a hodgepodge of overextended analogy, dubious psychology, and speculative biology, Steinbeck concocted an explanation of this relationship, dubbing his mélange a theory of "phalanx man." In choosing this term, he apparently took his inspiration more from the ancient military formation than from French socialist Charles Fourier's social units of the same name. Indeed, while Steinbeck was primarily interested in human societies rather than animal communities, he drew little from social thinkers and relied heavily upon biologists for his models. Steinbeck began with the observation that individual cells within a human body form yet another individual, the human. But a person is more than "the sum of all his cells. He has a nature now new and strange to his cells." Arguing more from metaphor than logic, Steinbeck contended that when individual people form groups like mobs, parties, or soviets, they too become parts of some larger organism; rather than remain an independent being, each person becomes "a unit of the greater beast, the phalanx."[18]

This phalanx theory was of course more a pipe dream than an actual theory, but it nonetheless had definite implications for human liberty. Under Steinbeck's scheme, free will virtually ceased to exist. Human beings effectively lost direction of their lives, for the phalanx "controls its unit-men with an iron discipline." Revolts might occur within a phalanx, but any rebel always and immediately became a member of yet another phalanx. The summons to join a group was an unappealable, unavoidable draft, for "when your phalanx needs you, it will use you." Likewise, one's phalanx would dissolve at some arbitrary time with no regard for its members' convenience or desires.[19] Thus for all practical purposes, Steinbeck built himself a deterministic world, with free will existing only in the uncertain moments when one was of no use to a phalanx, and with each phalanx likely to dissolve at any moment. This fatalism hardly bothered Steinbeck. Where others might understandably shy from the phalanx because of its determinism or intellectual vacuity, Steinbeck embraced it. For one thing, the theory gave some explanation for recent developments such as his mother's illness or even the rise of fascism. But during the early thirties, Steinbeck was a writer before all else, and it was as a novelist rather than as a grieving son or concerned citizen that he most relished his bizarre theory. With his deterministic phalanx he had latched onto a "tremendous and terrible poetry," a "gorgeous thing" that he could work into the "symbolism of fiction." In the months after he first formulated the group man thesis, Steinbeck was obsessed with it; he seemed almost a living caricature of the engaged artist, caring little for his surroundings or the people around him. Even in the midst of his mother's rapid decline, the phalanx was such a compelling theme that, with startling heartlessness, he could tell a friend that the "illness (which by the way is the beginning conception) is worth it—everything is worth it."[20]

Steinbeck utilized his phalanx symbolism in every major novel he published for the remainder of the 1930s. *Tortilla Flat* (1935), *In Dubious*

Battle (1936), and *Of Mice and Men* (1937) all had group themes and were all strongly laced with determinism. With these novels, he concentrated upon one aspect of the phalanx phenomenon and wrote about people who were trying "to get away from their individuality."[21] Lonely characters form groups, draw fellowship and support from each other, and do battle against their mutual unhappiness. The determinism Steinbeck emphasized here is not so much that his characters sacrificed their independence when they joined a group. Instead, the terrible poetry in these novels is more that the communities must certainly dissolve and that the protagonists are doomed to lives as unhappy as the ones they led before joining their groups.

In Dubious Battle is Steinbeck's most vivid depiction of that fate. The community in this novel is composed of migrant farm workers who strike against some California apple growers. Jim Nolan and Mac are Communists sent to organize the strike, men who enlist the help of a sympathetic physician named Doc Burton. Mac struggles to guide the strike along Party lines, but Doc understands groups and tells him this is impossible, for the workers have become a phalanx that is beyond even Mac's formidable manipulative skills. As Doc explains, the strike cannot move toward Mac's ideological goals because groups do not concern themselves with *any* ideas, whether about "the Holy Land, or Democracy or Communism." Instead, phalanxes utilize ideologies as slogans "simply to reassure the brains of individual men."[22] The strike is uncontrollable, and its failure is a foregone conclusion. Steinbeck's titles seldom lacked significance, and *In Dubious Battle* was no exception. The title comes from Milton's *Paradise Lost* and refers to Satan's decision to engage heavenly forces in a battle he would not win. The workers' strike was similarly dubious, for it was another hopeless assault on fate.[23] Steinbeck explained that he did not write the book to better conditions among California farm workers: "I'm not interested in [the] strike as [a] means of raising men's wages, and I'm not interested in ranting about justice and oppression." Instead, he believed that by its very nature humankind hates itself and is engaged in a perpetual battle in which some continually strive to oppress and demean others. Steinbeck saw his strike as an example of that ongoing battle, a "symbol of man's eternal, bitter warfare with himself." It was not a Marxist battle, and to underscore his message, Steinbeck had Doc Burton tell Jim Nolan that the strikers' true enemy was not some orchard owner, but immutable human nature. "Mankind hates itself,"

Doc told Jim, and *that* rather than capitalist exploitation was the source of the strikers' misery. "Man has met and defeated every obstacle, every enemy except one," Doc explained. But that last enemy was unconquerable, and the human battle both eternal and irresolvable.[24]

As he presented this theme in his novels of the mid-thirties, Steinbeck's voice was that of the detached observer. Though intellectually and artistically excited over the theme of an unalterable human destiny, he did not feel moved to speak out against that fate. Instead, he hoped that in writing books like *In Dubious Battle* he could act as "merely a recording consciousness, judging nothing, simply putting down the thing." Steinbeck carried this same detachment with him when he approached the actual world beyond fiction. In 1936 he refused to write an article on contemporary issues, fearing that such an assignment would lead him to meting out condemnation or praise. Even in politics he preferred to remain the uncommitted observer, "simply listening to men talk and watching them act."[25] As it happened, there were many opportunities to play the observer, for in an odd turn of events, *In Dubious Battle* gave Steinbeck the reputation as an expert on California's migrant labor. He received assignments for several articles on farm workers and took field trips far into the California interior. He found considerable tension there between workers and growers, thought the situation full of fine literary material, and began working on a new book based upon his observations. But before settling into this new project, Steinbeck first enjoyed the financial success of *Of Mice and Men* with a leisurely 1937 trip to New York and Europe. In the fall, he returned to gathering material for his new novel about migrant farm workers, and although he did not accompany Okies on their trek to California, he may well have worked for a time with transplanted Oklahomans in the California fields.[26]

The novel moved ahead with no indication that he would produce anything other than another detached portrait of humans coming up against the limits of their destiny. But Steinbeck's literary direction changed suddenly in February and March of 1938. He made additional trips into California's interior agricultural valleys, and there discovered a degree of anguish that surpassed anything he had ever seen. The migrants suffered not only from low wages and skimpy diets, but also from onslaughts of disease and flood. Local authorities only made matters worse, for at the growers' behest, they circumvented the workers' efforts to organize, as well as federal attempts to bring in food and medicine. *Finally,* after eight

years of running its course, the Depression registered upon John Steinbeck. Calling the situation "the most heart-breaking thing in the world,"
he became more caught up with contemporary events than he had been
thus far in the decade, and decided he could no longer continue to portray
misery as a necessary part of the human condition.[27] Putting aside his
former reserve, Steinbeck became a propagandist for the downtrodden.
He sang the workers' praises and railed against their oppressors. For one
such project, he revised some earlier articles, added several of Dorothea
Lange's photographs, and published the resulting pamphlet as a migrant
paean entitled "Their Blood Is Strong." With his new perspective, the
workers' adversaries now seemed "a fascist group of utilities and banks
and huge growers," and Steinbeck resolved "to help knock these mur-
derers on their heads." Steinbeck's pen had become his weapon, and he
took it up "to put a tag of shame on the greedy bastards."[28] He completed
the migrant novel as a 60,000-word indictment of repression in a lettuce
strike, and called it *L'Affaire Lettuceberg*. With none of the detachment
of his earlier novels, this was an intentional defamation of the California
growers, "a mean, nasty book."[29] Three years earlier he had not been
"interested in ranting about social justice and oppression." But after his
belated good look at Depression conditions, Steinbeck became obsessed
with justice and oppression, and began wholeheartedly ranting about
them.

We will never know if *L'Affaire Lettuceberg* was as nasty as Steinbeck
said, for he burned the manuscript less than a month after completing the
first draft. By doing this, he certainly saved his career from the burden of
a terrible title, but his stated reasons for destroying the book had more to
do with its contents. *L'Affaire Lettuceberg* seemed "a smart-alec book,"
one intended "to cause hatred" rather than help "people understand each
other."[30] Earlier, he had written of hatred as the eternal obstacle between
humans and happiness. Now he found that though he had joined the battle of human against human on the side of the underdogs, he was only
fomenting hatred and doing nothing to end the dubiousness of that battle.
Since hatred had been the problem, he destroyed *Lettuceberg*, turned to
a theme of love, and began writing the novel that became *The Grapes of
Wrath*. Throughout the decade he had written about groups that encouraged love between their members, but those communities inevitably dis-
banded. With *The Grapes of Wrath*, Steinbeck forged a group that could
unite all people in a lasting community of love, and that could retire

hatred from the human experience. In his central characters, the Joad family, Steinbeck created what he hoped would grow into a larger family embracing all humankind.

The community Steinbeck envisioned was one of harmony and unity. Accordingly he deemphasized political action in *The Grapes of Wrath*, for political instruments like strikes or unions seemed only to contribute to the contentiousness and belligerency he wanted to put aside. Steinbeck made his male characters the novel's political figures, and even gave one of them, Jim Casy, a brief glimpse of the universal community that was the author's ultimate goal. In Oklahoma, before the westward trek begins, Jim thinks that "maybe all men got one big soul ever'body's a part of." When they reach California, though, Casy turns his attention from spiritual unity to worldly battles; he becomes a spokesman for migrant rights and begins building a union. When the growers kill Casy, his mantle passes to Tom Joad, who is also more concerned with fighting than with harmony. These male characters are thus quite combative, and as Steinbeck unfolded his plot, he gradually got rid of them. Casy dies in the class struggle, Tom leaves to continue fighting it, and others die or simply fade away. By the novel's conclusion there are no strong men in the family, and leadership passes to the women. The men's flaw is that they are too political, too concerned with the vicissitudes of life's defeats and victories. As Ma Joad explains it, "man he lives in jerks." In contrast, women are more concerned with life's larger continuities than its intermittent struggles. To "woman it's all one flow, like a stream, little eddies, little waterfalls, but the river, it goes right on."[31]

The flow that Steinbeck's women perceive is the growth of familial affection to embrace more than just the usual family. At the novel's beginning, Ma was "the citadel of the family," protecting it from outsiders and prevailing against its own centrifugal forces. But on the road to California, Ma's maternal reflexes began involuntarily responding to the needs of other migrants, and the boundaries between her kin and other people started dissolving as the "families became one family, the children were the children of all." By the novel's end, Ma's motherly intuitions expand to encompass all humanity, and she feels the compulsion to nurture the whole race. It "use' to be the fambly was fust," she proclaims. But "it ain't so now. It's anybody." This was the growth of Steinbeck's intimate familial community, what he called the change "from 'I' to 'we.'"[32]

For his final symbol of universal family, Steinbeck turned to Rose of

Sharon, Ma's oldest daughter. As with the general dissolution of the Joads, Steinbeck arranged Rose of Sharon's story in order to show that it was not the biological human family he had in mind—her husband deserted her during the exodus, and her baby was born dead. On the second day after the stillbirth, Rose of Sharon and the few remaining Joads lose all their belongings to a flood and take refuge in a barn, where they discover a starving man. By this time the male characters are quite powerless and stand "helplessly gazing at the sick man." So, in one of the more contrived endings in any major novel, Rose of Sharon and Ma take charge. The two women look at each other, Rose of Sharon gasps and says "yes," and Ma hustles the rest of the family out of the barn. Following her own irresistible instincts, Rose of Sharon turns to the starving man, offers him her milk-laden breast, and smiles "mysteriously" as she nurses him. Steinbeck's editor could see how patently maudlin this scene was and wrote urging him to develop another conclusion. Steinbeck shot back a heated reply. Rose of Sharon's offering, he wrote, "is no fruity climax," and he insisted that the starving man "must be a stranger." To conclude his book, he needed some way to symbolize the intimacy and mutual succor he envisioned for his family of all people, and he believed he had found it in the nursing scene. Since this new family included *all* people, it was essential that Rose of Sharon have no previous connection with the starving man. "The fact that the Joads don't know him," Steinbeck steamed, "have no ties to him—that is the emphasis."[33] His new world would be one where the difference between stranger and intimate no longer existed.

By the end of the 1930s, Steinbeck thus left his characters with the prospect of tomorrows considerably brighter than those that awaited his earlier figures. With *The Grapes of Wrath* he modified his phalanx theory, giving groups the possibility of permanence and his characters a degree of control over their lives. Where his earlier protagonists had been almost completely at the mercy of an uncaring fate, his characters now possessed the ability to help bring about a brighter future. The workers of *In Dubious Battle* drifted into their strike, but Tom Joad chose to join a union and fight for migrant rights. Similarly, Rose of Sharon chose to listen to her inner drives and, by nursing the starving stranger, created a bond that would help build Steinbeck's universal community. Yet even with their increased abilities, Steinbeck's characters still had only minimal control over their fates, for the governing factors in their lives remained largely beyond their direction. Unruly forces of drought and economic collapse, more than their own designs, brought the Joads to the place that was to be the nursery for their new family, and the women's compelling maternal instincts, as much as their rational decisions, provided the nurture it required. In this manner, Steinbeck's characters could only stand within history's flow and help it along its way; they were not heroic figures who could stand outside its path and redirect it. In the early thirties, Steinbeck had acquired a fatalistic outlook when he wrote about an enduringly gloomy world, and when he later decided to write about a better world, he maintained his deterministic inclination. The future that Steinbeck placed before the Joads looked much more hopeful than it had for his earlier protagonists, but this was more because fate had taken a turn for the better than because the Joads chose what direction it would take.

Other social novelists of the thirties did much the same thing. Like Steinbeck, they began by composing a literature in which characters had little power over their lives and were instead in the clutches of uncontrollable forces. Where Steinbeck in his earlier works accepted this almost resignedly, the others complained virtually from the first about their characters' circumstances. Like him, they believed their novels were reflections of actual life, and they were as unwilling as he to relegate their characters to doom, for to do so would only suggest that real people had no deliverance from the Depression. So they gave their characters the certainty of brighter days to come and tools for coaxing along those tomorrows. But, as it was for Steinbeck, the ultimate source of their glowing future was fate rather than any of their characters' actions. They were writers of the Depression, a time when economic and political forces seemed more the masters of humans than subject to human mastery.

Indictments of America: Hopelessness and Violence

Late in 1939, James T. Farrell wrote an evaluation of the preceding ten years, the sort of article that has become standard journalistic fare at the end of a decade. Farrell was disappointed with the 1930s. Despite the Crash, the decade had seemed to begin well enough— there had been a flowering of radicalism and the time had appeared ripe for important leftward advances. Things had gone sour along the way, however. The Soviet Union turned out to be a repressive police state, and by decade's end, fascism, rather than socialism, seemed the coming order. Farrell was also disappointed with many American writers and intellectuals, for they seemed to have gone left too unthinkingly, naively sacrificing their independence of mind to toe the Party line. But for all his retrospective gloom, Farrell could see one bright spot. Most Depression writers, he believed, had performed the important service of holding American society up for critical judgment. If they had failed in other ways, at least they had "told us, in concrete terms, the cost of American civilization." Using their characters to illustrate capitalism's shortcomings "in terms of individual lives," they created sharp condemnations that "corrected many later-day myths." Though they failed to preserve sufficiently independent leftist perspectives, Farrell still thought writers had partially redeemed themselves by composing their bitter indictments of American society.[34]

Farrell was one of those authors. As he and other social novelists assessed it, American civilization demanded too high a price, and it eventually destroyed people. These novelists created characters whose lives were filled with a pervasive and inevitable doom, lives that could be nothing else given the existing social and economic system. In some of their stories, the social novelists concentrated upon protagonists (*not* heroes) who were capitalism's victims, and in others, they centered upon its Pyrrhic victors. But in both types of tales, they concluded that America's greatest myth was the promise of prosperity and happiness under capitalism. The social realists debunked that myth with a vengeance.

One group of authors wrote about people who could strive to get ahead rather than struggle to get the next meal. Farrell, John Dos Passos, Robert Cantwell, Edward Newhouse, and Josephine Herbst came from America's middle class, or at least the upper reaches of its lower class, and concentrated upon characters who began life far enough beyond poverty to have some chance of attaining success. But these protagonists all failed, even the ones who secured wealth and power. American society prescribed a set of nostrums like hard work and honesty that were supposed to lead to affluence and happiness. But the economic part of that promise usually collapsed, and those few who reached success were so drained that they could not enjoy their prosperity. Wealthy or not, the characters shared capitalism's only true reward, misery.

No one better exemplifies this group's critique of capitalism than Josephine Herbst. Born in Sioux City, Iowa, in 1897, her middle-class roots were similar to those of the characters she depicted. She graduated from Berkeley in 1919 and during the twenties joined the largely male ranks of lost-generation writers. She rejected the dullness and narrowness of Iowa for the excitement and traditions of Europe, touring the Continent with the likes of Ernest Hemingway and Max Eastman. When she returned to the United States, she lived in writers' colonies, where her neighbors included Edmund Wilson and Malcolm Cowley. Her first published article, a piece berating the literary provincialism of Iowa, found an appropriate home in H. L. Mencken's *American Mercury,* and her major novels of the twenties were criticisms of the Philistines' emotional coldness. Her life of the twenties was not without its political side, though, for when she visited inflation-burdened Germany, she spent much time in the company of poor Germans, viewing with distress the discrepancies between their lives and those of the comfortable burghers. During the thirties, Herbst became even more concerned with political matters, both in her life and in her writing. She traveled to the Soviet Union, investigated drought-hit families in the Midwest and plains, and visited Cuba to report upon its revolutionary peasants. She observed the Spanish Civil War firsthand and, together with her good friend Nathan Asch, wrote a one-act play supporting the Spanish Loyalists.[35]

Herbst used her Depression fiction to assess the middle class's burden under capitalism. As she described it in her Trexler trilogy, *Pity Is Not Enough* (1933), *The Executioner Waits* (1934), and *Rope of Gold* (1939), the load was tremendous and it destroyed people even if they attained prosperity. As her vehicles for this criticism, she created the Trexler brothers, Joe, Aaron, and David, men who mature in the late nineteenth century. Joe lacks the character necessary for success, plagued as he is with generosity and an inability to scheme. But still the glimmer of affluence lures him, for "he liked the shine of it and the spectacle and he couldn't separate himself from it." Wealthy people draw him into several swindles, but his only rewards are loneliness, poverty, and, finally, insanity. In contrast, Joe's brothers manage to wrench success out of the system, but at the price of a Mephistophelean exchange in which they sacrifice warmth and sympathy for their wealth. Moreover, they are among the few people who become adept at capitalism's requisite selfishness, rising on the economic ladder when most Americans are "more concerned with a way down than up." After finishing the first volume of the trilogy, Herbst explained that her intention in the project was to show that "the light by which that generation lived, individual initiative and 'more capital,'" was in reality "no light at all."[36] In the next two volumes, she succeeded at demonstrating her lesson, but at considerable literary cost. The certainty with which wealth defeated her characters also infused her plot with a certain melancholy monotony as each actor sadly and surely met his end at the hands of capitalism.

Where Herbst protrayed the failures of the middle class, Robert Cantwell and John Dos Passos concentrated upon more prosperous Americans. The two novelists pictured American society as a cavalcade of greed, and its upperclass stars as simply the greediest members of the troupe. Kenneth McArdle of Cantwell's *Laugh and Lie Down* (1931) climbs high in the world by toadying to his bosses and mercilessly driving those whom he bosses. Kenneth's guiding principle and the key to his success is "that personal integrity, that kindness, that everything that interferes with the acquisitive impulse is a stupidity, a luxury for simpletons."[37] Indeed, one would have to be a simpleton to miss Cantwell's point—villains and successes are the same people under capitalism. Dos Passos was a much better writer, and his *U.S.A.* trilogy (1930, 1932, 1936), besides being the best social fiction to emerge from the Depression, is an innovative combination of "newsreel" montages, biographies of actual people, and wide-ranging narrative. The most talented of the social novelists, Dos Passos was also the most experienced writer by the 1930s, for he had published a series of successful novels since the end of World War I. His books of the 1920s possessed a consistent critical edge that Dos Passos retained as he moved into "collective" novels, such as *Manhattan Transfer* (1925), in which he used individual characters to build a larger story about an entire city. In the late twenties Dos Passos began *U.S.A.*, a trilogy in which his criticisms became more political and his collective scope expanded to include all of American society. As Malcolm Cowley realized in 1932, the protagonist of *U.S.A.* is "society itself," which Dos Passos embodied in forty or fifty "characters who drift along with it." The American society of *U.S.A.* is affluent, shallow, and selfish, a place where the lure of wealth precludes principled conduct and awards only empty lives or early deaths as its prizes. One of Dos Passos's characters is J. Ward Moorehouse, a quintessential American, born on the Fourth of July with a grand desire to rise in the world. He achieves spectacular success through unscrupulous means, but corruption takes a continual toll and leaves Moorehouse a mental and physical wreck. Many of Dos Passos's characters end up as did Moorehouse, financially comfortable and morally bankrupt in the booming prosperity of the 1920s. Through such wrecked lives, Dos Passos strove to demonstrate what he called "the failure of New Era Capitalism."[38]

Edward Newhouse and James T. Farrell fashioned a different type of character. Their actors chased the carrot of capitalist success without getting so much as a taste of its bitterness. Gene Marsay is the protagonist of Newhouse's *You Can't Sleep Here* (1934) and *This Is Your Day* (1937). The one good episode in Marsay's life is merely "a kind of interlude" in a life that is otherwise "a succession of minor industrial accidents, discharge envelopes, headwaiters and tough foremen." Farrell centered upon a similar character in his major work of the thirties, the *Studs Lonigan* trilogy (1932–35). Enamored with realistic detail, Farrell strove to write "a thorough and exhaustive account of a way of life" but produced an exhaustingly tedious account of the dissipation of his protagonist, an Irish-Catholic Chicago youth named Studs Lonigan. Farrell purposely set his story just beyond Chicago's slums, for rather than society's economic casualty, he wanted to paint Studs as a victim of its "spiritual poverty," the set of empty quests that passes for values in America. Studs's father promises him "success and advancement," the Church pledges he will be "among the sheep and not the goats," and his peers assure him he will grow to be "a big tough guy." But all these promises fall through. Unemployed and a physical wreck in the midst of the Depression, Studs learns that even the assurance of an afterlife is empty. When he dies, neither heaven nor hell greet him; where Studs expected sheep and goats (and hoped to be among the former), there is only a black void.[39]

There were plenty of Lonigans in the Depression's social novels. Nelson Algren, Erskine Caldwell, Edward Dahlberg, and Richard Wright also created characters who could not achieve success in American society. But social novelists of this second group were largely from lower-class backgrounds, and their characters were for the most part also, in Dahlberg's words, "bottom dogs." On the lowest rung of the social ladder, such protagonists struggle for mere sustenance, and any thought of advancement is no more for them than a hopeless daydream. These characters are on the very margin of society, drifting people without homes, culture, or recreation.[40]

Richard Wright was the most capable author of these bottom-dog novelists. Born the son of Mississippi sharecroppers, Wright moved to Memphis upon leaving home, and then went on to Chicago in 1927. During the Depression, he worked in the Federal Writers' Project, joined the Communist Party, and contributed to various Party publications. As a black child in the Jim Crow South, Wright had grown up with a profound sense of the limitations imposed upon him, the inescapable realization that in America his color destined him to a life of poverty and victimization. After he arrived in the more affluent North, Wright found himself almost overwhelmed with the "desires that the Chicago streets, the newspapers, the movies" produced in him. But just as America's baubles were brighter in Chicago than they had been in Memphis, the racial barrier separating him from those lures was even more apparent than it had been in the South. Thus Wright entered the thirties with a reinforced awareness of a black man's unalterably low place in America, what he called "a new sense of the limit of the possible."[41]

It was with that sense of unconquerable limitation that Wright wrote some of the most eloquent fiction to come out of the Depression. He developed a string of characters who had only minimal control over their lives and who were almost completely at the mercy of their surroundings. Wright's greatest creation, Bigger Thomas, appeared in *Native Son* (1940), and Wright used the novel to illustrate the many ways in which American society trapped an unemployed black youth such as Bigger. Poverty, for example, forces Bigger's family to live in a foul tenement, but because Bigger has no more resources than the others in his family, he is "powerless to help them." It seems as though Bigger might finally have gained some power when he lands a job as chauffeur for a wealthy white family. The job proves to be no deliverance, however, for his employer is none other than the landlord of his filthy apartment. Bigger's first assignment is to drive the family's daughter around town and then get her safely home at the evening's end. This proves to be no small task, for she's something of a free spirit and is passed out drunk by the time the night's over. Rather than rouse the parents and risk their wrath for "allowing" their daughter to become drunk, Bigger carefully carries her up to her room, lays her gently on her bed, and appears to have resolved things quietly. But at that very moment, her mother unexpectedly comes in to check on her daughter, Bigger finds himself trapped in the forbidden territory of a white woman's bedroom, and he inadvertently suffocates the daughter as he uses a pillow to stifle her drunken moans. Circumstances have trapped him, this time in murder, and Bigger flees. But society is now more interested than ever in catching him and, with all the power at its disposal, quickly hunts him down and executes him in short order. Like the rest of Wright's protagonists, Bigger was black. Yet Wright believed his larger subject involved more than just racial issues. Doubtlessly the Depression helped lead him to this conclusion, for it made the despair that was a

constant part of black life an intimate part of the broader American experience. As Wright examined America, he came to believe that a whole host
of people were likewise trapped, "that Bigger Thomas was not black all
the time; he was white, too, and there were literally millions of him,
everywhere." From Wright's perspective, there was "a vast, muddied
pool of life in America," composed of people whom society so hopelessly
mired in poverty that they could never escape the bog.[42]

The other novelists who wrote about lower-class protagonists were like
Wright. Though they never matched the subtlety or complexity of *Native
Son*, they too created actors who were lowly, poor, miserable, and
doomed to stay that way. The economic system robbed these actors of
happiness and of the ability to determine the course of their lives. Jack
Conroy wrote about such characters from an autobiographical perspective. The son of a Missouri coal miner, Conroy failed to finish high school
and began work in railroad shops at fourteen. His hard-scrabble background gave his fiction a certain untutored power that often distinguishes
thirties novels from those of the preceding decade; yet his career shows
that there were important connections between the two periods, for his
early mentor was none other than that great iconoclast of the twenties,
H. L. Mencken. Conroy's protagonist in *A World to Win* (1935) is Leo
Hurley. Like Bigger Thomas, Leo is from birth "destined to share" the
worker's lot of "violence, death, backbreak," and Conroy grimly leads him
through just such a life. Similarly, Edward Dahlberg's Lorry Lewis grew
up in orphanages because his mother could not afford to care for him, and
he went from one terrible childhood experience to another; by the end of
Bottom Dogs (1929), he had resigned himself to a life of hopelessness.
Tom Kromer had in mind much the same message of despair when he
selected *Waiting for Nothing* (1935) as the tragic title for his largely autobiographical novel. After a long period of luckless bumming around the
country, Kromer's young narrator dismally concludes "that whatever is
before is the same as that which is gone. My life is spent before it is
started."[43] Even with their wandering plots and weak characterizations,
these novels have considerable power. The authors drew upon a sizable
body of painful personal experience and, in the Depression environment,
managed to recast that pain as a universal human experience. Crude and
often inept, the books still convey distress without whining.

Erskine Caldwell was a more polished writer, although he never
achieved the epic vision of a Steinbeck or the fine ear of a Dos Passos.

Like Lorry Lewis or Bigger Thomas, Caldwell's characters are doomed, but they are also bizarre and grotesque. In one short story, for example, Caldwell created Grady Walters, who kept a severely retarded black man, Blue Boy, as a pet; to impress visitors, Walters had Blue Boy show off some of his tricks: dancing, reenacting a pig slaughter, or masturbating. *Tobacco Road* was likewise set in Caldwell's native South and populated with a similar set of bizarre individuals. The characters in this novel have harelips and missing noses, drive their cars over a grandmother without the least remorse, and blithely fornicate in full public view on the front lawn. They are a notably libidinous crew, and the novel's sexual content led some audiences to consider *Tobacco Road* little more than a pornographic potboiler. Caldwell had something more in mind, however, and with his protagonist, Jeeter Lester, showed that there was a positive side to these benighted people. To be sure, Jeeter is no Tom Joad, for rather than coming to the aid of his family, he steals food from his own children. But Jeeter has a redeeming devotion to the soil, a visceral love of the land that leaves him "all weak and shaky" when he smells newly plowed ground. He desperately wants to plant things in the Georgia earth and knows exactly how he wants to be buried in it himself. Yet, as would befit the protagonist of a social realist novel, Jeeter manages to plant neither himself nor his seeds. Caldwell's character is consumed in a house fire, dying without having plowed a single furrow in the last seven years.[44]

Nelson Algren stood apart from Caldwell, Conroy, and the others, for he came from a more middle-class background. Holed up in college at Urbana, he graduated in 1931 and went looking for work—only to discover, to his surprise, that the Depression was on. While in college, he "had been assured that it was a strive and succeed world." But after a little fruitless job-hunting, he became convinced otherwise: "Everything I'd been told was wrong." Instead of universally rewarding people's efforts, American society produced "outcasts," and Algren soon began to write about those discarded individuals. He created characters like Cass McKay, a thoroughly selfish and unlikable youth inclined to robbery and rape. Cass's selfishness came naturally to an American outcast, for any ability "to see farther than the end of his nose had been dulled . . . into atrophy by hunger and cold and frequent humiliation."[45]

Cass was like Bigger, a person for whom America had no place and whom the country seemed quite willing to do without. Such lower-class figures were unlike Farrell's and Herbst's middle-class ones, for they were excluded from capitalism's acquisitive game even before the contest started. What linked these middle-class and lower-class characters was their common inability to regulate and control their lives. Whether reeling from the beatings they took or dizzy from gazing at unattainable heights, they led lives that were mostly drift with very little mastery. Edward Dahlberg, for example, took Lorry Lewis through two novels in which society pushed him about willy-nilly, and then Dahlberg left him on a street corner hopelessly fantasizing that he might "kick some go into himself" someday. Farrell developed Studs Lonigan as a more likable character than Lorry, but with a life that was just as uncontrolled; America had so enthralled Studs with those chimeras of masculinity, property, and heaven that he "never took time off to think of what he was doing."[46] In *U.S.A.*, Dos Passos built a whole nation full of such purposeless people, actors who drifted on the social winds, bumped into each other, and then ricocheted off in new directions. Dos Passos's final character, his archetypical American, was a homeless hitchhiker going no particular place. Dos Passos gave the man no true name but called him "Vag" (for the weary vagrant, *not* a carefree vagabond) and, through him, epitomized Americans—untethered figures in a society that specialized in casting people adrift.

Yet, for all their aimlessness, these American lives were hardly monotonous ones. The social novelists punctuated their tales of drift with episodes of incredible violence. Many of the characters were lower-class people without shelter or security, treacherously exposed to hazardous conditions. One of Kromer's impoverished young drifters, for example, tries to jump a speeding freight, falls under the train, and bleeds to death from the stumps where once his right arm and leg had been. Conroy similarly portrayed a coal miner trapped in a cave-in, a man who remains agonizingly conscious as the weight slowly crushes him to death. But the violence in these tales was not just the random lightning bolts of fate striking the precariously exposed poor. It was also like static electricity that built up with the movement of the characters until it suddenly arced between them. Social novelists had their actors kill and maim each other with frequency and relish. This was not so much the writers' introverted effort to exorcise injuries they themselves had received from the larger society, nor were these scenes merely the honest portrayals of life among the poor. Instead, the mayhem arose primarily from the authors' efforts to make their critique of America as dark as possible. In their presentations, life in the United States was not only violent, it was so stifled that this violence was one of the few avenues of self-expression open to people; with no way to make any positive mark on the world, Americans could only leave some scars on the faces of their fellow victims. Algren's Hooverville hobos batter each other constantly and get some fulfillment from the fighting. Standing over a defeated opponent, "you could look down and see dark blood bubbling over torn lips and know that it was you who had brought the blood up the throat and you who had ripped off those lips."[47] *There*, at least, one's actions had consequence. In Farrell's Chicago, violence is something like a necessary tonic. Two white men jump and severely beat two blacks, and one of the attackers explains that he must "sock somebody to make the day exciting and put me in good spirits for my date tonight." Steinbeck similarly described a chicken farmer who regularly attends the executions at a prison, for that is the only way in which he can experience any sense of profound emotion. Killing holds a like attraction for Wright's Bigger Thomas. Although Bigger commits murder, he has no regrets. For the first time in his life, he has rejected the hangdog passivity white society demands, and actually *acted*: "For a little while I was free," he tells his lawyer, Max, "I was doing something." Max makes the same point at Bigger's trial, telling the jury that American society has "so contrived and ordered the lives of men" that they are impelled to murder "through the thirst for excitement, exultation and elation."[48]

This theme of violence was dismal stuff, and it emerged in shocking ways. But violence constituted only the darkest side of a decidedly gloomy genre, and social novelists did not use it for mere shock value. Instead, they employed this furious brutality to bring a calculated bitterness to their social criticism.[49] The authors set out to assess the human costs of the collapsing American system, found the price staggering, and branded capitalism a villainous extortionist. Only a few people managed to achieve success, and theirs were hollow achievements, for they were forced to abandon humanity and warmth on their way to the top. The rest could not even enter the race for wealth and were forever destined to deepest privation. These fictional Americans were trapped in an intractable system that would only grant them lives of unreflective drifting interrupted with occasional self-expressive outbursts against their fellow prisoners.

Communism: The Appeal of Direction
and the Problem of Freedom

The Depression's social novelists did not stop at raging against an unjust society and portraying Americans as its helpless victims. Writing with real-life miseries of the Depression in mind, they were as unwilling as Steinbeck to say that those miseries would continue forever. Some of the authors did not move beyond social criticism to give their protagonists the comfort of hopeful futures, but these writers abandoned fiction before they designed escapes from the Depression's clutches.[50] The other social novelists shunned the notion that humans were destined to permanent anguish, for that sounded too much like predestination. They rejected any such formulation and instead strove to give their characters some way to influence the world. For this reason, Steinbeck forsook the automatons of his naturalistic phalanxes and turned to Rose of Sharon, a creature possessing both the ability and the freedom to nourish Steinbeck's universal human family. Other novelists similarly furnished their characters with the means and opportunities to make better worlds. Yet they portrayed most human actions as more the product of broad forces than of any person's free will. Time after time they conjured up futures that might bear the passing imprint of some character, but the final shape of those futures was beyond the individual's control.

In doing this, social novelists displayed a sense of history akin to Karl Marx's. Marx was as displeased as they were with conditions of his contemporary world, and he foresaw a time when those miseries would fall away. Like the social novelists, he granted that humans could (Marx even demanded they *should*) help bring about a more just world and influence its final dimensions. Ultimately, though, Marx believed that the new world would arise from great historical forces and take a grand shape that no individual could completely imagine. Thus for Marx, as for the social novelists, fate and hope were intertwined in the course of events. He and the novelists shared this optimism: so certainly was there a better world a-coming that no individual could derail it.

For those authors who gave their actors some escape from tragic fate, Communism was the single most frequently discussed solution to the problems of the Depression. Neither those discussions nor their kinship with Marx, however, were enough to make the writers into good Communists. They scrutinized Communism, found it alluring, but eventually rejected it. Jack Conroy and Edward Newhouse came the closest to embracing the Party in their fiction and to creating novels that mirrored the Party's proletarian formula. Yet even these two were not steadfast Party men. Though Conroy's characters accepted the Party, Conroy could not bring himself to do so. *The Disinherited* (1933) is his clumsy, disjointed first novel that nonetheless portrays Missouri coal miners as compelling, compassionate people. Conroy knew his material well, for he had lost his father and two brothers to the Missouri coal fields. His central character is an autobiographical figure, a young man who leaves the fields for industrial Detroit and returns home during the Depression; once back in Missouri, he becomes an organizer determined to lead his people to better lives. Conroy's skills had improved considerably when he wrote *A World to Win* two years later. This time he made his characters even more militant and active. They become Communist Party organizers and orchestrate the workers' discontent into a "prelude to storm," Conroy's phrase for the first rumblings that hinted of a coming revolution. But throughout these years Conroy paid little attention to Marxist ideology and cared even less for it; so repellent did he find the theorizing that "just to look at *Das Kapital* on the shelf gave me a headache."

Edward Newhouse probably had an easier time with Marx, and certainly had a closer affiliation with the Communist Party—he was a charter member of the first John Reed Club (a Party's organization for young artists) and an employee of both the *New Masses* and *Daily Worker*. For a while, Newhouse thought that Communism could produce personal happiness, and Gene Marsay, his protagonist in *You Can't Sleep Here* (1934) and *This Is Your Day* (1937), is a young man whom Newhouse led through hard times and finally into a full, happy life as a Party organizer. But after his second novel, Newhouse began to write about other characters who were less radical and less directed. Simultaneously, his faith in the Party began to falter as he learned about the brutality of the Moscow trials, and by the late thirties, Newhouse found himself "without any political molds to pour into." He quit the Party and its publications, started working for the decidedly unproletarian *New Yorker*, and shortly after the publication of *This Is Your Day*, began writing about people who drifted along without benefit of *any* guidance, much less the Party's.[51]

Other social novelists responded to the Party much as Newhouse and

Conroy did. Communism's emphasis on justice for the oppressed appealed to their democratic instincts, Marx's predictions of capitalism's collapse appeared to be coming true with the Depression, and the Communist Party was certainly the best organized of the country's progressive forces. Furthermore, the Party managed to make itself especially appealing with the Popular Front of the later part of the Depression, loosening its ideological rigidity and welcoming liberal allies. For all this, though, social novelists found the Party too demanding, its people too acerbic, and its art too homogeneous. Communism both attracted and repelled them, and their enthusiasm cooled markedly with the later thirties when they learned, as Newhouse had, more about the Party and its Russian comrades. Eventually they rejected Communism as a means for bringing management to a disorderly world and direction to their characters' lives.

Communism's attractions were numerous, and the Party could frequently rely upon the assistance of social novelists. Dos Passos had been a key figure in the Sacco and Vanzetti defense efforts during the twenties, working side by side with Communists on the defense committee. His activism continued into the early thirties, and in 1931, he, Herbst, and Dahlberg joined Theodore Dreiser's Communist-backed National Committee for Defense of Political Prisoners. Likewise, Algren participated in Party-led demonstrations and headed some of its fund-raising efforts for Spanish Loyalists. The Communists' sense of direction, so different from the decade's prevalent aimlessness, appealed to Farrell, and close to the end of his trilogy, he drew a stark comparison between Studs Lonigan's drunken, meandering heritage and the orderly marchers in a Party parade, people who with their purpose "were happy, happier than he was."[52]

Yet for all the authors' admiration for Communism, they were "confused liberals" who finally preferred the civility and flexibility of their confusion to the Communists' missionary zeal. Party members seemed brusque perfectionists with personalities too snappish and ideas too unbending to suit the social novelists. Algren resented the way in which Communists objected to his drinking, and he complained that they had "a rigidity, a kind of authoritarian attitude" that alienated him and other imbibing fellow travelers. Steinbeck found similar "waspish qualities" among the Communists he met in the California fields, and he ridiculed those organizers as "unhumanly virtuous men."[53] If the Communists were too prudish—a complaint suggesting that the novelists harbored some lingering biases from the 1920s—the comrades' ideas were also too obtuse. Herbst believed that the Party's unbending dogma and "phrases like the 'toiling masses' did not answer terrible questions." All about her "there were always people, real people," who were not abstract "masses" but who had unique problems that did not fit into any ideological pattern. Dos Passos also believed that inflexible doctrines stood in the way of truth, and with the Communists in mind, he warned Robert Cantwell that "sectarian opinions" erred by unquestioningly accepting "the formulas of past events" as patterns for the future. Never the most discerning of political thinkers, Steinbeck was baffled by the ideological shadings that were so vitally important to Communists, and he could not distinguish Stalinists from Trotskyists "except that the Stalinists were in power in Russia and the others were out. Anyway, they didn't like each other." By the end of the decade, Steinbeck found the modern world too preoccupied with such distractions, and, as traveling reporter Lewis Adamic had done, he took flight from it. Like the other novelists, Steinbeck believed that there were more important things to life than quibbling over political ideas. Sailing off to explore Mexico's Pacific coast, he found among "the simple good Indians on the shore" an undoctrinaire acceptance of life that seemed to him "a truer thing than ideologies."[54]

Social novelists were also attracted to, yet uncomfortable with, the Party's literary policies. They generally shared the Party's position that literature should assume an active role in the world, and they subscribed to the view that literature of the twenties had been an "art for art's sake." The thirties seemed like a time to forgo inward self-examination and look outward in social analysis. Josephine Herbst arrived at this sentiment at the Depression's beginning. In 1930, she attended the Communists' Second World Plenum of the International Bureau of Revolutionary Literature, held in Kharkov, Russia, and returned with considerable enthusiasm for fiction that dealt more with politics and reportage than with psychology and symbolism. Writers in her own circle seemed to be making this shift in their work, and Herbst approved. She displayed that satisfaction in her novels, creating a character who abandoned his earlier esthetic preoccupations for new political ones. All of Herbst's Depression novels were autobiographical, and one protagonist, Jonathan Chance, was modeled closely after Herbst's husband, writer John Herrman. Herrman was a former expatriate who returned to the United States with the Depression, joined the Communist Party, and took up radical politics and literature. In Herbst's novels, Jonathan Chance is also a writer who passed the twenties in a Bohemian café crowd that gathered "to discuss art and letters, to ponder over Joyce and Gertrude Stein." (In Europe, Edward Dahlberg had been one of Herrman's close companions in similar real-life café discussions.) But with the thirties, Chance's group leaves behind its wine and small talk to examine the closed factories; as did John Herrman, Jonathan Chance abandons Joyce to write about "the system that was creating top-heavy wealth for the few and misery for the many." This was an activist literature, and like Herbst, the other social novelists found it appealing. Eight of them joined her to sign a call for the Party-backed American Writers' Congress, numbering themselves among those who recognized "the necessity of personally helping to accelerate the destruction of capitalism." When the Congress actually convened, Algren, Dahlberg, Farrell, and Dos Passos were among those who addressed the assembly of capitalism's literary foes.[55]

Theirs was still not a solid front, however. Herbst, Farrell, and Dahlberg attended the Congress but ridiculed among themselves the solemnity of the proceedings. Not only did the Party seem too self-important, it wanted writers to do more than simply disapprove of capitalism. Its program for proletarian literature demanded that the novelist become an actual combatant in the class struggle, one who demonstrated Party doctrine through formula stories and rallied others to the cause with prescribed militant appeals. Social novelists shied from this role. Dos Passos was willing to sacrifice some freedom of action to work with the Party toward their shared goals. But he refused to write the sort of fiction that Party leaders wanted, and he used the Writers' Congress to tell them so. To impose formulas on literature was to have writers "give up their freedom of thought," he lectured the Congress, and to insist that novelists follow the Party's "minute prescriptions of doctrine" was to engage in "boss rule thuggery."

Herbst also shuddered at the prospect of those directives and thought herself strong enough to write without them. She argued that those authors who accepted the line were pitiful weaklings, for "dogma to them was the needed arm, not anathema." For the same reasons, Farrell found himself pulling away from the Party and drifting toward anti-Stalinist literary leftists such as William Phillips, Philip Rahv, and others of the *Partisan Review* orbit. His disenchantment with the Party surfaced in his 1936 *Note on Literary Criticism*, a work that still stands as one of the most

eloquent and informed discussions of Marxism and intellectual independence to emerge from the period's left-wing literary debates. Though Farrell remained a committed progressive, he saw in the Party's esthetics a
disturbing inclination to forge literature into a political weapon in which
truth was subordinated to doctrine. Such a process turned his own literary goal of "a true recreation of social relationships and human beings"
into a commodity "less important than the merely formal ideology." Dos
Passos agreed and, in a letter to Edmund Wilson, suggested that those
writers who were "more interested in getting at realities than in being on
the right side" should be wary of orthodox Communism. Herbst likewise
thought the Communists too easily sacrificed accuracy to ideology, and
she was miffed when her assigned interpreter at the Kharkov conference
translated her actual speech into one that he thought she *should* have
given.[56]

Thus for social novelists, the Party's esthetics not only compromised the
truth, its policies also inhibited expression where the authors demanded
free reign in their writing. But the social novelists found still another
shortcoming in proletarian literature. Like many other liberals, they were
inclined to regard Marxism as a "vulgar materialism." To them, it appeared to exclude freedom of action; Marxism, especially the Communist
Party's version of Marxism, seemed to say that all human behavior origi-
nated in existing material conditions and unfolded in precise accord with
Marx's predictions. The Party's literary program appeared just as bereft of
free will, demanding that characters act only as official doctrine said they
should act. It was, Herbst lamented, "a deterministic construction of
man's role."[57] The social novelists wanted to create a literature in which
people had free will and the ability to govern the flow of events. Although
they never satisfactorily achieved this goal in their own fiction, they rejected the proletarian formula because it portrayed human behavior as the
product of historical forces rather than of individual free will.

Of the novelists, Richard Wright best revealed this dual fascination
with, and rejection of, the Communist Party. Leery of the Party during
the early part of the Depression, Wright eventually attended a meeting of
its John Reed Club. He came home with piles of literature and, in those
writings, discovered a group of writers who seemed engaged in "an organized search for the truth of the lives of the oppressed and isolated."
Wright decided to enter that search himself, became a member of the
Club, and joined the Party in 1933 or 1934, finding in both organizations

the sense of belonging that Party activities sometimes brought to thirties intellectuals. Over the years, though, Wright noticed that Party members seemed increasingly close-minded. The party refused to recognize his individual desires, gave him assignments on the basis of its needs rather than his qualifications, and let him know "it was not wise to be seen reading books not endorsed by the Communist Party." In addition to this disregard for his own cherished freedoms, the other Party members seemed paralyzed into ideological rigidity. They were more involved in shoring up the Party line than in the search for truth that he had once thought was their quest. It took a full eight years for Wright to renounce the Party, but when he did, it was because he had come to feel that he was perhaps the only member with a preference for the objective truth. Wright quit the Party and its dogma in 1942, proclaiming that "there is a need to think and feel honestly, and that comes first."[58]

Like other social novelists, Wright advocated a social role for literature, but the Communists' literary proposals eventually looked too restrictive. His first few years in Chicago were what he later called his "cynical period," Bohemian days of debunking all sorts of sacred cows: God, business, and the revolution. But Wright came to regard his work as too aloof, "too lacking in reference to social action." After joining the Party, he began writing pieces about social action, some even calling for revolution. At first, Marxism seemed to him a marvelous writer's tool, for he believed that good literature had to move beyond the simple description of human activities, find the pattern in those occurrences, and then mold the future to fit the pattern. When he gave his fellow black authors a "blueprint for Negro writing," he told them that they must have some sort of general hypothesis—such as Marxism—in order to avoid becoming stuck at the level of mere narrative. In one of the most perceptive analyses offered by any of the social novelists, Wright realized that "anyone destitute of a theory about the meaning, structure and direction of modern society is a lost victim in a world he cannot understand or control." Yet for all Wright's understandable respect for the insight and the leverage that a theory can provide, he would not lastingly embrace Marxism. Wright held that literature should ultimately correspond to the actual world, not the hoped-for one. Having praised Communism in his blueprint, he went on to caution that "Marxism is but the starting point. No theory of life can take the place of life."[59] By the end of the Depression, he came to believe that Party officials, with their inflexible proletarian literature, had lost all sight of life's actual complexities. Under their direction, literature could only become as aloof as it had been during the cynical Bohemian days.

Communism demanded too high a price. To the social novelists who gave their characters some release from misery, it provided an unsatisfactory escape. Like Richard Wright, they sooner or later found Communism personally and esthetically noisome. The Communists seemed boorish and intolerant, requiring loyalty of thought and action where Wright and the others cherished independence. Social novelists of the Depression wanted freedom for themselves and free will for their characters. But the Party demanded discipline, and its literature prescribed a deterministic role for humans.

Weapons of Liberation

Social novelists saw Americans as engaged in a battle against oppression and hunger, and they refused to arm their characters with Communist weapons of class warfare. They nonetheless sought the solace of assured victory and turned to the arsenal of American liberal tradition for some well-worn weapons: education, civil liberties, and community. The novelists believed that these would enable their characters and the real people whom they represented to become the masters of life, directing destiny where they had earlier been its pawns. Yet for all the power these weapons were supposed to give their protagonists, social novelists did not provide any means for their actors to lay hold of the arms when they were needed. Education was meant to be an invaluable tool, but only certain people proved able to learn; civil liberties were supposed to help people in their fight, yet the freedoms came more by geographic chance than through human initiative; communities were intended as instruments of dominion but were impossible to steer toward any particular goal. Not content to leave their characters unarmed in ugly worlds, the authors provided what they thought were powerful weapons. But they left the keys to the armory in fate's hands.

James T. Farrell believed that an educated mind was the essential tool for solving humanity's problems. Born to an Irish-Catholic family in Chicago, Farrell first attended parochial schools and then went on to the University of Chicago, where he became interested in writing. Politically active during the 1930s, Farrell supported a variety of strikes and was once arrested, along with Newhouse and Dahlberg, for picketing a department store. An adamant anti-Stalinist by 1936, he publicly denounced the Moscow trials and, in 1937, traveled to Mexico with John Dewey to observe the proceedings of the Leon Trotsky defense committee. Farrell's close association with naturalism led many people to conclude that he was a strict determinist. But Farrell insisted that he was not, and held that humans could govern and direct their lives with trained minds, the necessary instruments for manipulating the world's workings. Farrell's central caveat was that the mind must remain free to follow all courses of inquiry, or else humans would lose their only means for possibly controlling events. In Farrell's estimate, there were two great threats to his cherished freedom of mind, Catholicism and the Communist Party. An unreflective acceptance of Church doctrine was, just like the swallowing of Party policy, "a means of intellectual suicide."[60] Intellect was humanity's only possible tool for directing destiny, and dogma, whether sacred or profane, dulled the mind and lessened the chances that people could influence fate.

Danny O'Neill was the most autobiographical of Farrell's Depression characters, and by using his mind, Danny gained some control of his life. Studs Lonigan had unquestioningly accepted the dogmas of his world and then commenced a life of meaningless drifting. But Danny went on to the University of Chicago, read Thorstein Veblen (*not* Marx), and experienced "an elation of intellectual discovery and stimulation" that Studs never knew. Church schools had taught both Studs and Danny that "the world was good and just, and that the good and just were rewarded." With his trained intellect, Danny weighed those teachings against the actual world of poverty and injustice and came to realize that "all his education in Catholic schools, all he had heard about and absorbed, had been lies." But rather than let Danny molder in disillusionment, Farrell gave him a glimpse of "a better world" unburdened with Catholic dogma. Danny's education allowed him to direct his life, and though Studs could only drift, Danny "would destroy the old world with his pen; he would create the new."[61]

Farrell designed Danny as the solution to Studs's world. But there was a flaw in Farrell's design, for Danny was *too* different from Studs and the others of Irish-Catholic Chicago. Throughout his childhood Danny stood apart from the other boys, rejected from their games, teased because of his glasses, always "different from the other kids." Farrell intentionally created Danny with this difference, what he called "an irreducible core of inadaptability to the world he knows."[62] Therein lay the difficulty in proposing Danny's pathway as a release from Studs's world. Danny managed to escape because the historical accidents of his birth and upbringing made him never completely a part of that world. He could not help getting free any more than Studs could avoid being stuck. In short, Danny was as fated as Studs was, only he was destined to break the chains of Irish Catholicism and give some direction to his life, while Studs was ordained to remain shackled and have no control over his existence.

Where Farrell thought that education could help Americans fight oppressive social forces, Dos Passos believed that individual freedom was the key to freedom from those forces. Born the illegitimate son of a powerful New York attorney, Dos Passos attended Choate and Harvard and was one of the literary Americans who served as ambulance drivers in World War I. By the 1920s, he had become an accomplished novelist and written plays as a member of the New Playwrights' Theater. Dos Passos was consistently an advocate of individual liberties, and the Sacco and Vanzetti case convinced him that capitalism was the biggest American threat to those liberties. Capitalism suppressed and silenced the two Italian anarchists, denied them a fair trial, and seemed responsible for many of the country's other ailments. (Dos Passos was hardly alone in his outrage over the case; joining him on one protest picket line were traveling reporter James Rorty and painter William Gropper.) In 1928, he traveled in the Soviet Union and examined its alternative to capitalism. But by the mid-thirties, he had come to believe that Soviet-style collectivism offered little protection for individual freedoms, and that the only hope for securing them lay in the Jeffersonian principles that seemed to have proliferated in the early days of the United States. Dos Passos's position became an openly nationalistic one, and by the time he wrote the third volume of his trilogy, *The Big Money* (1936), he was critical of both capitalists and the Communists, painting the radicals as ineffectual bunglers and condemning the plutocrats as men who had "taken the words of our fathers and made them slimy and foul." In 1934 he declared that the country needed a "passionate unmarxian revival of Anglo Saxon democracy," and through his narrator's voice in *The Big Money*, Dos Passos pledged to "bring back (I too Walt Whitman) our storybook democracy."[63]

Dos Passos's use of the word "storybook" revealed more than he intended, for his democracy worked more by the magic common in children's stories than by any concrete process. Democracy was to be the solution to the complaints of *U.S.A.*, but there was no way for humans to nurture it and then employ it to tame unruly capitalism. Dos Passos's position was one of faith, and his program scarcely more than a Whitmanesque singing of that faith. He gave no hint of how democracy's guarantees of individual freedom would help his characters, nor of how individualism would keep them from once again mindlessly pursuing prosperity. It would just do so, somehow. Moreover, in Dos Passos's scheme, people had no power to secure their individualism by encouraging democracy. It simply grew by itself in the United States, where there lay "latent spores of democracy . . . in the local American soil," untilled seeds that occurred naturally and sprouted only in their own good time. There was no reason to worry about the survival of those seeds, for they had weathered earlier threats, "and there's no reason why they shouldn't survive monopoly capitalism."[64] Dos Passos's solution to the quandaries of *U.S.A.* was a democracy that would eventually and inevitably guarantee people their individual liberties, yet it was a democracy that they had no power to cultivate. Humans were no more in control of their lives than they had been throughout *U.S.A.*, but at least now the fate awaiting them was benign.

Among other social novelists, there was little sentiment for individualism and no echoes of Dos Passos's cry for a nationalistic brand of it. The other writers shared Dos Passos's concern for personal liberty, but they did not follow him to the point of rejecting collectivism for individualism.[65] For Cantwell, Wright, Herbst, and Steinbeck, *community* was the answer to Americans' Depression problems and the means by which their protagonists escaped misery. Through communities of varying sizes, these writers granted their protagonists a sense of identity, the satisfaction of family-like affection, and a love for others that would replace the hatred responsible for social evils.

These four writers usually placed their characters in some sort of crisis, created emerging communities around them, and then suggested that those communities could ease their actors' suffering. Steinbeck's Joads began as a displaced family who put their own welfare before that of others. But as they endure that harrowing trek to California, their notion of family gradually grows until they come to consider all people their kin. Cantwell emphasized a similar sort of concern in *The Land of Plenty*. Taking a factory in the Pacific Northwest as his setting, Cantwell created such bonds between the workers that they could silently, mysteriously, and almost instantaneously communicate with each other. This communication system quietly broadcasts the news of one worker's serious injury, and during a strike, that same system enables the workers to walk out suddenly in one unified body, each sharing a common emotion of excited pride. Cantwell's protagonist is Johnny Hagen, a young worker with an unhappy home life. As Steinbeck had, Cantwell replaced this character's biological family with a larger family-like community. Johnny grows closer and closer to his family of strikers, getting from them the warmth he seldom receives at home. Johnny's full adoption into that larger family occurs at the novel's mawkish conclusion; after the bosses have killed Johnny's father, the leader of the strikers moves into the father's empty place. With Johnny in tears, the leader tenderly "put his hand on his shoulder, 'Come on, son,' he said gently, 'don't cry.' "[66]

Richard Wright thought that the country could use more of this kind of empathy. As a black in racist America, he came to believe that the nation's problems arose chiefly from an unfounded hatred of people for one another, hatred that sundered a fundamental unity tying all humans to each other. It seemed to him that this "problem of human unity" deserved more attention than even hunger or poverty, that it was indeed "more important than life itself." This "common bond uniting men" possessed much the same power of instant communication that existed among Cantwell's workers, for Wright's ideal world would have "a continuous current of shared thought and feeling circulating through the social system, like blood coursing through the body." If people were not alone, were not cut off from each other, then hatred would presumably have no place to grow. In *Native Son* he chose to describe this unity on a small scale, the bond that begins to grow between Bigger and his lawyer, Max. Before the trial Max and Bigger have a conversation in which Max seems to take a sincere interest in Bigger's life and thoughts. For the first time ever, Bigger senses that he might not be alone in the world, comes to hope that "in that touch, response of recognition, there would be union . . . a supporting oneness, a wholeness which had been denied him all his life."[67] It seemed as never before that there could possibly be some relationship besides hatred between Bigger and the white world, and hence the possibility that if whites had only extended him Max's kindness earlier, then Bigger might not have murdered.

Josephine Herbst's release through community was similar. In the early

twenties, she had yearned for the same sort of primal flowage Wright and
Cantwell described, for "currents, down under, that no eye can see." In
the thirties, the possibility of reaching these currents seemed stronger to
her, and by 1933, she thought she could see the emergence of a "new
group society." It appeared to her that up until then the United States had
been largely an individualistic country, a land of entrepreneurs whose
unswerving allegiance to capital produced the Depression. But the tide
had turned and for the better. People were beginning to think that they
could best insure their well-being not as individuals but as members of
groups. The 1930s had therefore become a time when an individual's personal sentiments were "haphazard, trivial, inconsequent compared with
his feelings experienced as a member of a particular group."[68]

Herbst's central character in the Trexler trilogy is Vicky Wendel. Vicky
travels a route strikingly similar to Rose of Sharon's, for she loses her baby
and husband and then tries to take the whole of humanity for her family.
Her husband leaves her because he becomes a cold ideologue, allowing
Communist dogma to replace the "fellowship of man for man" that had
first drawn him to the Party. But Vicky avoids his error. She travels to
Cuba as a correspondent and visits the country's revolutionary peasants.
These insurgents are engaged in a battle for justice and have committed
themselves to a fight that could eventually help all oppressed peoples.
They have a certain ideology to be sure, but they are driven by their love
for humanity and not by some abstract dogma. From them, and especially
from one of their leaders, Vicky receives the strength to give herself to
that same larger community. The leader "had looped his life to an entire
world; was she less able than he?"[69]

In this manner, Herbst, Wright, Steinbeck, and Cantwell offered their
characters some escape through communities. But these communities
were not effective political devices for achieving direction in a universe
filled with unruly forces. Rather than solutions to the characters' plights,
the communities were either failures or unfulfilled promises. Cantwell's
strike falters under the onslaught of the company police, and his workers'
community evaporates as its members flee before the charge. Bigger's
relationship with Max likewise fails to provide the promised release, for
rather than offering the kinship and "deeper awareness that Bigger sought
so hungrily," his lawyer remains remote, "upon another planet, far off in
space."[70] Max insists upon discussing Marxist abstractions, and Bigger
goes to his death as lonely as he has ever been. Steinbeck's characters

were not so quite lonely at the conclusion of *The Grapes of Wrath*, for he arranged the nursing scene between Rose of Sharon and the starving stranger. But the possibility of any material benefits from Steinbeck's family of all humans remained an unredeemed pledge; the novel concludes with the Joads in worse condition that ever, literally with only the clothes on their backs. Herbst's story also ends with an unfulfilled promise. The distance between Vicky Wendel and the Cuban rebels is simply too great for bonds to grow between them during her brief visit. Though Herbst tried to fabricate some sort of connection between the middle-class Vicky and the Cuban peasants, Herbst was unable to do so. The greatest similarity between Vicky and the rebels is one of loss—she loses tears over her troubles and they lose blood because of theirs.

These communities failed in yet another sense. The writers did not give their characters a means for controlling fate but simply made fate into a brighter thing. They proposed to bring their characters closer together, to mesh them so that the distance between the self and the other became infinitesimal. Since few creatures willingly harm themselves, and since there would be little distinction between the self and the community, people would supposedly stop hurting each other. If the communities were as large as the universal ones that Herbst, Wright, and Steinbeck proposed, then *all* oppression would end. But just because people achieve a unity that makes their lives easier and warmer, this does not mean that they have attained the ability to direct or examine their circumstances. Wright had seen this in Chicago's black neighborhoods on the night of Joe Louis's sensational victory over Max Baer, his white opponent. The crowds in the streets were ecstatic, centuries of white oppression seemed insignificant given the new sense of black invincibility, and there was "a feeling of unity, of oneness." That unity had no purpose, however, and was instead what Wright characterized as a "wild river," completely unharnessed and without direction. This was the problem that lay at the heart of these community novels, for the actors had little sense of purpose behind their coming together. Bigger sought Max's understanding not to get out of jail but to make his stay in jail less lonesome. Similarly, Steinbeck's migrants reached out to each other much as Cantwell's workers did, uniting "without knowing why," and acting out of something closer to instinct than reason.[71] Their unity brought them no control or free will but instead melted them into loving communities. These groups might do some good, but they worked largely like analgesics, reducing pains in the social body, pains such as racial or wage oppression. They did nothing to provide society with a new life or to keep new disease from infecting it. Rather than giving humans control over destiny, Herbst, Cantwell, Steinbeck, and Wright made destiny more benign while warming it with the fires of fellowship. The goal of human control over life remained as elusive for these authors as it was for Farrell and Dos Passos.

Fate: A Habit of Mind

I n the 1960s, Nelson Algren took a retrospective look at the 1930s. As he compared the two decades, it seemed to him that the novelist's lot had been a much easier one in the Depression years. These were the early sixties (before Algren knew much about Vietnam), and they seemed to him tiresome years in which to write. The times offered few compelling topics, for the social forces of the day appeared neither particularly villainous nor particularly praiseworthy. In contrast, the thirties seemed to have been a less ambiguous period, when the issues had been clearly drawn "between human rights and property rights," and when it not only had been easier to write, but it had also been "easier to be right."[72] Algren's hindsight was doubtlessly too kind to the thirties, for creating a good novel was probably no easier then than at any other time (and the difficulty of getting a living in the Depression may well have made it harder). But in expressing his preference for the thirties, Algren neatly summarized the social novelists' concerns and unwittingly revealed their shortcomings.

Depression America held few ambiguities for these writers, and, as Algren indicated, economics was a vital contemporary issue for them. Capitalism had ridden roughshod over Americans' rights to sustenance and independence, and the authors penned novels that were grim portraits of its victims. Many of their characters were hungry and destitute, and the few who achieved some physical comfort became spiritual cripples in the process. These were stories packed with woe and suffering, in which capitalism was the culprit. In this way, morality, economics, and art were all intertwined, for the novelists believed that there were good and bad economic relationships, and hoped that they could correctly praise the one and damn the other in their books. The very suffering of the

Depression seemed to call upon a writer to make these distinctions, and some of the novelists achieved a balance between their moralizing and their writing. Wright and Dos Passos, for example, wrote novels that were compelling and imaginative. But for most of the social novelists, as for Algren, it was so *easy* "to be right" that they were not successful in linking their judgments with their art. The issues of the moment were so clearly drawn between property rights and human rights that the writers often offered no more than stereotypical portraits of evil oppressors and inno- cent victims. The times may have made it easier for Algren and the others to be right, but the Depression did not encourage their originality or their subtlety.

There was another way in which writing was easy during the thirties. As writers who had absorbed the American naturalist tradition, they were both familiar with its principles and uncomfortable with its deterministic implications. But the Depression made it easy to see human will as sub- ject to environmental control, and the social novelists never managed to fabricate a full alternative to the naturalism that they found so chafing. As optimists, they were not content to rage aimlessly, and like Steinbeck, they wanted some sort of deliverance for their protagonists. They duly examined the Communists' alternative to capitalism, for it promised to make people like one of Wright's characters, "focused and pointed" oppo- nents of capitalist oppression.[73] But Wright, and the other social novelists like him, came to believe that Communism was too focused and pointed, for the Party's official line prescribed human conduct and excluded free will. In this way, social novelists strove for the security that capitalism could not offer and the self-determination that Communism seemed to lack. Their great quest during the Depression was *both* for better worlds and for the ability to govern those worlds.

Ultimately they chose security over self-determination. In their desire to show that neither the Depression nor capitalism would endure, the authors tended to misplace free will.[74] Reluctant to portray their charac- ters as hapless, miserable victims, yet accustomed to portraying humans as destiny's pawns, they gave their protagonists better, but not more con- trollable, lives. These Depression writers never fully managed to change the way in which they portrayed human behavior. With their talk of free will and their adamant rejections of Communist dogma, social novelists suggested that a new sort of character would be necessary if their fiction moved beyond immediate social criticism to portray a new society. Rather than being society's passive victims, such protagonists would redirect it along paths of their own choosing. Yet the social novelists created few such characters. As they composed their condemnations of capitalism, they retained the habit of seeing human action as the product of broad forces beyond individual control, and they never completed the literary transition from passive, weak characters to active, heroic ones.

As Algren indicated, these Depression novelists repeatedly chose the easier course. In part, these choices were made because some of the authors were not especially gifted and even perhaps because some of them were lazy. But there is yet a final consideration that helps explain their inclination to emphasize historical necessity rather than human volition. The thirties were insistent years, and the crisis seemed to demand an artistic interpretation that lessened the grip of the present by depicting the future as necessarily better. The Depression was like a mighty storm in which American society foundered. In the urgency of the moment, it seemed most important for social novelists to get their characters into lifeboats and of little significance that the boats had no rudders with which the actors could steer. Moreover, while these castaways of capitalism could not select their own courses, they were destined for better futures because the novelists laced their books with deep currents that would draw them unfailingly toward brighter tomorrows. The authors intended to release Americans from their miserable fate and give them the free will to control their lives. But they wound up giving their characters brighter, yet unmoldable destinies. With their haste and habits of mind, the social novelists neglected freedom· and refurbished fate.

Overleaf: Joe Jones, *We Demand,* 1934. (Butler Institute of American Art.)

FIVE

Born-Again Painting:
The Depression
as Redeeming Catastrophe

ockwell Kent liked to tell allegorical stories. His account of the Depression began, as tales often do, on a cold and stormy evening. Kent sat warm and comfortable beside a blazing hearth, his windows shut tight against the driving rain. Contentedly musing about his painting, he gave little thought to the world outside. Then came a knock at the door. Kent asked who it was, and above the howling of the wind and the confusion of voices came the reply, "America." The artist opened his door to find a tattered, bedraggled crowd, refugees from the Depression's tempest. Among the throng were an old woman symbolizing the country's impoverished elderly, children personifying its futureless youth, and a brutally beaten representative of America's suppressed labor movement. Their spokesman was an unemployed worker who asked Kent, "Can't art somehow help us . . . can't you do something about this Goddamned, senseless, cruel waste and misery?" Kent stood speechless before the spokesman's continuing tirades until finally the crowd shuffled out. Soon a puff of wind came down the chimney, filling his room with smoke. To clear the air, Kent threw open the windows. Upon looking outside, he found that the rain had stopped and the stars had begun to reappear.

From this allegory, Kent wove his explanation of the Depression's effect upon his life. Secluded in his artistic retreat when the crisis struck, he was surprised to learn of its severity. As reports of distress filtered in, he eventually felt compelled to abandon isolation, take up his brushes and aid his beleaguered fellow citizens. The storms of the decade seemed less severe once he emerged to face them, and he was relieved to see a few bright spots here and there among the clouds. Once he was thus smoked out of his "privileged sanctuary," Kent protested the decade's suffering, attained a new sense of purpose in his art, and came to feel "as though reborn."[1]

Other painters had similar sensations of rebirth during the 1930s. Most of these artists claimed that they had once aspired to the "ideal" art career—a detached life devoted to perfecting technique and pursuing beauty, a life led in some remote retreat such as Kent's sanctuary. The Depression dashed any such hopes, proving with their own hardships that the artists were not immune from worldly problems, and demonstrating with its horrible vistas the irrelevance of idyllic paintings. Describing themselves as roused from esthetic reveries, these artists abandoned any pursuit of detached grandeur and committed themselves to social realism, a school of art devoted to delineating and criticizing the actual world. They surveyed the social mess symbolized in Kent's crowd and answered his unemployed worker's plea by painting vivid protests of the oppression, hunger, and despair that plagued ordinary Americans of the thirties. But the Depression did more than propel painters toward a didactic and representational form of painting. In the midst of the larger calamities, and beset with their own personal tragedies, social realists began to despise the sequestered life. They craved both the comfort of knowing that they did not suffer alone and the sympathies of their fellow sufferers. As they painted the plights of everyday people, these artists came to believe they had found among those masses not only a down-to-earth lustiness that seemed to enliven their paintings, but also a welcome they had never before experienced. With the 1930s, social realists saw themselves as regenerate artists, painters whom the Depression redeemed from a former effeteness and brought into communion with "the people."

Philip Evergood: A New Start for Art

Philip Evergood (1901–1973) was a model social realist. The Depression taught him that his purpose was to protest the suffering of the thirties and that his place was alongside those who suffered. Evergood's father was a Polish Jew who painted landscapes, and his mother the daughter of wealthy British parents. When Evergood reached school age, his mother's well-to-do family brought him to England from New York so that he could get a proper education. After Eton and then some time at Cambridge, he rejected the genteel life and, in a decision that alienated him from his mother's family, abandoned them "to live more agreeably . . . as an artist." He first studied art at the Slade School in London, then came back to New York where he worked under "Ash Can" painter George Luks.[2]

By the late 1920s, Evergood had returned to Europe in search of a style and a topic. He respected the flattened perspective and religious scenes of El Greco and painted a number of his own flowing Biblical compositions of Job sitting on the dunghill or Jacob wrestling with the angel. The same fluid style emerged in other paintings of the late twenties, imaginative renditions of classical themes, paintings of centaurs and men, an antique urn, or *Harem Girls* (c. 1927; Figure 1). During this time, he studied the works of post-impressionists and cubists with an appreciation for their technical and stylistic innovations but eventually decided they had little to offer him. These continental genres seemed incapable of rendering the subject he came to prefer—everyday life in the United States. In selecting this topic, Evergood decided that contemporary America was a vast, vital land that was "a fitting subject for the brush of a painter." As products of a different cultural environment, European styles were either too abstract or too urbane for so vibrant and so crass a subject, and he therefore rejected those styles. He gradually turned away from wavy lines and mythical subjects like those of *Harem Girls* and strove to create less flowing images of American workers and their quite different kind of clothing—"the down-to-earth robust rawness of a steel worker's boot, or his wrinkled salt-caked sweater, or his grimy blue jeans." With this move away from mythic scenes, Evergood hoped he had joined the ranks of painters who were "not too effete to describe life," artists such as Pieter Brueghel and Hieronymus Bosch.[3] Evergood's claimed association with such macabre fantasists is revealing, for though he wished to describe life, his intent was not to render it in the literal manner of a Norman Rockwell or an Andrew Wyeth. Instead he chose for himself a species of fantastic expressionism that approximated the cartooning of George Grosz, a combination of caricature and symbolism that permitted Evergood to portray the actual world while freely editorializing about it.

In this way, Evergood's interest in earthy subjects emerged even before the Depression. Although this was at first a purely esthetic concern, it soon became a social one. He returned permanently to the United States in 1931. The thirties brought hard times to the American art community, and Evergood worked as a handyman to support himself. He scraped by with difficulty yet managed the time to paint and search for his desired subjects. The hard times made ruggedly dressed models easy to come by, and he found scores of them when he chanced upon a large shanty town one cold winter evening in 1932. In a snowy vacant lot, there were fifty or so shacks built from cardboard, crates, and mattresses. A group of men, black and white, ignored racial differences to huddle together around a fire. They had nothing. Their food was from garbage cans, their fire was built of driftwood, and even their names were makeshift—Old Foot, Bean Pod, and Terrapin. They welcomed Evergood into their circle; he talked with them and bought gin to ward off the chill. To Evergood, these men were interesting characters with colorful backgrounds, but it was their present misery that most impressed the young Eton-educated artist: "Their tragedy hit me between the eyes because I had never been as close to anything like that before." Then he "got a brain wave." It occurred to him that rather than a mere visitor to the Depression-stricken, he "should be involved in my work with this kind of thing." He ran home to get his drawing pad and pencils, quickly returned to the camp, and sketched the men until dawn.[4] This was the night that ultimately brought Evergood to social realism, for in those people who were the Depression's castoffs, he uncovered all the grimy clothes and ugly life one could ever want to paint. But he also found himself in sympathy with their plight *and* warmly accepted in their circle. By painting such people, he could not only wrestle with life's raw side, he could also protest their circumstances and bask in their fellowship. Having earlier abandoned his family for art, he now spied a way to compensate for that loss by using his art to adopt a new family.

It thus seemed to Evergood that the Depression had occurred at just the right time in his personal career, giving him not only a host of good subjects but also a sense of belonging. He further believed that the crisis had struck at a fortunate time for all of American art, helping to direct it down the engaged, worldly path he had chosen. Sometime in the past, Evergood thought, American artists had taken a wrong turn. They had become engrossed in modernist techniques and had virtually denied the need for any comprehensible content or message in their works. This was "the bearded and bohemian era in American art," when the artist retreated to "his garret amid ivory tower dreams." Isolated and bemused, he produced little that had any relevance to the actual world. For all his dreams, though, the artist still had to eat. Since museums collected only dead masters and the public had no use for nonrepresentational art, there was but one place to market his work: the wealthy would buy his paintings if they were pleasingly decorative and sufficiently abstract. Only able to sell to a select minority who considered him a charmingly unkempt Bohemian, the artist "grew the herbage and sang for his supper." In Evergood's description, it was as though American art had betrayed itself. An unconscionable sell-out was in progress, and by the late 1920s, it was so far advanced that there was very little true art left in the country.[5]

Then came the Depression, and the art market fell soon after the stock market crashed. Evergood saw that his fellow artists were hit "devastatingly hard," for there was even less room for their skills in the now tottering economy, and many of them "felt the chill which the fear of starvation brings to people." The tragedy that had hit Evergood between the eyes also seemed to hit his colleagues in the stomach, shaking them out of their ivory towers and showing them that they were not in the least bit isolated from earthly problems. To Evergood, all this was a blessing in disguise. The Depression freed the painter from pandering to rich patrons, persuaded him that he should abandon abstractionism for realism, and convinced him that his true home lay with the workers who suffered just as he did.[6] Evergood thus saw the Depression in large epochal terms, a historical perspective that he offered with the greatest sincerity but that was not very accurate. Pre-Depression American art had not been as thoroughly abstract or patron-tied as he described it; many painters were realists and existed on the very edge of poverty. But Evergood thought that the crisis had vindicated both his style and his activism, and like one who had won a victory, he was inclined to exaggerate the strengths and numbers of his former opponents.

Evergood devoted an entire canvas to this vision of the Depression's liberating effect upon American art. Like a predecessor, French realist Gustave Courbet, Evergood depicted the artist as the linchpin of a new social scheme, a figure who is both humble craftsman and ideological redeemer.[7] In the lower portion of his own painting, *Artist in Society* (1936; Figure 2), Evergood showed what the art world had once been. Towards the bottom of the canvas he placed a group of old, wealthy patrons who disdainfully examine a canvas. Their painting is obviously ornamental rather than meaningful art, for it rests in an over-large and too-ornate frame and appeals to the likes of this bejeweled and bejowled crowd. To the right of these rich dilettantes are symbols indicating how constrained and lifeless art becomes when it panders to such patrons. One painter works with his neck and arms in a stock, showing that he is more of a prisoner than a retainer; as a creative person, he is more dead than alive, and the coffin in which he rests symbolizes the decay that has already beset his work. Slightly higher on the canvas lie two other artists, already dead; the stigmata on their feet show that these men have been crucified upon the cross of effete art. One final symbol of death—the large skeleton—rests upon a massive, impenetrable wall that separates art from the people. In the bottom left corner, Evergood placed a group of ordinary Americans, walled off from the art community (such as it was); these workers are deprived of art's elevating influences and so must seek their solace in alcohol.

Having demonstrated in this lower half of the painting just how bad things had become, Evergood moved on to show the Depression's redemptive effect in the upper half of his composition. Here the artist stands unshackled, a brawny, smiling man free to move as he will. Where he was once a figure separated from the people, he is now integrated with them, wearing a workman's hat and shirt, and like the plumber and the miner, proudly carrying the tools of his trade. Since the people now have art in their midst, they too are happier and their faces are a sea of smiles. Together with the artist, they avoid the Dust Bowl symbols that a young boy points to, and all march toward a future somewhere over the misty horizon. There was, of course, more imagination than actuality to *Artist in Society.* That painter's broad shoulders arose more from Evergood's insistence upon art's virility than from any muscle building involved in fine painting. Similarly, there is no obvious reason why the plumber and miner should accept the artist as their fellow laborer, much less receive him with the adoration displayed upon the faces in Evergood's crowd. With all its fantasy, this was Evergood's ideal vision of the Depression artist and his society—once the sickly prisoner of the wealthy, the artist had become a free and robust member of the masses, and those masses in turn benefited from his influence.

Evergood thought that a definite style of painting must accompany this new social relationship. He believed that the unshackled artist should recognizably depict the world and shun abstract depictions, and accordingly, Evergood pledged himself to utilize "the forms in nature such as men, trees, buildings."[8] When he painted these sorts of natural subjects, however, he did so in his own "peculiar calligraphy" and avoided what his fellow social realists called "naturalism," a thing quite distinct from the literary naturalism that influenced novelists like John Steinbeck. Evergood and the others understood "naturalism" to mean painting that aimed to give pure literal renditions of the objective order. This intention seemed wrong to them because they believed that one must not simply copy the objective order; any such exercise made the painter more of a passive transcriber than an active interpreter of his world. Not wanting the artist "to be found by nature as the naturalist is," Evergood thought painting should be the product of an active, engaged mind that offered up a translation of nature upon the canvas. To execute his own paintings, he began with forms from nature, and then used "the imagination entirely in composing a design."[9] Therefore, in a painting such as *Dance Marathon* (1934; Figure 3), he began with a common enough scene of the day, the type of dance contest upon which author Horace McCoy based his 1935 novel *They Shoot Horses, Don't They?* But rather than simply reproduce a scene from one of the many dance marathons, Evergood added his own touches; he distorted the faces, foreshortened the perspective, and added unusual objects to achieve the effect he wanted. Particularly striking are the distortions Evergood made in the human bodies, producing images that are bizarre and perhaps even repulsive. The figures in *Dance Marathon* are contorted into awkward positions, with fractured faces and large, clumsy hands. Despite their appearance of poor craftsmanship, these primitive-looking images were a product of Evergood's conscious design rather than his technical inability. Since he believed that "the physical presence of rickets due to malnutrition surely has a moral and spiritual counterpart in personality," Evergood thought that no one could live through the Depression "without being in some way warped or twisted." His marathon dancers looked the way they did for a specific reason—their drooping bodies and long faces were translations of the despair and fatigue that permeated the thirties.[10]

Besides showing how strange the world could be, Evergood also wanted to hold it up for judgment. He usually included a political message in his Depression paintings, striving for an art that would make "assertions about life and society." His assertions varied somewhat from one painting to the next, but the general theme was that innocent people were the victims of a corrupt economic system, and that the system's deterioration during the 1930s had only heightened their misery. Evergood's verdict was that capitalism extracted too high a toll from its workers, and with his art he protested that cost.

Since his protests would be lost if his messages were obscure, Evergood foreswore any "abstruse, mystic or inverted type of symbolism." Instead, he searched for symbols "that can be understood easily."[11] The ones he found were often effective and arresting. The dance marathon, for example, became a metaphor for capitalist society. The chief symbol in Evergood's cartoonlike composition (Figure 3) is the spiderweb pattern of the dance floor: the dancers are caught in a web from which they cannot escape, and just like American workers, the more they struggle or dance within it, the more they become its exhausted victims. In the upper left corner, a death's hand clutches money to symbolize the exchange that capitalism offers its dancers or its workers—small wages now and death later. With tacky hats perched over the exhausted faces, Evergood's painting suggests that gaiety and pleasure could only be hollow and transitory under capitalism, while the applause from a chubby-fisted, spike-braceleted audience shows that any praise for one's efforts under capitalism is actually a barbaric adulation of one's self-destruction.

This is a powerful, direct painting, and Evergood's symbolism is just as explicit in another canvas, *American Tragedy* (1937; Figure 4). Here his subject was the same organizing crusade that excited so many other intellectuals of the 1930s, including traveling reporter Louis Adamic. In a movement away from craft unionism, John L. Lewis and others had formed the CIO and won recognition in the auto and steel industries. Part of that campaign was a strike against Republic Steel near Chicago, and on Memorial Day of 1937 police attacked a group of strikers and their supporters, killing ten and wounding another eighty or ninety. *American Tragedy* was Evergood's portrayal of the massacre, a set of images he derived from contemporary accounts and a newspaper photograph. He set his scene before a fortress-like steel plant, pictured the police as brutal company goons, and showed the strikers as innocent victims of police brutality. Throughout the scene, cruel-eyed police indiscriminately beat people and shoot into the fleeing crowd. On the right, a policeman clubs an already fatally wounded man. On the left, another officer shoots point-blank into the back of a fleeing woman, while at his feet sprawls the body of a black man, who is obviously not a subversive person for he still patriotically clutches his American flag. Some of the actual picketers probably carried tree limbs or pipes, and Evergood gave them a decidedly sympathetic rendition by portraying his single limb-wielding demonstrator as a small, pregnant woman whom a man (the father of her child?) tries to shelter from the police charge. Photographs of the incident offer little indication that such a woman was actually in the center of the melee, but Evergood added her for his own special effect: ". . . making her pregnant, I thought, would kind of accentuate the horror of the whole thing." *American Tragedy* was an angry indictment of the Chicago police, and Evergood's anger was the product of a brutal beating he had received at the hands of their New York counterparts. While he was participating in a strike of WPA art workers, the New York police attacked the demonstrators, ripped Evergood's clothing, broke his nose, and tore his ear. His bitterness over this mistreatment inspired both his labor solidarity and this particular canvas. "I don't think," Evergood observed, "that anybody who hasn't been really beaten up by the police badly, as I have, could have painted an *American Tragedy*."[12]

Evergood's symbols were clear and his assertions forceful. Capitalism trapped Americans and forced them to dance to its tunes, and if they organized against it, the system beat them back with all the brutality at its disposal. The country was full of great suffering, the tottering economy was responsible for that anguish, and Evergood's paintings protested the outrage. Evergood believed that by producing such works he had not only joined the masses but was also working for their cause. With remarkable audacity, he bragged to those everyday Americans that here was a person "who is fighting for you and dying for you, who is working for you." When they encountered such an artist, they should no longer regard him as effete or "look on his face with hate." Whether or not the public actually respected his work, Evergood desperately wanted to be loved for his art and for his imagined ("dying for you") sacrifices. Positively aglow with his newfound sense of belonging and dedication, Evergood proclaimed he and his colleagues were no longer "separate from humanity," and that they had now become "one with mankind."[13]

Much as Evergood desired Americans' affection, he sought it more as their leader than as their comrade. Evergood believed the social artist had joined the masses as they marched toward the future, like the painter in *Artist in Society;* yet Evergood wanted to be in the vanguard of that march, not in the ranks. Just as the painter in *Artist in Society* (Figure 2) took a position near the head of the column, looking back at his followers, Evergood saw himself as a captain rather than a private in the people's march. From that vantage point, he intended to illuminate the pathway with the light of his artistic insight. Given the terribly "turbulent world" of the moment, people were avidly searching for "an understanding of their relation to society and the universe," and Evergood was ready to give it to them through an "art devoted to understanding America."[14] With brush and pencil, he would show them that the corrupt economy was responsible for their plight, and so impress them with its vileness that they would never again allow it to defile their country.

Evergood needed an income while leading and educating the people, and he found it in the New Deal art projects. As both an employee and client of the work-relief agencies, he saw them not as government charity but as "help from the people," who, crying out for understanding, agreed to support the artist in exchange for his assistance. For his part, the artist promised that if the people would "stand back of him and see that he gets a steady job," then he would fulfill their needs with " a great People's Art." In Evergood's fanciful conception, the people thus paid the artist to compose *their* art according to *his* notion of what it should be. With the Depression, Evergood believed, "the people" had replaced the wealthy as art's patrons, and since "the people" so sorely needed the artist's guidance, they gave him carte blanche to create as he would. Unlike the old days when the artist was his patron's beneficiary, the new people-patrons "now see *him* as a benefactor."[15] Thus with the Depression, Evergood not only attained a sense of artistic purpose and social leadership, he also came to have the comfortable feeling of being a paid benefactor.

As the thirties progressed, the anger and protest in Evergood's paintings gradually faded. In the years following World War II, his work retained a certain satiric disenchantment with American economics and society. Nonetheless, at the end of the 1930s, he moved toward more contented scenes and away from angry protests, toward the upper portion of *Artist in Society* and away from its lower portion. One example of this trend was *Music (The WPA Band)* (Figure 5), a canvas he outlined in 1933, completed in 1938, and retouched in 1956. Here there are no pitched battles between police and workers, nor do people dance to someone else's tune. Instead, the people peacefully make their own music. Players of all races and ages harmonize and do so with looks of obvious satisfaction upon their faces. These are plainly people from different social classes, for orchestra members wear the costumes of both the rich and the poor; but they cooperate with each other, and the conductor looks as though he came up from the workers rather than down from the wealthy. As the anguish of the thirties seemed to ease, Evergood also produced yet another type of non-protest painting more frequently. His fascination with visual incongruities grew, and he increasingly painted pictures of odd-looking objects or eccentric-looking people. Since many of the country's social ills seemed to wane, he felt more at liberty to indulge himself with paintings of the bizarre scenes that so intrigued him.

Other social realists had careers similar to Evergood's. For the most part, they were young men at the start of the thirties, likewise just establishing their individual styles. The Depression nourished Evergood's inclination to face life, and it led the others to share his determination to paint a harsh and ugly world. Shocked at the collapse of the art market and the country's widespread suffering, artists came to believe that painting of the recent past had been sadly frivolous, isolated, and without worldly significance. But they also came to feel as Evergood did, that for all its hardships the Depression was a godsend for American art, a painful but therapeutic slap in the face that snapped painting out of its former triviality and aloofness. Aroused and awakened, they resolved to meet the grim world about them, portray it in their work, and deliver their judgments of it. Like Evergood, they believed the Depression brought unwarranted agony to working people, and they painted bitter protests of that suffering. In the very workers they portrayed, the artists discovered the contact with objective experience that art seemed to need, and in their assumed role as the people's spokesmen, they found a comforting sense that they were of value to humankind. The social realists complained loudly when social conditions were bad and, like Evergood, turned away from protest when the Depression eased with the decade's passing.

Social Realism

"Social realism" was the name that a number of Depression artists used for their particular school of painting. Like Philip Evergood, other members of this school composed pictures of the negative aspects of life under capitalism, choosing as their subjects scenes of labor strife, the suffering of workers and the poor, and the greed of the wealthy. Such pictures dominated their work, but they also painted, as Evergood did, some uncritical works about daily life or even occasional allegorical pieces, especially toward the end of the decade. Chiefly interested in producing didactic images and lessons about the everyday world, they were inclined to paint pictures of readily recognizable objects and events. Like Evergood and Kent, the principal social realists were articulate men who achieved considerable recognition within the American art world. Born largely between 1894 and 1910, many of these artists drew their first breaths in Europe and later accompanied their families to the United States. Their parents were often either artists in their own right or they provided environments that could nourish a child's creative inclinations. An urban group, most of the social realists studied and eventually worked in the nation's large cities, especially New York. They were inclined to be leftist activists, joining progressive artists' organizations such as the Artists' Union and American Artists' Congress, and frequently rising into the leadership of those organizations. Most of these painters were poor during the Depression and qualified at one time or another for work on government art projects. Though involved in such agencies, their chief concerns were not with the bureaucratic workings of the New Deal projects; their creative urges, and the control of their output, were more their own than the government's. As people who had often studied together in their youth, and as highly visible members of the New York art community, the social realists constituted a true artistic and intellectual community, drawing inspiration from and critically examining each others' work.[16]

Social realism arose within specific European and American art traditions. The larger realist movement had developed as a nineteenth-century European crusade to bring painting away from romantic ideas and idealized settings. Realists like Courbet were visual innovators in that they took ordinary people as their subjects, and ideological reflectors in that they displayed some of the socialist sympathies that emerged in the wake of the revolutions of 1848.[17] By the end of the nineteenth century, a group of American painters was cultivating realism and continued to nurture it well into the twentieth century. Following the lead of Robert Henri, members of this "Ash Can" school (painters like George Luks, John Sloan, and George Bellows) forsook the conventional genteel depictions of beautiful landscapes or virginal maidens. Rather than adopt the placid and orthodox motifs that permeated the established American art academies, Henri and his students scandalized art circles by concentrating on urban working people, taking as their subjects such vulgar things as street scenes, prizefights and open-air markets.

Where academic artists used clean lines and soft shades, the Ash Can painters preferred loosely drawn shapes and sharp lighting contrasts.

With their emphasis upon ordinary subjects and exaggerated designs, the Ash Can painters set precedents that the social realists would follow; indeed, many social realists were like Evergood, either befriended by, or the students of, Ash Can painters. [18] The social realists also absorbed some of their teachers' political predispositions—Henri was a thoroughgoing democrat and Sloan an active Socialist. But where the later social realists readily displayed their political views on canvas, the earlier Ash Can painters produced few political paintings. Instead, the Ash Can pictures of urban slums are usually noncommittal or even a little sentimental. This does not mean, however, that political or critical pictures emerged only with the Depression. Social commentary had existed in American graphic arts virtually since the first English settlements. Well before the 1930s, political *cartoons* and satirical *drawings* were standard features in newspapers, magazines, and campaign broadsides. Members of the Ash Can school composed some of the best left-wing cartoons of the early twentieth century, often publishing in the *Masses* where John Sloan was art editor. The younger social realists worked within this heritage of political graphics, some taking their inspirations from cartoons in the *Masses,* and others such as William Gropper publishing in subsequent leftist journals like *The Liberator* and the *New Masses.* Yet it was only at the dawn of the thirties, just when Evergood started looking for vital working-class subjects, that American artists began to bring protest and social commentary to "fine" art—oils or other works intended for outlets such as museums or galleries. [19] Even such a painter as Rockwell Kent, a Socialist since the early twentieth century, only introduced a protest theme in his serious work in 1927 when he portrayed Sacco and Vanzetti as Christ-like martyrs.

If the social realists inherited a good deal from the Ash Can school, they also felt the influence of developments in Mexico. During the 1920s, several Mexican muralists, including Diego Rivera, José Clemente Orozco, and David Siqueiros, produced class-conscious murals celebrating the Mexican revolution. These murals evoked considerable excitement in the United States, prompting John Dos Passos to write a laudatory essay about them for the *New Masses.* The social realists shared Dos Passos's enthusiasm for the Mexicans' social criticism and clear social messages. Both Ben Shahn and George Biddle worked under Rivera, and Biddle, in a telling phrase, said that during his studies he had "sucked to the pulp" a book about the Mexican muralists. Raphael Soyer sketched Rivera at work, attended Lewis Mumford's slide talk on Orozco, and marched in protest when Nelson Rockefeller ordered the destruction of Rivera's radical mural in Rockefeller Center.[20]

The Mexicans' paintings intrigued the social realists, but the Americans did not become muralists. Although Depression murals are perhaps the best-known art format from the thirties, they should not be equated with social realism. Paintings of local history or hulking symbolic figures, the murals were seldom as openly political as were the social realists' canvases. Murals in public places like post offices had an important Depression message, though, for their staid historical themes suggested that there was an unshaken continuity to human affairs, and their bulky men and women were a strong hint that Americans were large enough to withstand the onslaughts of the present. Many American muralists received the same types of government aid as did the social realists. As highly visible productions, however, the large panels came in for a good deal more censorship than did easel pieces, censorship that ruled out most of the political messages Evergood and the others were so determined to paint. Consequently, the social realists usually concentrated upon smaller, and less regulated, easel paintings. When all was said and done, murals constituted only a small fraction of the decade's total artistic output. The social realists composed only a handful themselves, and in the largest of the government art projects, the ratio of smaller works to murals was forty to one.[21]

If the social realists respected Rivera and Orozco, they held no such regard for abstractionists. The social realists usually described themselves as an embattled minority, struggling to preserve realism in an art world that abstractionism both dominated and decimated. Their perception, however, was not very accurate. "Modern art" certainly stood out because it was such a departure from past styles, and a number of Americans had experimented with it well before its introduction at the 1913 Armory Show. After World War II, modernist influences became more prevalent in the United States, but the American art community had been under the art academies' style for generations, and by the 1920s, it had not yet shaken off its academic drowsiness.[22] All the social realists' allegations to the contrary, abstractionism did not rule at the Depression's onset.

Besides social realism, there was another active and vocal school of representational painting in thirties America—regionalism. Where social realists complained about America's Depression conditions, regionalists—Grant Wood, John Steuart Curry, and Thomas Hart Benton—suggested that the country was in good shape. These regionalists painted largely rural scenes, and though their works were occasionally satirical or iconoclastic, they usually praised the fecundity of the earth, the joys of planting, or the stability of rural institutions. In many ways, their efforts were visual equivalents of the celebrations of rusticity contained in the writings of a group of contemporary southern writers, the Nashville Agrarians.[23] Like the regionalist artists, Evergood and the other social realists wanted to paint American topics, and both groups preferred to work in the United States rather than in Europe. But the two genres should not be lumped together, for the regionalists were frankly celebratory and occasionally nationalistic, while the social realists believed that critical dissent had more validity during the thirties.[24]

Evergood, for example, held that "the advocates of regionalism and nationalism are doing untold harm to art in America" by allowing the problems of the day to continue without protest. According to social realist Joe Jones, regionalism arose out of Depression anxieties, apprehensions that Thomas Hart Benton or Grant Wood erroneously tried "to console . . . with ideas of national superiority." Moses Soyer feared this might make art subservient to the state, which in his perspective would lead to "artistic suicide. Witness Nazi Germany." For their part, the regionalists were no more inclined to be kind to the social realists. Benton and Wood had even less sympathy than did Evergood for abstractionism, even though Benton had earlier painted as a modernist and Wood respected many of modernism's technical innovations. They came to feel that it was both decadent and unAmerican, a European import that Americans should pass beyond. Since the social realists were inclined to use more distortion than the regionalists, Wood and Curry believed that Evergood and the others had probably remained too long in the abstractionist fold. Benton also considered the social realists little more than radical dogmatists. Their leftist orientations seemed to him yet another type of European decadence, a Marxist form this time, and one that obstructed art's free growth by forcing it "into the stereotypes of a propagandistic pattern." The social realists were hardly as Marxian as Benton imagined, nor were the regionalists the proto-fascists that Soyer and Jones imagined them to be. Artists in both camps produced good paintings that were laced with both abstractionism and social commentary. Yet to the artists involved, it appeared as though there was a large ideological and topical gulf separating the two schools, and they spent the decade exchanging potshots across it without managing to bridge the chasm.[25]

Salvation by Catastrophe

The American art world was something of a guild at the time of the Depression. Young painters studied under older ones and measured their own development against the examples of their predecessors. The schooling typically included strong doses of art history, and as products of such training, social realists constantly reexamined the development of twentieth-century American art. In their deliberations, they usually concluded, as Philip Evergood had done, that American painting had nearly atrophied into an aloof and abstruse thing before the Depression saved it. There was a personal side to this sense of deliverance, for the social realists viewed themselves as novice members of a smug fraternity and believed that as the Depression had redeemed the larger brotherhood, so it had saved them individually from a barren art.

One social realist who had learned his art history was Moses Soyer. Moses was born to a Jewish family in central Russia and, along with his twin brother and fellow social realist, Raphael, he came to the United States in 1912. The brothers studied at the National Academy of Design, where they learned plenty of genteel motifs; after a sketching class under Robert Henri, however, they opted for realism's more earthy depictions and left the Academy. Moses studied for a time at the Educational Alliance Art School, where Evergood was one of his fellow students. Coming to social realism with the thirties, Soyer joined the Works Progress Administration/Federal Art Project (WPA/FAP), helped organize the Artists' Union, and was a founder of the Artists' Congress.[26]

Soyer could see few bright spots in recent American art. Earlier in the century, Ash Can painters had managed to infuse painting with the vitality of their urban scenes. Then, just when things seemed to be developing as Soyer would have had them, European abstract art arrived with the 1913 Armory Show, bursting, as he said, "like a bombshell in the midst of Artistic America." The show was beneficial in that it opened painters' eyes to new esthetic problems and possibilities, but it also destroyed Henri's nascent realism, for artistic concerns seemed to shift from content to form. Abandoning the broad audience that representational works had been acquiring, American art embraced abstractionism and, Soyer believed, "degenerated into shallow, unimportant decorations aimed to delight the eyes of the rich patrons." In saying this, Soyer exaggerated the connection between artists and wealthy sponsors, for most painters struggled along from one sale to the next just as he did. Nonetheless, it appeared to him that, in their effort to please the rich, artists had sealed themselves off from life and elected to spend the twenties in what Soyer called "a sheltering bohemia." Demonstrating little appreciation for the subtle concerns of modernism, Soyer claimed that since such paintings had virtually no content, they helped promote among artists an intellectual atrophy that seemed typical of the 1920s—an era he arrogantly labeled one of "mental bankruptcy."[27]

With the turn of the decade came the Depression, accompanied by "violence and despair." Soyer nonetheless believed that the Depression was beneficial for American painting. It showed artists the precariousness of their supposed dependence upon the wealthy and their error in assuming that art could stand apart from life. With plenty of painfully chastising lessons, "the Depression resulted . . . in a new grasp of values[,] in a new outlook on things on the part of artists." As Soyer described it, these artists with their "bitter awareness of a stricken society" shook off their former outlooks, rededicated themselves to meaningful art, and "created the school of Social Realism."[28]

Peter Blume's art history encompassed a longer span of time, but it retained the same dark element of pre-Depression isolation. Like the Soyer boys, Blume was also born a Russian Jew; his family later immigrated to the United States, and Blume grew up in Brooklyn. By the 1930s, he was living in Connecticut where he was Malcolm Cowley's neighbor and busily at work; he painted some post office murals, composed a major antifascist canvas, and joined the Artists' Congress. When it was his turn to address the Congress, Blume said that artists had in the past occupied important social niches as mouthpieces of the medieval church and state. With the rise of bourgeois society, however, they were no longer transmitters of ideas, but simply decorators who hired out to wealthy patrons. Yet this too passed. Unlike Soyer, Blume thought that painters no longer had even the questionable company of the rich by the eve of the Depression; artists had retreated into "a cloistered world of their own—into a Bohemia." In monkish isolation, they abandoned the actual world and soared to an ethereal plane, "higher and higher into the stratosphere, far from the sight of mother nature." Fortunately, in Blume's view, the Depression brought this sordid business to an end, for "it took more imagination than even artists possessed" to concentrate on esoteric issues "in the midst of unemployment, breadlines and bank failures."[29]

Blume and Soyer shared an obvious antipathy towards the rich. There was a populist ring to their statements, doubtlessly derived from their working-class origins and the resentments that these two immigrants had acquired as their families struggled to gain a toehold in the United States. But the larger metaphors that emerge from their art histories have more to do with religion than with populism, and their discussions speak more of sin and redemption than of economics and politics. They described American art as beset with two particular kinds of evil. One was wealth. Rather than simply an economic status, wealth had certain moral connotations for Blume and Soyer. Excessive riches suggested excessive materialism, the sin of worshiping false gods. If the artist painted to please the rich, or even associated with them too much, there was the danger, Soyer and Blume apparently felt, that the sinfulness of the rich might rub off upon him. A second evil was isolation. In accord with Judaic tradition, they argued that one must be at work within the world and take an active role in fulfilling its designs. The unwary painter might fall into transgression if his images were about figures that had nothing to do with the world. Thus there were the sins of riches and aloofness to shun, and in Soyer's view, the two were intimately associated with each other, for the wealthy corrupted the painter by demanding abstractionist paintings from him. Fortunately, Blume and Soyer agreed, the 1930s had ended the threat of either sin, for the Depression made both wealth and escapism impossible.

Other social realists echoed Blume's and Soyer's sense of salvation. In particular, they believed that painters of the 1920s had been as Philip Evergood portrayed them in *Artist in Society*, walled away from the world and walled in with the wealthy. To Joseph Hirsch, artists of the twenties had been beguiled by postimpressionism, a style concerned with the "world of sunlight, where no one seems to have wept or starved." The affluent were the only possible audience for such pieces, which only compounded art's remoteness, for the rich seemed more interested in the worldliness of decoration than in worldly significance. For them the art-ist's product was, Stuart Davis said, nothing more than "a commodity for speculation or a costly triffle." To Louis Guglielmi, this had been a time of "spiritual and moral bankruptcy," when the general decadence of the 1920s corrupted the artist and he produced little more than a "super-deluxe framed wallpaper to decorate the homes of the wealthy." Those patrons were a disgusting lot—arrogant, contemptuous, and haughty— and William Gropper portrayed them with precisely these characteristics in his painting Art Patrons (1939). His patrons are immense, so gone to fat that they occupy more of his canvas than does the piece of art that he showed them examining. One of the figures holds a catalog between her-self and the painting, demonstrating that she is not perceptive enough to approach art on her own; instead she must rely upon some other person's analysis. Most striking of all is the pose Gropper gave his patrons. Their noses stick high into the air with all the priggishness Gropper could evoke.[30]

The demands of such patrons virtually vanished with the Depression, and for this the social realists were thankful. The painters were not, how-ever, so glad to do without purchases from wealthy clients. Even the best of times had been hard, for like other American artists, the social realists relied less upon their own creative efforts and more upon moonlighting, working spouses, or tolerant parents for an income. The Depression cur-tailed not only art sales but also these other forms of support, and along with countless other Americans, the painters faced truly desperate cir-cumstances.[31] As Guglielmi described them, "the early thirties were coldly sobering years," a time when there was "a frightening lack of money" and one scraped by on the narrowest of margins. Ben Shahn, for example, once had to make the rounds among a large number of his friends before he finally collected enough money merely to keep the heat on in the apartment he and Walker Evans shared. Shahn's begging was all the more difficult because he simultaneously had to dodge other artists whom he feared would ask him for help. Such poverty was widespread among the social realists, creating what Evergood called "a desperate sit-uation for the artist," and producing such hardships that, in Moses Soyer's words, "the misery of the artist was acute." Nor was this desperation solely economic. Some of the social realists had begun their careers with the expectation of concentrating primarily upon esthetic problems, and even though they praised the Depression for exposing the vanity of those expectations, they were still quite shocked by the sudden change it forced in their life plans. Stuart Davis wrote that the Depression demonstrated with devastating bluntness that his work could not be aloof from the problems of the world, "shaking those psychological and esthetic certainties which had once given force and direction" to the work he and the others had undertaken. Poor and bewildered, Guglielmi and his crowd found themselves with few physical or psychological assets, no longer otherworldly, but "helplessly a part of a devastated world."[32]

If the Depression impoverished social realists and quashed their career aspirations, it also assaulted their esthetic sensibilities. As they told their stories, the hideousness of the country's Depression vistas only compounded their misery. Their training seemed to leave them poorly outfitted for the world that came to pass, for they had spent years refining their appreciation of the beautiful, only to be brought up against the sheer ugliness of the times. Evergood, for instance, described the artist as a person whose education had equipped him with special "antennae" that could "pick up waves from the social and human ether"; but the Depression messages received upon those antennae were so disturbing and so grotesque that they could only be translated into the misshapen figures of a painting like *Dance Marathon*. To Soyer, the visual environment was more than something the artist merely *received*. Instead, it positively *assaulted* "his perception . . . with a suffering on a tremendous scale; the faces of men—even the face of the land—reflected violence and despair." Shahn believed that this was especially painful for the artist, because the very nature that drew him into creative work also made him a "perceptive, thinking, sensitive individual." Guglielmi echoed Shahn's assessment, describing the typical painter as "a highly sensitive person." Within Guglielmi's art, there are numerous hints that his own sensitive soul was sorely troubled over the decade's devastation, for death images increasingly emerged in his poems, and in his paintings, coffins and funeral wreaths began appearing regularly. George Biddle took an odd sort of comfort from such pieces, for he believed that it would have been unforgivable for the artist to have been anything less than aghast over the Depression's horrors. If the painter had "not been appalled, shocked, wounded by the tragic and unnecessary wastage," then in Biddle's estimate, he would not only have been stupid. dishonest, and inhuman, "as an artist," he would have been "completely without sensitivity, completely blind."[33] The thirties made it impossible to wear the blinders of aloofness, and the painters were thankful because this helped to redeem art. But it also meant that nothing stood between the artist's delicately trained eyes and the Depression's chilling sights.

The Depression was thus an agonizing experience for the social realists, and as normal humans, they sought some relief from the agony. As Biddle realized, there comes a time when pain becomes too acute, when the "sensitive being must find some escape, or sublimation, for the horror he feels about him." To ease his own terror, Rockwell Kent first tried to escape. Older than the other social realists, Kent studied under Henri and Bellows before beginning a successful career, one that provided a considerable income even at the height of the Depression. (Such security, of course, made retreat more of a possibility for him than for the others.) Throughout his life, Kent had a peculiar affinity for the arctic, finding an "utter peacefulness" in Greenland's wide stretches of ice and snow. But Depression America had little of the peace he craved; instead it was a "chaos" of unemployment, misery, and mismanagement that even the hefty shutters of his mountain estate could not keep out. So, like traveling reporter Louis Adamic, he abandoned America for one of the world's backwaters and, in 1934, set sail for his beloved Greenland in an unabashed "escape from discord into harmony." By any normal criteria, Greenland is a boring place, yet in these trying times the uneventful landscape was just the thing Kent felt he needed, and he painted pictures of it to "show what Heaven is like." But there was a problem. As a longtime radical who had cast his very first vote for Socialist Eugene Debs, Kent had always been more interested in *making* a paradise on earth than in finding it in some remote corner. His old enemy, capitalism, appeared to be weakening with the thirties, so that the Depression, despite its chaos, held out a promise that the monster just might fall. Not only "powerless to resist the continued and multiplying encroachments" upon his peace, Kent became, he said, "*unwilling* to resist them." He returned home to throw himself into political demonstrations and to paint protest art. Recasting his self-image, Kent began to describe himself not as a fragile esthete who retreated from the world's turmoil, but rather as an artist who met the confusion and conquered it with his work.[34]

As Kent eventually did, so the other social realists also confronted the Depression. Of Biddle's two methods for coping with the terrors of the thirties, they likewise chose sublimation over escape, setting down to work rather than going into hiding. Certainly, they believed, the Depression had brought confusion and hard times, but it also brought renewed energy and direction. Biddle contended that the Depression had produced an "invigorating effect on American art," infusing artists, including himself, with a "new vitality." Such sentiments were reinforced on many fronts, such as the John Reed Club, where members like Biddle, Evergood, Gropper, and Raphael Soyer could hear the thirties heralded as "a field of untold artistic experiences" that would "give art new life and vigor." Louis Guglielmi and Joe Jones were similarly enthusiastic, for though both granted the Depression's harshness, they described it as an exploding and enlivening force in the formerly stagnant art world. Jones believed that there was an "eruption that is in the making," a liberating concussion that would shake up abstract and genteel artists, proving to them that *there are important things to paint.*" Guglielmi likewise held that "the economic upheaval and the consequent tragedies" were not fatal blows to his own or others' painting; rather than devastating, the upheavals and tragedies instead combined to become "an erupting and directing force in art."[35]

To Jack Levine, it was not the decade's destruction so much as it was "the ferment, the power of the 1930s" that had "opened my eyes" to the esthetic potential in social commentary. Moses Soyer believed that for all its misery, the Depression had been something of an ethical revolution for painters, giving them "a new grasp of values." Surely the times were hard, Guglielmi allowed, but this made him all the more determined to create works that were "saturated with hope," paintings that gave "people a reason to live out of the debris of our years." Jones was certain that such crisis-inspired work would produce "something finer than we have known," and Levine spoke of a general thirties "feeling that things were going the right way." Summarizing these responses to the Depression, Davis listed two distinct phases in the typical artist's reaction. At first, the painter felt the pain of losing both his artistic detachment and former patronage, for he "saw his world crumble and experienced disillusionment and despair." But there followed a second stage in which the painter came to feel well rid of the earlier art world and "found a new orientation and a new hope and purpose."[36]

Kent had called them reborn artists, and the others shared his perspective. The most recent episode in American art had been a dark and evil time, and they had been lured by its temptations. But the thirties brought redemption to their craft, making it both more lively and less remote.

Most assuredly it was a traumatic rebirth, given the Depression's agonies, but they gloried in their newfound salvation—even though it was a salvation by catastrophe. Convinced that art had found its proper course, they set out as Davis said, painting amidst the ruins with a vigorous sense of hope and purpose. With this sense of beatitude and wholeness, the artists' reorientation was strikingly similar to the traditional conversion experience.[37] The crisis seemed to bring a unity to art and to the artists' own lives, ending old romantic dichotomies between life and art, action and contemplation.

Regenerate Art

Simply being reborn was not sufficient for the social realists. Once the Depression brought them away from older, decadent ways of painting, they were compelled to identify and execute a newer, virtuous art. Accordingly, they hammered together an esthetic canon for their regenerate art. This doctrine proved "regenerate" in both the adjectival and the verbal senses, for it simultaneously *identified* regenerate art and told the artist *how to* regenerate his work. To comply with the code, orthodox art needed to be a harmonious blending of content, form, and message. The creed demanded that a piece's content come from the objective world, and the doctrine proscribed purely conceptual or emotional art. Since each painting was about the external order, it should have a form that bore obvious—though *not* exact—correspondence to the outside world. Finally, the work must make a point, preaching a secular sermon in an arresting, unambiguous visual language.

Social realists believed that art should grapple with actual experience. Anything less would be dishonest, for, in Moses Soyer's words, the Depression allowed "no honest opportunity for disengagement." Levine, for example, hoped to convey an urban slum so authentically that he would become the "steward of its contents."[38] More often than not, though, the other artists believed that a good painting should depict a slum's residents rather than its buildings and streets. Moses Soyer proudly referred to himself as a "humanist," by which he meant that humans were his favorite subject. Jones likewise thought that "people and their problems" stood as "the greatest and most interesting things in life" and were therefore the best topics for an engaged, redeemed painter. Levine adhered to this principle throughout his life, and when he addressed other artists on "humanist" doctrines, he told them that "man is the legitimate and prior concern of man." Along with such declarations, realists stressed that emphasizing human subjects did not mean that the artist should take *himself* as a topic, for that would be to launch upon a Thoreauvian exploration of inner frontiers and so abandon realism for romanticism. The human message had to be public rather than private, and, as Levine explained with a typically curious metaphor, the painter must never use a canvas to bare "his soul like a peeled shrimp."[39]

The social realists' paintings reflected these ideas. With the Depression's arrival, the artists moved away from spiritual allegories and toward earthly subjects, abandoning flowing forms and broad splashes of colors for more closely delineated forms. In the late twenties, Evergood's topics and his style were remote and otherworldly. Some of his paintings were like *Harem Girls* (Figure 1), a panorama of flesh in which voluptuous women sprawl luxuriously beneath exotic palm trees, onion-domed buildings, and the watchful eyes of their keepers. The colors here are swirled around the canvas in broad brush strokes, and the faces have only the briefest of definition. Though less sybaritic, his biblical works from the same period were likewise mythical, suggesting that humankind's greatest concern was its battle with spiritual forces. But by the 1930s, Evergood's characters were wrestling with quite different forces, the earthly and material ones that could trap people into a decidedly unluxurious dance marathon. Furthermore, his brushwork became sharper, so that the faces are more carefully elaborated. Rendering the world's details more exactly did not seem enough, though, for Evergood began placing more and more of those people into his canvases. He had had this inclination for some time, and early works like *Harem Girls* certainly suffered from no shortage of figures. But by the mid-thirties, Evergood was adding even more individuals, so that a piece such as *Artist in Society* became almost saturated with people.

Evergood's painting moved from splashiness toward more careful delineation with the Depression, and Ben Shahn's work reflected the same drift. In a portrait of Walker Evans made very early in the thirties, Shahn used virtually no straight lines, pictured Evans with double-jointed limbs, and gave his roommate large bulging eyes. But by 1936, he was producing images like his *Years of Dust* poster (Figure 6). Shahn's new subject is a squint-eyed and stiff-jointed farmer sitting amidst the straight lines of his porch and clapboard house. Rockwell Kent's pictures also changed with the thirties. His pieces always had some of the sparseness of a woodcut about them, but during the thirties, an earlier mythic element dropped from his work. In a 1929 work called *Almost*, Kent had depicted an ever-questing human figure, striving, always striving, upward toward a spiritual light just above its head. But in his 1936 piece *And Now Where?* (Figure 7) there is no suggestion of striving in either title or image, and the figures have their eyes cast down to the earth rather than up to the heavens. Throughout their lives, the Soyer brothers painted moody portraits of plain people with rheumy eyes, folks who seem constantly on the verge of either sighs or tears. But the Soyers also changed with the thirties, for then, as during no other time in their careers, they portrayed their sad-faced subjects in street settings rather than in the studio. Guglielmi also changed; he stopped painting pleasant park-like scenes and began showing people enduring the humility of relief or struggling with their poverty. Speaking on his own behalf, Guglielmi described his style as having moved "from an honest translation of the French [impressionist] painters" and toward " a more literal and objective representation of life about me."[40] Even Peter Blume journeyed toward representationalism in his work. In the twenties, Blume utilized cubist motifs, but during the thirties, he left this behind for the realists' more literal translations of the world.

With their affinity for recognizable images, social realists had little use for abstract painting. To them modernism asserted that painting should be a series of shapes independent of nature and that its contents should not be modeled after the objective world. This seemed mistaken, and Biddle spoke for the rest when he argued that there was no other option for artists but to "accept nature as the necessary subject matter" of their work.[41] This realist imperative was an insistent and powerful part of the creative environment in Depression America. Fine illustrations of that compulsion are Stuart Davis's verbal contortions as he tried to prove that his painting dealt with the objective world in the same way Philip Evergood did. Although Davis's pictures *were* abstractions, and therefore quite different from the works of the more orthodox social realists, he stood with them in other aspects. He was enrolled in government art programs and served as a president of the Artists' Union, as an editor of its magazine, *Art Front,* and as a charter member and national chairman of the Artists' Congress.[42] In its own way, an abstract painting could be as didactic as any representational one, and modernism certainly seemed allied with progressive forces when Hitler attacked modern painting and when Picasso's *Guernica* proved helpful in raising funds for Spanish anti-fascists. But Davis labored to prove that "abstract art is a realistic art," and he used several arguments in the effort. One of his tactics was to confuse the issue, arguing for the *reality* rather than the *realism* of his work, saying that it was "a real thing, equal to but not a replica of the subject in nature." At another point, where other social realists claimed that their works were of the world because they attacked social problems, Davis held that abstract art was likewise "a direct progressive social force"; his abstract painting accomplished this, he contended, by liberating people from their "familiar reality" to consider "the new lights, speeds, and spaces which are uniquely real in our time." Davis struggled to forge some connection between his painting and the objective world, but demonstrating that direct correspondence between modern art and actual objects eventually proved too difficult a task. By 1940, he tired of the effort, abandoned relevance, and declared, "There's nothing like a good solid ivory tower for the production of art."[43]

The other social realists disdained abstractionism. But they also believed that the artist should avoid "naturalism" and creatively interpret the world with a moderate amount of distortion. Louis Guglielmi voiced this notion most clearly. The son of Italian parents, Guglielmi immigrated to New York in 1914, studied at the National Academy, discovered the impressionists and Cézanne, and painted in their manner until he came to social realism with the Depression. By the 1930s, the actual world with its ugliness seemed to him a much better subject than did impressionist beauty. Yet he refused simply to copy the objective order into his paintings and proclaimed "I reject the need to hold a neurotic mirror to a disordered world." Mirroring the world without any interpretation would be an "illusionary realism," and a canvas produced in that manner was nothing more than "a winding-sheet for the sick and disillusioned." Moreover, Guglielmi realized that mirroring probably is impossible. Like James Agee, he recognized that every piece of art is ultimately a construction of the creative mind and, as such, is quite distinct from any object it might represent. "A work of art is contrived and it is autonomous," Guglielmi wrote; it is not some mere translation of the world but is instead "the artist's assimilation and sublimation of the individual experience." The painter's duty, his "creative responsibility," was to avoid passive transcription and be ever innovative when picturing the world.[44]

Guglielmi tried his best to fulfill that responsibility. Intrigued with the

drama of city streets and "the unseen life hidden by blank walls," he
strove to give these scenes something besides a strictly literal rendition.
To achieve his goal, he used "fantasy in an otherwise orderly and objective
representation," employing distortion or unusual objects for "poetic suggestion and the haunting use of metaphor."[45] In *The Hungry* (c. 1936;
Figure 8), Guglielmi began with a realistically stark picture of city streets
and then added various visual metaphors to convey the despair of people
whom the Depression had thrown out onto those streets. To the right, he
placed a man in a classic position of dismay, his head hung low and his
arms clasped tight about him, virtually the same pose Dorothea Lange
captured in her photograph "Man Beside Wheelbarrow" (chapter 3, Figure 2). On the left side of his canvas, Guglielmi painted a couple with
sunken, worried-looking faces. They push a baby carriage, but this carriage holds no child who might symbolize the future and their hopes for
it. Instead, the carriage contains only a few meager belongings the couple
has salvaged from their past, a past that has left them walking the streets.
Then, to make the scene still more wrenching, Guglielmi used fantasy to
show how hungry people existed in the "unseen life" away from the city's
streets. He opened an imaginary hole through the wall behind the couple
and revealed a relief office with a stooped supplicant, hat in hand, asking
for aid. But even in welfare there was no hope for Guglielmi's hungry
people, for the clerk is a huge and inhuman figure, towering above the
applicant with a look on her face that says there will be no relief from this
relief office.

Other social realists agreed with Guglielmi's principles. They believed
that the artist should distort and fantasize, avoiding what Raphael Soyer
called "the danger of naturalism." The world of the 1930s needed recognizable depiction, but it also needed the painter's interpretation. In
adopting this position, they brought their own genre close to expressionism, a type of art that freely and obviously distorts and so lends itself quite
well to social commentary. In describing the position, Shahn referred to
the mirror analogy Guglielmi had used, and he argued that it was the
painter's duty to "refract" rather than simply reflect a given scene. When
Shahn worked as Rivera's mural assistant, this sentiment led to a disagree-
ment between the two painters. Shahn thought that Rivera added too
much detail to a painting, making it crowded and cluttered. He agreed
with Rivera's premise—that the actual world was one of clutter rather
than order—but rejected the Mexican master's conclusion that a painting

should likewise convey disorder. Art's job was to be involved with life, and Shahn insisted that it rearrange life if necessary. Levine agreed that paintings should not be literal copies of the world and produced his own pieces in which humans had oddly misshapen bodies that flowed into and around their surroundings. Levine explained that when he created these paintings he would intentionally "distort images" to convey his belief that there was a certain "drama" or dynamic interchange between "man and his environment."[46] In this manner, Levine, Shahn, and the others sought a pictorial distance from the world they confronted, painting the objective order but from a perspective that allowed them to interpret it rather than transcribe it.

Social realists not only felt free to rearrange the world, they dearly wanted to pass their verdicts upon it. This desire had come upon the Soyers early in their careers. Moses recalled how he and Raphael had been infatuated with protest art from the moment that Henri introduced them to illustrations in the radical magazine *The Liberator*. To their delight the brothers discovered that the people who made the drawings "were not afraid to moralize," and with those artists as examples, Moses and Raphael set about becoming moralizers themselves. The Soyers were not alone in this, and Joseph Hirsch also wanted to show right from wrong with his paintings, and declared his intention to "castigate the things I hate and paint monuments to what I feel is noble." Levine made a similar determination when he weighed the artist's duty to comment upon a scene against the artist's desire to make a pleasing image of it. It was clear to Levine that "justice is more important than good looks," and that the artist's primary responsibility was to "sit in judgment" upon his world. These were not idle words, for Levine painted according to his principles; in most of his canvases, good looks have been sacrificed to a set of ugly, contorted images that indict a long list of American injustices.[47]

The judgments Levine and the others delivered were usually leftist ones. They despised capitalism for what it had done to art and to America and, like Moses Soyer, approved of paintings that were "kind to the poor and dealt cruelly with the rich." Given such sentiments and Communism's high profile in the 1930s, the social realists easily developed associations with the Communist Party. Joe Jones actually joined the Communists, and one of his Party comrades was artist Bernarda Bryson, Ben Shahn's wife. William Gropper was a long-time radical, whose credentials included membership in the IWW, and who had accompanied Theodore

Dreiser on a 1927 pilgrimage to the Soviet Union. Likewise, if the Party needed to, it could count upon Stuart Davis for consistent support, at least up until the Russian invasion of Finland in 1940. Rockwell Kent also supported the Communists; he contributed money to the Party and served as titular head of a group backing its 1936 presidential ticket. The Party's John Reed Club attracted social realists, and they were equally drawn to its successor, the American Artists' Congress. Davis actually became chairman of the Congress, and Biddle thought that its founding was the most significant American art event since the Armory Show. Finally, those social realists on WPA often joined the Artists' Union, where Communists held important posts; Evergood served a term as the Union's president, and Shahn and Davis helped produce its magazine, *Art Front*.[48]

Even with such ties to the Communist Party, the social realists were not its devoted followers. Despite their Communist associations, most of the artists seldom were anything more than cooperative fellow travelers. Party discipline simply did not set well with the social realists, for egotism ran high among them—Rockwell Kent felt compelled to write *two* exceedingly long autobiographies. Though a thorough understanding of Marxism was hardly required for one to join the Party during the thirties, the social realists were ideological innocents in comparison to most Party members. And they balked at exchanging their innocence for Party dogma. Even Davis, who made chameleon-like changes to accommodate the fluctuating Party line, refused to accept the Communists' position that ideological content was more significant for art than was skillful technique. Raphael Soyer had similar difficulties with the Party. He cherished the John Reed Club as an organization that helped him obtain "a progressive world outlook," but when it came to accepting esthetic direction from the Club, Soyer "did not let it influence my art." Although Party members such as Bernarda Bryson were in the leadership of both the Artists' Union and Artists' Congress, they were elected more because of their readiness to do thankless jobs than because of their Party loyalty. Willing to exploit the Communists' readiness to work, and sharing some of the Party's positions, the social realists were still more inclined to make scatalogical remarks about the Party than they were to praise it. One Union member thought the Party's district committee was "full of shit," and Ben Shahn was of a similar mind. When Shahn became *Art Front* editor, the Party sought to discipline and direct the magazine through him. This outraged Shahn, and he exploded: "I wouldn't submit my used toilet paper to you. I share the economics of this thing with you, but not my work."[49]

Censorship and creative control were anathemas to the social realists, and they parted with the Party when it seemed too ready to control their paintings. Yet if Communism was suspect, social realists were certain that fascism was the greater danger to creative freedom. To some extent this was a mere commonplace in the Artists' Congress or other Popular Front circles. But like Lewis Mumford and other independent intellectuals of the thirties, the social realists sincerely believed that fascism had a hazardous potential for cultural standardization. To express their hatred, Gropper, Evergood, Shahn, Blume, and Kent took up their brushes and lambasted the fascists in paint. Raphael Soyer also found fascism's growth one of the decade's greatest causes for anxiety and painted his own canvas in support of the antifascist forces fighting in the Spanish Civil War. When the fascists ultimately triumphed in that war, Biddle thought their victory one of the worst aspects of "these ghastly, honor-soiled days" and wondered openly if the concerned artist might not have preserved creative liberty and "served Loyalist Spain more efficaciously by dropping bombs" than by painting.[50]

Stridently independent, the social realists protested fascism and other social evils with paintings that were frequently hideous or repellent. It is tempting to regard them as odd people possessing some perverse affinity for the ugly and to view them as artists thus peculiarly suited to work during the Depression. Moses Soyer sounded like he might fit this description when he reviewed a 1934 exhibition of children's art. He found that the youngsters had captured the world with sufficiently vivid and realistic techniques, "truthfulness of observation, clarity, and boldness of execution." But more exciting to Soyer was that these children, even at their tender ages, produced art displaying the frightful "social conditions around them." He selected two paintings for particular praise, rejoicing in their lack of childish innocence. One was a picture of mounted policemen violently breaking up a workers' demonstration. To Soyer's eye, "the swirling movement of the masses, the charging horses, the brutality of the police" were all well observed and finely expressed. The second picture was the opposite of the first, showing quiet misery rather than violent turmoil. This painting seemed successful because it engulfed the viewer in its despair, conveying "a mood of hopelessness, of sadness, of unemployment."[51] Soyer was pleased, but not because the children had adopted some warped celebration of ugliness. Instead, he was gratified because they had learned right from wrong and then become full-fledged moralizers in their own right. This was precisely the same thing that Soyer and the social realists hoped to accomplish in their own work. Hirsch had said that he wanted to castigate the evil and build monuments to the good, but with the suffering and turmoil of the thirties, he and the others found more to castigate than to memorialize. They painted protest pictures and usually painted two types of them. One kind was like the child's picture of unemployment, showing unhappy people who had come to their despair by some unspecific route. Paintings of the other sort were more like the child's rendition of police brutality, lodging specific complaints about Depression conditions.

Many of their specific protests were against lynching. Unlike the widespread urban breadlines, lynching was hardly a new phenomenon with the thirties. White Americans had long demonstrated a sickening penchant for illegally executing black people in swift "justice" for a host of imagined crimes. But outrage over lynching grew with the thirties, encouraged by the speedy convictions—legal lynching, really—of the Scottsboro "boys" (black youths unjustly charged with rape), reports of racism such as those that John Spivak wrote, and plays like Paul Peters's and George Sklar's *Stevedore* (1934). As part of the larger outcry, Evergood, Gropper, Jones, and Marsh each produced paintings that condemned lynching. Though they usually showed the victims with open sympathy, the artists' chief concern was with the barbarity of the lynchers. In *This Is Her First Lynching* (1934; Figure 9), Marsh demonstrated this emphasis when he eliminated the victim altogether and concentrated upon caricaturing the crowd. The spectators look upon the lynching with ghoulish enthusiasm, avid fans of something that to them seems more like an exciting sports event than the taking of a life. Marsh underscored the viciousness of the act by distorting their features so that they are almost as inhuman as the lynching itself. Unsatisfied with their own iniquity, they eagerly corrupt a young child, holding her high and teaching her to appreciate what is for them only a pastime. With such works, Marsh and the others protested the evil of lynching and employed a strong visual language intended to move the viewer to act against the terrible custom.[52]

Like these lynching protests, the realists' paintings of strikes were also an art of criticism and complaint. Working Americans pressed for fair wages and better conditions throughout the 1930s, and there were any number of strikes the painters could use as models: San Francisco's general strike, the campaigns of Minneapolis teamsters, or the CIO's great push in the auto and steel industries. These efforts involved considerable violence, for management often hired armed thugs as strike breakers, and sometimes stockpiled private arsenals (Republic Steel became the nation's largest single consumer of tear gas). In *American Tragedy* (Figure 4), Evergood included symbols such as a pregnant woman and an American flag to tell the viewer that the strikers were the good guys— safe, unthreatening, and worthy of sympathy. But his primary message had more to do with the brutality and outrageousness of Republic Steel's police. Like Evergood, the other painters who depicted strikes gave less attention to showing the workers' virtues and more to stressing the viciousness of their opponents. Gropper's *Youngstown Strike* (1936; Figure 10), with its bright colors and swirling forms, might almost have been the first painting that Soyer described in his review of the children's art exhibit. The company's men in this picture are hulking figures armed with clubs. Though there are many strikers and only a few of these sinister-looking men, the clubs have apparently taken a toll upon the crowd: one victim lies prone and unconscious, and another is being helped from the fray by his comrades. Gropper did not depict the strikers as completely passive victims, for the central figure is heaving something (a brick?) at his adversaries. But the strikers are far from winning this encounter; most of them can only manage to gesture in frustration or gape in horror at their assailants. Hirsch painted a similar strike picture, full of turmoil and terror, and entitled his work *Landscape with Tear Gas* (1937).[53] The police and company thugs in such pictures are evil men, symbols of an economic system that would wage war against workers rather than treat them justly, and the artists repeatedly rebuked that capitalist system.

Yet only a few workers were in any position to go on strike in the Depression. With the high unemployment rates, jobs were hard to come by, and many workers had no choice but to be docile. Given such circumstances, social realists were inclined to see worker complacency as more of an indicator of forced silence than a sign of satisfaction. When the social realists painted scenes of labor peace, they did not laud the nobility of work or the workers, nor did their leftist inclinations lead them to imitate Soviet renditions of gallant proletarians.[54] Instead of celebrations, the social realists painted protests of the circumstances under which Americans toiled and the toll those situations took upon people. The artists singled out women workers for special treatment; although women suffered as much as men, their pain seemed to need more advertising because they were often invisible sufferers, doing piecework at home for the needle industries. Evergood's *Toiling Hands* (c. 1939/1957–58) shows a sad-eyed woman slaving at her sewing machine, a job that pays so little she can not adequately clothe her own emaciated child. Gropper repeated the scene in *Homework* (c. 1938), a painting of a woman miserably sweating over another sewing machine. For these women, work under capitalism was a slow draining of one's vitality. But it could be immediately deadly, Gropper showed in his painting of male laborers, *Roadworkers* (c. 1936). In this painting, a member of a road crew has collapsed, either from the heat or an accident, and another worker tends his lifeless form. Through such paintings, social realists portrayed work not so much as a way of getting a living, but more as an uncertain means of postponing death.[55]

They further represented the worker as damned to an ever-subservient role, unable to bridge the tremendous gap that separated him from his bosses. Jones portrayed the dichotomy between dockworkers and their overseer in his river scene *Roustabouts* (1934; Figure 11). The supervisor stands not only over the men as they work, but distinct from them, his natty hat and tie contrasting with their work clothes, his form running to fat while their leanness hints of hunger. Moreover, they are black, while he is white, a difference that might never be insignificant in the United States. Levine believed that work in such a capitalist system was so overtaxing that the worker belonged more to the employer than to himself. Accordingly, Levine insisted that "the symbol of work can never express the working man." In his canvases, Levine painted evening scenes in order to catch "the man *not* at work," during those few moments he is "for a time a free man." A worker thus suffered as she or he toiled and, at best, experienced only brief reprieves from the servitude.[56]

Sympathetic to capitalism's victims, the social realists were antagonistic to those who were its beneficiaries. Gropper's *Art Patrons* are prigs and snobs, and this is in large part because of their wealth. Shahn similarly ridiculed the wealthy in his mural *The Passion of Sacco and Vanzetti* (1931–32; Figure 12). He viewed the Sacco and Vanzetti trial as a mockery of justice, sharing the common belief that Sacco and Vanzetti were tried, convicted, and executed more on the basis of their radical politics and Italian origins than any evidence pertaining to their guilt or innocence. In Shahn's perspective, genteel America was responsible for their death, and he conveyed that view in his painting. After the convictions, an outside judge and the presidents of those citadels of the establishment, Harvard and the Massachusetts Institute of Technology, were appointed to review the trial. Their job was to look for judicial bias or other improprieties. Ignoring considerable evidence of a miscarriage of justice, the committee vindicated the highly questionable trial, and so sealed the fates of Sacco and Vanzetti. Shahn drew the committee members in top hats, their badges of wealth, and portrayed them as men of distorted perspectives who sanctimoniously pay their respects at the coffins of their victims. The building behind them appears to be a courthouse, for the presiding judge raises his hand to administer an oath. But in American architecture, it is difficult to distinguish court buildings from banks, and Shahn drew upon that ambiguity to suggest that capital rather than justice had executed the two men. With his title—*The Passion of Sacco and Vanzetti*—Shahn said that these men died as Jesus had died, for the sins of others rather than for their own transgressions. Jack Levine was no less hostile towards the wealthy, and in his own portrait of a rich man, *The Millionaire* (1938), he included some cartoon symbols, a plump cigar and a tuxedo, which were standard idioms for the decadent capitalist. But he omitted the usual bloated waist and added touches of his own. He gave the eyes a cold, ruthless stare, painted the mouth as twisted by the habit of speaking out of both sides of it, and made the hands over-large, symbols of clutching greed.[57]

Hunger and the Dust Bowl were two other recurrent themes in the social realists' repertoire. Determined that Americans' empty bellies should not go unnoticed, the artists produced pictures of emaciated people, and many of the paintings carried stark titles, such as *Starvation*. Joe Jones liked the vividness in such titles, but preferred to add a bit of sarcasm to the ones he chose for his own paintings. In 1937, he selected the title *Luncheon* for a painting that depicts not the adequate formal meal usually implied by the word *luncheon*, but instead a very meager *lunch*. With another title, he posed the question *Who Could Ask for More* (c. 1938) and, with the sparsely spread table in the picture, gave his answer—*anyone*.[58]

As one of the more visually vivid of the Depression's calamities, the Dust Bowl proved as great an attraction for social realists as it was for documentary photographers. The social realists' works in many ways resembled those of Alexandre Hogue, a southwesterner who had grown up on a 50,000-acre ranch in the Texas Panhandle—an area that in the thirties became the heart of the Dust Bowl. Hogue's paintings were explicit reactions to agricultural conditions of the Depression, and he accurately attributed the dust to too much plowing of the native grasslands. Unlike the social realists, who considered the Dust Bowl as part of their larger critique of American society, Hogue lamented it more because the plow had devastated the land he loved. His symbols were trite, as in *Mother Earth Laid Bare* (1938), a scene of plow-induced soil erosion in which the shape of a naked woman has emerged among the gullies. The social realists included people in their works more often than did Hogue, and where his pictures were largely mournful, theirs were more often accusatory and political.[59] Shahn's Resettlement Administration poster, *Years of Dust* (Figure 6), is a good example of how their Dust Bowl pieces tried to evoke sympathy for the drought's victims. The viewer comes face-to-face with the plight of a single man, his dejection symbolized with the ubiquitous Depression image, the head-in-hands position. In the background lies his devastated farm, and over his knee rests a paper, its headlines proclaiming what is hardly news to him—western dust storms are forcing farmers to flee their homes. It was wrong, Shahn and the others were trying to say, that such scenes should occur, and Shahn went further to tell his viewers what they could do to help: support the Resettlement Administration.

These were paintings showing the suffering of drought and work, or the brutality of lynchings and labor repression. Taken together they comprise a list of specific things the painters thought wrong with the country. But there was another side to social realism, one in which the artists dealt more with the psychological than with the physical consequences of the Depression. In this, they were like the second young painter Soyer had seen at the children's exhibit, for they too produced static pictures with little action, pictures of idle, melancholy people. With these works the artists did not make explicit moral judgments like "lynching is wrong," but rather presented more general messages like "we ought not allow such despair." The list of social evils was equally unspecific, for while people in the pictures were frequently poor and jobless, it was not apparent how they came to their plights.

Rockwell Kent's 1936 lithograph, *And Now Where?* (Figure 7) was one such scene of unspecific despair. A couple stands at the top of a hill, their few possessions gathered about them. They have the surrounding countryside in complete view, but no one direction holds out more promise than any other. Their stooped shoulders indicate their weariness, yet it is impossible for the viewer to tell how they came to the hilltop or what he should do to help them. Hirsch's *Seller of Apples* (1934) is a piece along the same lines, a painting that marked an early point in the process that raised the apple peddler into a standard image of the Depression. Hirsch's man stands slouched and depressed-looking, his hands in his pockets and his crate of apples on an empty street where there is little promise of making a sale. The peddler is unemployed, but the strongest message in the picture is the man's sadness over his condition. Jones painted several similar canvases, among them *Man Power* (c. 1937) and *Nothing Better to Do* (c. 1937), showing men for whom society had no place, people who were willing but wasted workers.[60]

Moses and Raphael Soyer virtually specialized in such pictures of sad people. As Raphael described his paintings of the thirties, they were of "silent, nondemanding figures rather than the demonstrations, clashes with the police" that other social realists more frequently produced. Instead of criticizing specific injustices that poor Americans endured, the Soyers chose to protest "the debilitating boredom of their lives," a boredom that steadily whittled away at Americans' strength. In technique, these "brown paintings of the unemployed" are nearly as drab as the lives they depict, utilizing muted colors, indistinct features, and vacant eyes to convey the dismay of their subjects. The Soyer brothers' paintings show Americans with nothing much better to do than dimly hope for better times. For example, Raphael's *Transients* (1936; Figure 13) cluster in a mission, their numbers so great that they fill a large room, and the details become indistinct toward the back. While a few men pass the time reading or in conversation, most can only stare blankly; to underscore their tedium, Raphael painted his own yawning face into the background. Their boredom really *is* debilitating, for one of the men is lame and uses crutches, and many of the others have faces that resemble death's heads. The Soyers were well aware that such paintings were not as forceful as Evergood's *American Tragedy,* and as Raphael admitted, the twins were "by temperament" more inclined to paint subdued rescue missions rather than violent repression.[61] But though they were quiet men, the Soyers did not refrain from critical comment upon the social order. They were just as much painters of protest as were the other social realists, and although the mental despair they depicted was not as visually dramatic as the Depression's physical suffering, those onslaughts could be just as injurious.[62] Moreover, the Soyers' people are, for all their weariness, not quite resigned to their circumstances; the men of their paintings remain *transients* in the Bowery rather than its permanent residents. Such people had few weapons with which to battle the Depression, but they nonetheless continued to struggle without surrender, to hope for better times without accommodating themselves to the present. In the very fact of their effort lay the heart of the Soyers' protest—these people were miserable over their conditions, and those conditions were therefore intolerable.

In contrast, Reginald Marsh's Bowery figures became accustomed to their circumstances. Born in Paris to artist parents, Marsh grew up in a New Jersey artists' colony and was considerably more affluent than the other social realists. A Yale graduate, he worked as an illustrator for a New York newspaper while studying with Luks and Sloan. By the 1930s, Marsh was good friends with Evergood and the Soyers, and he and Raphael frequently employed the same unemployed man as a model. In the early years of the Depression, Marsh produced pictures like those of the other social realists. *Bread Line—No One Has Starved* (1932) and *This Is Her First Lynching* (1934; Figure 9) were both from this early period and portrayed standard protest motifs. But by mid-decade his interest in social protest began to wane, eased out by his lifelong fascination with the human body. In *End of the Fourteenth Street Crosstown Line* (1936; Figure 14), for example, he showed a picket line of striking employees, a typical enough protest theme. But Marsh placed his picket line in the background and gave primary attention to the brawny bodies of construction workers in the foreground. Like the other social realists, Marsh believed in concentrating upon human subjects, but his interests took an increasingly anatomical bent. In 1931 and again in 1934, he enrolled in medical school to study anatomy, and dissected cadavers as part of his course work. Throughout the thirties he was fascinated with Coney Island and burlesques, delighting in their open displays of human flesh, especially female flesh. By the mid-thirties, the problems of the Depression no longer attracted Marsh so much, and skin-filled scenes edged out his earlier protest motifs, just as his muscular road crew pushes in front of the picketers in Figure 14. As his friend Evergood realized, Marsh ceased to be critical of the scenes he depicted. The men in his later Bowery pictures were poor, but they had become acclimated to their circumstances, settled into almost domestic routines. Evergood compared Marsh's derelicts to his own and said, "there is a difference in Bums." He saw that Marsh's poor were tragic figures, lost men representing eternal hopelessness. In contrast, the men in Evergood's paintings "were not congenital Bums but transient Bums . . . my Bums were Bums because the social system had made Bums out of workers."[63]

The social realists were complainers, painting criticisms of the physical and psychological injuries that the Depression inflicted upon Americans. To suggest that the decade's miseries were a natural part of the human condition, as Marsh came to do, seemed to be apostasy. With their redeemed art, the social realists hoped to face actual life of the 1930s, legibly portray it, and go on to give their evaluations of it. For Evergood and the others there was only one correct evaluation: capitalist America was a sinful society, one that starved and beat its workers and then turned them into bums.

A Niche for Art

During the 1930s, social realists searched for a social niche, some place where they could find emotional support, creative freedom, and artistic stimulation. The wealthy offered no satisfactory haven, for the rich were responsible for capitalism's Depression debacle, they placed apparently inordinate demands upon the artist, and they seemed to have withdrawn their patronage when it was needed most. Ultimately the social realists selected for themselves a place among the everyday Americans whom they painted, among "the people." Much like the traveling reporters, social realists believed the country's Depression-stricken offered just the sort of solace they wanted—a warmth the wealthy lacked, plus a combination of respect and inspiration that no rich patron seemed to possess. "The people" also provided financial support for artists, sponsoring through their government the various art programs of the 1930s. To the social realists, those programs indicated that art had at long last located an enduring and meaningful social station, for "the people" appeared to have an abiding need for the artist's leadership.

Most of the social realists were no strangers to deprivation. Sons of immigrant or working-class parents, these men had aspired to move beyond the poverty of their childhoods. But during the Depression, these prodigal sons returned to explore their roots and paint scenes similar to the ones they had experienced as children. Many were of immigrant stock, yet their explorations arose not so much from old-world nostalgia as from empathy with poor people of all ethnic backgrounds. Louis Guglielmi, for example, hailed from "the people," and during the thirties he hoped to return to them. When he immigrated to New York at the age of eight, his family settled in a tenement neighborhood in Italian Harlem. As he grew up and began his art training, Guglielmi came to recognize the constraints of poverty and sought "to escape this environment." His immediate goal was "what seemed sunnier—the middle-class world," and Guglielmi began producing "French paintings" that he hoped would be marketable and catapult him into the sunnier world of the upper class. But then came the Depression, showing him that the rich were a secure source of neither support nor inspiration. Deciding that his attempt to escape had been foolish, Guglielmi worked "to regain the roots of earlier years and repudiate the upper crust of society." The members of that upper crust seemed to have been cold and remote patrons, but when he left them and returned to New York's poorer neighborhoods, he found that "the loneliness of the artist began to dissolve in the understanding of the people." "The people" were an audience that wanted his renditions of everyday life, and Guglielmi responded by painting pictures such as *Wedding on South Street* (1936), a slice of life, "an almost literal reporting of the marriage custom among the poor." By returning to such scenes, he felt he had discovered a "source of inspiration" that charged his work with "the richness, the vitality, and the lusty healthiness inherent in the people." Besides being appreciative and inspiring, these people were also good patrons, for through their government, especially the WPA/FAP, they "provided a weekly check."[64]

Other social realists agreed that "the people" became their source of inspiration and appreciation. Shahn believed that with the Depression and the federal art projects the artist was "no longer hygienically sealed from the ordinary public." As Shahn's phrase indicated, no matter how clean or pleasant they were, his earlier inspirations now seemed quite sterile, too. With its grittiness, the Depression had led him to the lives of ordinary people, "an inexhaustible source of art motifs." Hirsch was even more appreciative of "the people," for they seemed to him not merely his new subjects, they were his spiritual saviors, too. In his words, this was an intense feeling, a veritable "faith in the common ordinary man"; the faith infused Hirsch's Depression-era paintings in a way that he likened to "the emphasis by El Greco, in his day, on his faith in the church." Moses Soyer was not quite so worshipful but still believed that when social realists took on the worker as their "new ally," they acquired someone who had "a deeper inner understanding of art than the superficially cultured wealthier class." Unlike wealthy people, who knew something about ornamentation and perhaps ivory towers, the worker came "into contact with objects of nature" and so had an intimate, almost innate, appreciation for social realism.[65]

In addition to these willing subjects and a comprehending audience, the social realists thought they also acquired a satisfying sense of social identity by aligning themselves with "the people." This was no nationalistic impulse, but was instead a desire to identify themselves as members of America's lowest classes. Soyer believed that he had rediscovered a home with the workers, a sense of belonging "just as any worker who produces with his mind or with his hands belongs." Indeed, he went on to say, "One would be utterly blind in these days of race hatred, depression, and the [New Deal symbol] Blue Eagle not to align himself with the class to which he feels he belongs." Somewhat older than Soyer, Rockwell Kent had established *his* sense of working-class identity a few years earlier. Immobilized by his middle-class proclivities, Kent had come to regard himself as superfluous, one of life's onlookers rather than one of its builders. Developing what he diagnosed as "a real inferiority complex," Kent was plagued with self-doubts, fears that he "could only overcome by becoming a workman myself." To find himself he went to Maine's Monhegan Island where the sparse off-season economy had no room for anyone but common laborers, and there Kent earned his way by cleaning privies and building houses. So great was his need that even the task of cleaning privies gave him "a great, proud feeling—to belong!" and he continued to revive himself with occasional infusions of manual labor throughout the rest of his life.[66]

Joe Jones relished the working-class persona as much as Kent did, but Jones came by it more naturally. Jones appeared never to have left the people, and other social realists lionized him for that appearance. The product of a St. Louis working-class family, Jones honed his technique as a youngster by making pornographic drawings on public buildings—until unappreciative officials sent him to a reformatory. At age fourteen, he joined his father in the house-painting trade and continued his self-taught art instruction throughout the 1920s. By 1934, this exuberant, brash, worker-artist was a Communist, lived in a houseboat propped up on a levee, and supervised a mural project. Jones eventually left St. Louis and came to New York, where his boisterous manners, slum pictures, and talk of paintings that could "knock holes in the walls" made him the darling of the social realist set. He seemed equally confident of his pictures, too, for rather than using them to beg for acceptance by "the people," Jones said that he painted "to express my solidarity with them." Herman Baron, his friend and the director of an important social realist gallery, described Jones's New York career as a "meteoric success." It was no wonder that his house painter so quickly became the man of the moment in such circles, for he was much more than a credible painter of social realist pictures; he was an authentic working stiff who was as lusty and forceful as the other painters thought a worker should be.[67] Even his name—Joe Jones—had a good proletarian ring to it. In Jones the other social realists found a more than serviceable representative of the people, and accordingly they welcomed him into their company.

Part of the social realists' mythos of "the people" was that they had become the artists' patrons through the various government art programs of the 1930s. All the major social realists were on at least one of the projects, enrolled for periods ranging from a few months up to five years. Most commonly, they were with the programs on an on-and-off-again basis between 1933 and 1939. By far the largest of the projects was the Works Progress Administration/Federal Art Project (WPA/FAP), and it employed over half the major social realists at some point during the decade. The WPA/FAP hired artists on the basis of their need, imposed few restrictions on the type of work they produced, and was responsible for over 173,000 different pieces. This government aid was an important aspect of social realism's growth, for it allowed artists to create when there were few other sources of income, and perhaps it even kept some from abandoning their art altogether. But the wellsprings of social realism lay in the artists' individual reactions to the Depression, *not* the government programs. WPA/FAP allowed them immense creative freedom, and the artists usually came to their genre well before they joined WPA/FAP or other programs. WPA/FAP corresponded very closely to the program that artists had been demanding through the Artists' Union and its predecessors, and the Union and WPA/FAP shared at least one major aim, supporting artists while giving them creative license. In WPA/FAP bureaus outside New York City, and in the Treasury Section or the short-lived

Public Works of Art Project, there was some direction of artists' work. But it was the type of direction that social realists found more repressive than inspirational. For example, Rockwell Kent painted a post office mural for the Treasury Section in which he showed Puerto Ricans receiving a letter from Alaskan Eskimos, a message calling for mutual independence and urging them to "change chiefs." This suggestion of colonial rebellion outraged Treasury officials, Kent had to threaten suit to get his pay, and the message was eventually censored.[68]

Despite such occasional tussles, the social realists praised the New Deal art agencies. It seemed to the artists that with these projects, especially WPA/FAP, American art had at long last come to its proper sort of support, a people's patronage. Kent surveyed the programs and declared that "our people as a whole had, through government, become art's patrons." Evergood agreed with him that the nation's "collective wealth and patronage" finally stood behind the artist, and thought that artists now had "help from the people" who with the 1930s had enthusiastically given themselves over to "patronage of the arts." Stuart Davis relished the freedom of expression that the people granted through WPA/FAP and believed that with that independence painters had achieved their long-sought freedom "from the need to scramble for favor in the cutthroat chaos of irresponsible private patronage."[69]

The word "patron" has two general meanings, and the social realists were certain which one was more applicable to the type of patron they wanted the public to be. In its most common use, "patron" denotes some sort of sponsor, one who supports, protects, and exercises control over a retainer. The patron in return receives things of value, like paintings. The word "patronizing" stems from this sense of "patron," and there is a definite superior-to-inferior aspect to the relationship; the artist must please his benefactor or be out in the cold. But there is another use of "patron," one referring to someone such as the library user or the steady customer of a store. Here the patron still has something like a retainer in the librarian or store clerk, for both librarian and clerk must satisfy the patron to insure their livelihoods. Yet there is not so much of the inferior-to-superior relationship surrounding this form of patron, for both librarian and clerk seem to be providing practical services or needed goods, whereas the artist's product has an appearance of being impractical and superfluous. This second usage of "patron" is much closer to what the social realists had in mind when they spoke of their new patrons, for rather than condescending benefactors, they wanted "the people" to be something more akin to satisfied customers or contented library users.

Ultimately, however, no standard usage of "patron" quite fits the relationship that the social realists envisioned between themselves and "the people." In an odd twist of thinking, the painters hoped to become the leaders and directors of those Americans who were their patrons. In *Artist in Society* (Figure 2), Evergood pictured the sort of association they had in mind—the artist of the thirties was a leader of the masses where the painter of the past had been a subjugated vassal. The painters saw themselves as more than ordinary leaders, though, and conceived of themselves as articulate moral and political guides. Kent believed that "the people" knew what they wanted but lacked the skills for voicing their demands. Those toiling Americans came to Kent and the others, asking the artists to become "the spokesmen of their time." Always interested in emotions, Moses Soyer thought that he and the other social realists had become the public's emotional spokesmen, expressing "the life, the misery and the hopes of the people of their time." Similarly, when Guglielmi returned to the ghetto, he saw himself as more than a recipient of warmth and inspiration. He intended to guide the poor as "a spiritual leader with a command of the medium to speak with." Eventually Guglielmi even believed that "the people" were following him, for "at last the artist is being seen and listened to." To Gropper, leadership meant more than merely being a benign spokesman. It included telling one's followers *what to think*. Thus he told his friend Evergood that "we painters of the people must not only tell them the truth in human justice and rightness, we must convince them." Biddle was even more straightforward in his advocacy of manipulation: "Propaganda? Of course. Education? Art is always more convincing than fireside chats." So Biddle took Shahn around to CIO headquarters to sell the workers on art that would in turn sell the CIO to the country. Yet those workers were not quite sure they liked the sort of pictures that the painters wanted to make for them. Talk of propaganda and the proletariat sounded subversive, and the union wanted none of it. But Biddle saved the day: "I didn't speak the truth. I talked in terms they could understand." He told them art was good salesmanship, argued that the social realists were proposing not propaganda but an extensive advertising campaign with pictures, and he left certain he had convinced them.[70]

All such talk about leading "the people" and sharing their identity was more the painters' desire than anything they every achieved. They desperately wanted followers and an audience, for without them, the artists' protests would go unheard and injustice unconquered. As Jones put it, if the painter has no disciples, then his solitude "leads him to believe there is no hope." Yet for all their hopes, the social realists did not attract their longed-for followers. Perhaps they could never attract such devotees, for there are few reasons why the populace should choose to place itself under the leadership of men who make visual images. Arguably the politician or social theoretician could better address problems of hunger or injustice than a person who paints pictures. It is also difficult to imagine how the social realists hoped to become propagandists or secure wide audiences, for they showed little inclination to abandon their individual canvases for the broader circulation potential of prints or posters. Moreover, for all their rhetoric about coming close to "the people," social realists did not paint pictures that the masses wanted to see. Pictures of oppression or despair, such as Shahn's *Years of Dust*, had little to say to the people whom they depicted, for those victims knew all too well that they were unhappy. Instead, the artists' messages often aimed at some third party, striving to demonstrate a social problem like racism or hunger. But audiences usually find the negative aspects of life to be offensive, inappropriate subjects for art. Most of the persons represented in the social realists' paintings probably acted like the Sacco-Vanzetti Club of New York's Little Italy did when it was offered the opportunity to buy one of Shahn's Sacco and Vanzetti paintings for ten cents on the dollar. Club members viewed the works, found them grotesque, and forthrightly rejected the offer.[71]

The people-patrons existed only in the social realists' minds. They were the painters' vision of what ideal art sponsors should be, offering inspiration, identity, and security, and in exchange asking for nothing more than enlightenment. The social realists aspired to be the unrestrained spokesmen for these pliant patrons, airing the masses' grievances through paintings of protest and looking after their best interests. Behind the artists' work there was a deep concern about the crises of the 1930s, and they sincerely wanted to bring art around to confronting such worldly tragedies. But they also wanted to carve out a secure social niche for themselves. The Depression had convinced them of both the extent of injustice in American society and the precariousness of what they took to be the painter's former reliance upon the wealthy. Accordingly, the rebirth in art they sought not only entailed worldly relevance but also included the artist's independence. By recasting their patrons as ever-supportive and never-demanding, the social realists were actually reaching out for creative autonomy and security.

Social Realism's Passing

The heyday of social realism passed with the 1930s. A few painters like Evergood and Shahn continued to criticize American social maladies up through the 1960s, and others never completely abandoned social commentary. But with the end of the decade, paintings of social protest no longer held the dominant place in these artists' works, nor did they command such attention in the American art world. Although the problems of hunger, inequality, and repression continued in varying degrees after the Depression, social realists infrequently chose to denounce such ailments. They continued to paint, yet abandoned protest.

The departure was not as great as it may seem, for social realism was never a revolutionary art genre.[72] For all their anger, the social realists were hardly good radicals. They lodged few complaints against capitalism's museums and galleries, as long as their own paintings were shown there; they did not wish to overturn the world of "fine" arts, but hoped to refashion that world so that they and their work would find acceptance in it. Nor were the social realists very interested in revolutionary egalitarianism; rather than every man acting as his own artist, they envisioned themselves as the exclusive providers of the art that "the people" needed. Evergood and the others were more protesters than revolutionaries, mad at circumstances of the moment but without anything like a blueprint for the future. Indeed, though the future they wanted would include a better deal for artists, it was otherwise quite indefinite. Evergood's *Music* (Figure 5), for example, is characteristically vague. Here there is harmony between different peoples, but otherwise Evergood was not at all clear about what social principles should guide the future or where power should lie. He gave no hint as to what ideological tune his musicians played, when the most desirable parts were assigned, or how the players came by their conductor. His foggy tomorrow was in part a product of the limitations of art itself, for while one can paint pain or abuse with some ease, it is virtually impossible to use the brush to build economic models or project social structures. Evergood and the social realists were quite capable of showing that capitalism had made a mess of the thirties, but they lacked the means to portray some suitable replacement for capitalism.

In part, the Depression's protest painting also passed because the Depression itself passed. As economic conditions eased with the coming of World War II, there were fewer American scenes that attracted the social realists. But overseas, topics like fascism and the war itself did entice them. Hirsch secured himself a slot as a war correspondent and illustrator, composing scenes of combat and its consequences. Gropper and Evergood dearly wanted to go to war, for they hoped to witness and record the defeat of the Nazis against whom they had railed for so long. They jumped at the chance when the War Department recruited them to make a pictorial record of the fighting in North Africa, and then were bitterly disappointed when the government canceled the project because of their earlier radicalism. Together with the Soyers, Gropper finally found a forum for his war work in an exhibition by a group called Artists for Victory.[73]

If the social realists' styles changed, so did their topics. Given the relatively few antecedents in American art, they had been required to be stylistically innovative as they combined protest and realism.[74] They continued this inventiveness during the late thirties and into the forties, prevailing against "naturalism" as they increasingly warped their renditions of the objective world while commenting less upon it. Shahn's distortions grew as he painted figures with greater and greater emphasis on pure form. Similarly, Evergood and Guglielmi moved closer to fantasy after the thirties, Evergood placing a person on the back of a flying flamingo in one painting, Guglielmi imprisoning figures in a bell jar in another. By the 1940s, Guglielmi was on the verge of abstractionism, describing himself as "working toward an individual esthetic within the modern form."[75] Jones never went so far as to describe himself as a modern artist, but he became intrigued with realistically portraying wheat fields during the mid-thirties and, by the end of the decade, was composing paintings that resembled the regionalists' rural celebrations more than his earlier pictures of slums and hungry children. For social realists of the Depression, "humanism" had usually meant that a painting should depict some instance of human suffering. Most continued to produce paintings of people, but with time, the element of suffering slipped out of their pictures. Marsh made the most obvious shift, moving from paintings of anguished humanity to ones of well-toned human flesh. Gropper and Evergood demonstrated some of the same concerns by mid-decade, Gropper painting a strip show and Evergood a satirical beach scene.[76]

But there was another topic that held their attention more than even the most curvaceous of bodies. As happened with the documentary photographers, the social realists' interest in humans developed into an interest in "character." With the later thirties and into the forties, the social realists concentrated more upon the personality and peculiarities of the individual in the picture, and less upon his social conditions. Hirsch's *Two Men* (1937) was one of these mellow paintings. In this picture, the artist showed no suffering and lodged no protest. Instead, Hirsch created a close study of two interesting-looking characters, men wrapped up in an animated conversation. Another of these pieces is Evergood's *My Forebears Were Pioneers* (1940; Figure 15), based upon a woman whom he had seen in the aftermath of the great hurricane of 1938.[77] The old woman in the painting is a startling sight, sitting placidly amidst the wreckage of her life. There is no clear protest in the picture, and the social message, if Evergood even intended one, is obscure. The woman's Bible and pioneer ancestry may comfort her in her distress, or they may keep her from realizing the seriousness of her circumstances. Her dog may be hiding his head in distress, or he may be just resting on the ground. The moralizing of earlier social realism is absent here, for rather than emphasizing what is right or wrong about the woman and her circumstances, Evergood's canvas suggests that his view is simply one of the many visual incongruities that life serves up. Evergood chose to paint this scene merely because it seemed odd, and Gropper increasingly took up the same sorts of subjects. In 1937, Gropper made a trip across the United States, and as he traveled west, he became more interested in anecdotes about his subjects and less concerned with the effects of the Depression on them. In Youngstown, Ohio, Gropper depicted police brutality in a steel strike, but when he reached Elk City, Oklahoma, he portrayed a barefoot boy in bib overalls with the adult responsibility of getting medical help for his grandfather, who had childishly injured his hand playing with firecrackers. Shahn likewise became infatuated with such people when he traveled around the country. Enchanted with the odd folks he met, Shahn found that rather than their conditions, it was "the individual peculiarities that were interesting." Shahn began incorporating those characters into his paintings, shifting away from protest pictures and beginning to explore the eccentricities of individual Americans.[78]

The Depression led these artists to call for a reborn art, one that was more engaged, secure and independent than they believed earlier art had been. In answering their own call, they created a new genre, social realism, and they developed within it a set of techniques for protesting Depression conditions. They took comfort in their newfound contacts with ordinary people and hoped that they had located a social niche as the spokesmen for those people. But as the crisis passed so did their driving concern with a rejuvenated art, for the improving economy helped lessen their sense of insecurity and soften the dismal scenes that had inspired their social criticism. Perhaps social realism's demise lay in its very origins, for from the beginning Evergood and the others had lodged two contradictory demands. They insisted that the artist have both the freedom to create and that he create in a certain way—that he be free to work without the constraints of academic or Party dogma, and that his works must protest his surroundings. With time, freedom won out over protest. They left their common core of social criticism to explore a myriad of individual styles and topics.

1. Philip Evergood,
Harem Girls, c. 1927.
(Zeitlin and Ver Brugge.
Courtesy of Denenberg
Fine Arts.)

2. Philip Evergood, *Artist in Society*, 1936. (Estate of Philip Evergood.)

3. Philip Evergood, *Dance Marathon*, 1934. (James and Mari Michener
Collection of American Painting, Archer M. Huntington Art Gallery, University
of Texas at Austin.)

4. Philip Evergood, *American Tragedy*, 1937. (Private Collection. Courtesy of the Terry Dintenfass Gallery.)

5. Philip Evergood, *Music (The WPA Band)*, 1933/38, 1956. (Chrysler Museum, Norfolk, Virginia. Gift of Walter P. Chrysler, Jr., in memory of Jack Forker Chrysler.)

YEARS OF DUST

RESETTLEMENT ADMINISTRATION
Rescues Victims
Restores Land to Proper Use

6. Ben Shahn, *Years of Dust,* 1936. (New Jersey State Museum. Gift of the New Jersey State Federation of Women's Clubs, Junior Membership Department.)

7. Rockwell Kent, *And Now Where?* 1936. (Akron Museum.)

8. Louis Guglielmi, *The Hungry*, c. 1936. (Renée Gross. Courtesy of the Jane Voorhees Zimmerli Art Museum, Rutgers University.)

9. Reginald Marsh, *This Is Her First Lynching*, 1934. (Augustus M. Kelley. Courtesy of the Whitney Museum of American Art.)

10. William Gropper, *Youngstown Strike*, 1936. (Butler Institute of American Art.)

11. Joe Jones, *Roustabouts*, 1934.
(Worcester Art Museum, Worcester,
Massachusetts.)

12. Ben Shahn, *The Passion of Sacco and Vanzetti*, 1931–32. (Number 12 from the Sacco and Vanzetti Series of 23 paintings. Collection of the Whitney Museum of American Art. Gift of Edith and Milton Lowenthal in memory of Juliana Force.)

13. Raphael Soyer, *Transients*, 1936. (James and Mari Michener Collection of American Painting, Archer M. Huntington Art Gallery, University of Texas at Austin.)

14. Reginald Marsh, *End of the Fourteenth Street Crosstown Line*, 1936. (Pennsylvania Academy of Fine Arts.)

15. Philip Evergood, *My Forebears Were Pioneers*, 1940. (Georgia Museum of Art, University of Georgia.)

Moses Soyer, *Artists on WPA*, 1935. (National Museum of American Art, Smithsonian Institution, Washington, D.C. Gift of Mr. and Mrs. Moses Soyer.)

SIX

Conclusion: Hope and the End of Alienation

he Great Depression was a terrible time. Yet it provided the essential creative stimuli for American social artists and writers. In an environment of unemployment and hunger, people such as Philip Evergood, Nathan Asch, Dorothea Lange, and John Steinbeck produced some of the best work of their lives. They began with great political and esthetic visions, hoping to create works that would challenge the capitalist order and become vital elements of everyday life. These were noble aims, but Lange, Evergood, and the others never quite attained their goals. The anger that had so infused their political messages gave way to a more sanguine feeling that things were going along satisfactorily, for confidence and consolation replaced their earlier reprimands and admonitions. In a like manner, their high artistic hopes produced only sporadic esthetic achievements; despite some notable exceptions from figures like James Agee or John Dos Passos, these works of the Depression generally fail to satisfy. As a group, only the documentary photographs remain compelling over the years. Most of the rest of the pieces are wooden, dated, and trite. Social art of the 1930s never achieved its full potential, and fell short of its creators' political and artistic intentions. Beginning with the promise of a considerable bang, social books and pictures of the Depression usually fizzled.

There are many possible reasons for this performance. One is that most art of any age is largely mediocre art. In any group of artistic products, there are more hackneyed and clumsy works than truly inspired pieces, and Depression art was no different. Furthermore, there was an urgency about the Depression that was as draining as it was demanding. Perhaps these painters, writers, and photographers simply got tired, and the fatigue hobbled their efforts. These are plausible explanations, but even more compelling ones emerge if we remember the artists' motives, goals, and backgrounds. Most of these women and men were politically naive when the Depression came upon them, with little insight other than that things *should* be better in America and with little of the experience that might enable them to say *how* to make things better. They were more consistently social wishers than social planners, and so they tended to hope for indefinite futures more than to design achievable steps towards specific futures. Esthetically, the task they set for themselves was tremendous. They wanted nothing less than a reshaping of the parameters that had defined Western art for perhaps as long as six centuries. They sought an end to the alienation of art and the artist, to bring art to society's center stage and the artist into the bosom of his community. This was a Herculean task, given the accretion of centuries. To achieve such redefinitions of art and the artist was so large a job that perhaps no one could have accomplished it; certainly these writers, painters, and photographers did not. Their contributions to American culture were significant, for with a considerable raw power they hinted that there was reason to be optimistic despite the gloom of the Depression. But neither the hope nor the power made theirs an enduring movement.

The End of Alienation

As James Rorty, Ben Shahn, and their colleagues surveyed the Depression's onslaught, art and the artist seemed cut off from America. The artist and his work were *apart*: from any broad audience, from the warmth of human fellowship, from events of the world, and even from the very content of that world. If this standing had been acceptable in the immediate past, it was no longer tolerable. The time had come, they believed, to end this alienation, and they all sought to bring art and artist closer to life and to the things of life. This was an audacious quest that infused their art with not only energy but also a certain relevancy, for the end of alienation is a goal many have sought in one form or another for much of the nineteenth and twentieth centuries. Yet for these artists of the thirties it was not always a clearly articulated mission, and even the more perceptive among them failed to grasp the sizable dimensions of the project that they had undertaken. It was most likely a futile quest, too. One suspects that neither these artists nor the rest of the creative community will achieve full social integration in the foreseeable future. In some ways, to be a modern (or postmodern) intellectual or artist in the United States is to be alienated by definition, is to be at once both alone and free. A shared world vision had prevailed during the Middle Ages, but when that unified perspective eventually collapsed, creative people lost their accustomed place as its cultivators. Yet new independence and new liberty accompanied that loss; for all their moaning over alienation, few of the Depression's social artists would have exchanged their liberty to regain a sense of belonging.

There were at least three separate aspects to the alienation under which they chafed. One of its dimensions was historical or anthropological. In earlier times, or among more primitive contemporary societies, the artist seemed to have held a position of recognized social importance. The oldest art objects had been votive or totemic, and all members of a tribe recognized their importance and significance. It is, for example, virtually impossible to separate Egyptian art from Egyptian belief. Similarly, the earliest Western literature—Homer or the Old Testament—was more of a common collected record than any one individual's wisdom. Thus there had been a seamlessness to the relationship between art and society, but somewhere along the way the artist and his audience, created thing and community belief, got separated from each other. Social artists of the thirties badly wanted to end that separation. Another portion of their alienation involved Cartesian dualism. Descartes, the seventeenth-century French philosopher, had argued that there is a necessary distinction between the mind and the body, a wide gap that separates the spirit (and its activities) from the outside physical world. This suggested that the artist's creations, as products of the mind, were cut off from that objective world, with no connection whatsoever between themselves and the world. To artists of the thirties this seemed mistaken, not only because their works appeared to exist in the objective world, but also because their immediate objective world was forever insisting its way into the mind. To them, mind and body, art's contents and the world's contents, were of the same stuff. Finally, theirs was an alienation in the Marxian sense. Like Marx, they believed that capitalism had corrupted some important relationships, not only taking work's nobility and rewards away from the ordinary worker, but also profaning art in the process. Under capitalism, art became a mere commodity, a thing to be sold or traded for private profit rather than valued for its beauty or message. In Marx's vision, the worker does not merely hire his time to the capitalist; he loses that part of himself that he invests into the product and that profits the capitalist more than himself. The social artists likewise felt that they put themselves into their works, and that part of the self was ripped away each time capitalism forced them to place their art in a market system that treated those creations as mere speculative commodities.

For the social realists, art and the artist thus seemed alienated, cut off in ways that were simultaneously historical, Cartesian, and Marxian. Their complaint reflected a larger thirties discontentment, one that emerged in quite disparate intellectual circles. For Agrarian writers like John Crowe Ransom, and for Regionalist painters like John Steuart Curry, art had lost its necessary contact with the soil (frequently the southern or midwestern soil), and they labored to reestablish that contact through their works. Proletarian writers like Mike Gold or Clara Weatherwax thought that American art could be improved, and sought to infuse thirties writing with both the class struggle and working class allegiances. Whether from Communists or Regionalists, the echoing call came for art to abandon any ivory tower pretensions and confront the actualities of daily life. There were a few voices that did not join the chorus for relevancy, and they belonged to New Humanists like Irving Babbitt, men who advocated an unapologetic dualism. The New Humanists saw art as a part of some transcendent spiritual realm and believed that the artist's duty was to preserve their work and the spirit from life's grubby compromises. But such dualistic positions were rare in the 1930s, and the New Humanists did not harmonize well with their contemporaries.

The social realists were much more in tune with the times and believed that art and life were intimately connected. They saw no place for any romantic dichotomies wherein the artist is a privileged messenger from "higher" realms and aloof from activities of the world. Nor would they allow any Thoreauvian retreats from life. Instead, their belief and their program saw the artist *in* society, the very title that Philip Evergood had chosen for one of his paintings. Art for them was part of actual goings-on, and they rebuffed those less involved artists who painted impressionist scenes, wrote of the Old South, or photographed wild Yosemite. Moreover, they believed that life was for art to act upon rather than to contemplate, and in their own works, they engaged their environment by protesting its Depression tragedies. They further applied this belief to their lives outside their work. Unlike Thoreau, who had not only withdrawn from society to Walden Pond but also signed off from most of society's organizations, these poeple were joiners, members of the Photo League, Writers Congress, and Artists' Union. There was also among them a persistent and almost frenzied activism that led them to picket lines where the police clubbed them, towns where the locals ran them out at gunpoint, and, in Evergood's case, a sit-in during which the authorities nearly ripped off his ear.

They confronted life, and since it so often turned violent, they understandably viewed life as generally tough—and particularly tough during the 1930s. Dos Passos thought that the present decade was much more demanding than the twenties had been, but it seemed possible to him that "we can at least meet events with our minds cleared of some of the romantic garbage that kept us from doing clear work then." Whereas artists might have been able to get by with remoteness in earlier times, that was no longer the case: "We must deal with the raw structure of history now, we must deal with it quick, before it stamps us out."[1] Other social artists agreed that this was an imperative task, and, like Dos Passos, they felt themselves up to it. Some of the painters believed that dealing with life's rawness involved questions of their own virility. Joseph Hirsch explained that "the real men of art" had always been "keenly aware of the world around them," and he believed that his thirties work made him a member of that manly crowd. Rockwell Kent likewise thought that men who took up painting were too often expected to renounce "whatever common, ordinary decent manhood they possess" and acquire something like a priestly celibacy. But the Depression had led Kent to realism, and so, he felt, saved his work from both continence and effeminacy.[2] For John Collier, even this was not enough, and he left the "decadence" of painting for the seemingly greater realism of photography. Although John Steinbeck did not travel the migrants' path from Oklahoma to California, he still let stand the popular impression that he had been strong enough to face the harrowing trip himself rather than "merely" writing about it. For Steinbeck, Hirsch, and the others, life *was* demanding, and they saw themselves as a special breed, men to match those demands. Their works conveyed this grittiness in their very texture, repeatedly reminding the reader or viewer that the artist possessed the strength necessary to confront the floods, droughts, and strikes that were his subjects. Like Ernest Hemingway or Dashiell Hammett, these Depression purveyors of social realism cultivated the American image of life as an essentially raw experience, and of the artist as a breed apart, a man sufficiently strong enough to subdue life.

This attitude doubtlessly contributed to some of the stylistic and esthetic innovations that accompanied social art and literature of the thirties. In order to meet the times (and assert their own abilities), a number of the artists left behind romantic styles and developed more direct and realistic forms of expression. Dorothea Lange, for example, moved from an adequate but uninspired studio protraiture into the location photography that proved to be her forte. Ben Shahn likewise moved into a more literal style that suited him better than his earlier wavy expressionism, and Josephine Herbst turned to the social descriptions that more closely fit her talents than did the largely psychological portraits she had drawn in her earlier novels. Here was a form to fit the artists' talents, and a form that nicely accommodated the artists' intense concerns for their subjects. Though the executions are often clumsy, these works convey the sense that the artist sees himself involved in something larger than the self, an engagement akin to that found in Vietnam-era artists who saw themselves as participants in "the movement."

The intensity is high, and these works usually convey it to the audience. But, again like many products of the Vietnam era, it was an engagement with life of the moment, and the art is often dated. Some works manage to transcend the moment and float above the chronological moorings of their topics. Richard Wright's *Native Son* is one such piece, a novel about a black youth of the Depression, but one that continues to hold readers with a well-crafted plot that leaves readers *feeling* the protagonist's panic. Yet many other works are more like Evergood's *Dance Marathon* (Chapter 5, figure 3). Here again the subject is trapped people, but unlike the characters in Wright's novel, these characters are caught in a uniquely thirties phenomenon, the dance marathon. Before the viewer can appreciate the painting, much less experience some of Evergood's sentiments, he must know that during the Depression there were desperate people willing to dance themselves past the point of exhaustion for the chance at a few dollars. Both the novel and the painting are powerful and full of objective experiences, but Evergood's painting no longer "works" because it is about a part of life that has passed.

Depression artists and writers wanted to bring more of the stuff of life into their works and so lessen the distance between their creative efforts and the objective world. They also hoped to diminish the distinctions between themselves and their audiences, to overcome a persistent sense that artists are apart from those who experience their work. Rather than telling audiences how to think or feel, the painter or writer would travel with them in a mutual exploration of life. This notion was a departure from some prevailing notions of the proper relationship between the artist and his viewers or readers. During much of the nineteenth and twentieth centuries, the artist was perceived to be above or beyond his audience, possessing an almost mystical access to the elevating powers of "culture." One turned to the artist for refinement and improvement, reading a book or studying a picture to acquire taste and elegance. In some ways, the artist *was* rather like a priest, and it was that expectation against which Rockwell Kent had rebelled; as keeper of the keys to some higher realm, the artist was supposedly unsullied by the crudeness of ordinary life.

Over time, it seemed as though this difference between artist and audience had developed into an open conflict. As society and audiences became more bourgeois, the artist became more Bohemian. He assumed a position at society's very edge, attacking the center for its smugness and shallowness. He challenged the great middle classes with abstractionist works or with intentionally bizarre behavior that equally affronted their genteel expectations. *This* artist was not someone the middle class accepted as a guide to spiritual improvement. But whether the well-mannered and carefully pressed pastor, or the smock-and-beret-class hooligan, the artist seemed irrevocably alienated from his audience. His messages and his life were things apart from the daily lives of his readers or viewers.

But the Depression's social artists and writers had had enough of this separation. They wanted to close any gaps between themselves and their audiences, and this desire helped give their art a characteristic openness. For all its inadequacies, Depression social art is *accessible* art, neither esoteric nor precious. Never was there a social novel or a travel report so delicately executed that it seemed to speak about a world apart from that familiar to the ordinary reader. Nor did an appreciation of social realist paintings or documentary photographs require any special training; they drew their metaphors and messages from the vernacular. Consider Dorothea Lange's picture of the hunched-down man in "Man Beside Wheelbarrow" (Chapter 3, figure 2). Immediately one perceives this man's sadness and—almost effortlessly—Lange's commentary: this man's back is against the wall and his livelihood (represented in the wheelbarrow) has been turned upside down. There are no occult secrets to understanding such a work, nor does one have to be emotionally precocious to comprehend (and maybe even feel) the emotions of the artist. Steinbeck's anger registers clearly in *The Grapes of Wrath*, as does Evergood's outrage in *American Tragedy.* If the emotions were obvious, so was the content, for such experiences as the Okie migration or police brutality were straight from the headlines. These were immediate topics, and the social artists refused to indulge in the romance of other thirties painters and writers. One could forget agriculture's plight by looking at Grant Wood's canvases of lush Iowa hillsides, or journey with Margaret Mitchell into Scarlett O'Hara's Georgia plantation. But in a time when a large part of the American public was down and out, Josephine Herbst chose to discuss destitute Iowa farmers, and Erskine Caldwell wrote about Georgia's rock-bottom poor.

Since objective hardships like droughts or strikes pressed so heavily upon people, the social artists found it easy to believe that Depression audiences would be interested in their work. But that impression probably reflected the artists' hopes more than any actual gap-bridging that might have occurred. There were only two novels from the lot that became best sellers, Steinbeck's *Grapes of Wrath* and Caldwell's *Tobacco Road,* and even these were not received quite as the authors had intended. Readers tended to pity Steinbeck's characters more than admire them, and to laugh at Caldwell's people rather than take them seriously. American audiences may have been more attuned to Margaret Bourke-White's sensational photography, and Bourke-White's popularity doubtlessly contributed to the soaring success of *Life* magazine. But other, less melodramatic, documentary photographers encountered more ambiguous audience reactions. In 1938, a sizable number of the Farm Security Administration photographs were exhibited at the First International Photographic Exposition in New York City. This was a salon show with a (considerable for the times) admission price of forty cents, and the FSA exhibit stood alongside other photos of more standard, nondocumentary fare: nudes, landscapes, and still lifes. The FSA exhibit included a comment box where viewers could register their reactions to the documentary pictures, comments that were dutifully recorded and filed. Most of the commentators reacted as the photographers had intended, expressing their shock that such poverty could exist in the United States or indicating their solidarity with the New Deal. But a number of the viewers wanted more traditional, less engaged, art photography; these people tended to find the documentary photographs ugly, poorly crafted, and esthetically worthless. One such observer wrote that these were a "lousy bunch of prints." To him, the subjects were "very sordid and dull for exhibition," and he concluded by calling for "more nudes." But more nudity would have offended the bourgeois expectations of another viewer, who reacted negatively to the half-naked four- or five-year-old boy in one of Walker Evans's Alabama tenant pictures: "Object very much to picture of boy without pants. Shameful to hang it."[3] This was of course but one exhibit of a limited number of photographs, but it suggests that at least a portion of the Depression audience wanted something other than what the documentary photographers offered.

We have still fewer indications of public reaction to the social realist paintings, but even these show audience ambivalence or rejection. For example, when that Italian men's club was offered a virtual gift of Ben Shahn's Sacco and Vanzetti painting, the club members decided the painting was ugly and refused to have it in their meeting hall. These kinds of responses suggest that, despite the artists' wishes, social art was not something that consistently appealed to Depression audiences. Art and audiences seem to have remained alienated from each other regardless of the artists' hopes.

Their desires to end alienation also led the artists to imagine themselves as members of the larger American community. Repeatedly they fancied themselves to be coming closer to, and perhaps even joining, "the people"—that broad mass of ordinary folk in the land. More than just the pursuit of good communication with an audience, this was a search for belonging. To the writers, painters, and photographers, their kind seemed cut off from experience, and they sought to commune with those warm ordinary people who seemed in touch with life's intricacies and actualities. Thus it was more than a set of new subjects that Evergood discovered in that wintry shanty town; he found companions who willingly accepted him into their campfire circle. Anderson was similarly drawn to the men who became his drinking partners, for though he had come to St. Louis to write about its economy, the men's companionship and acceptance seemed of greater importance. For Anderson, Evergood, and the others, this was more than a poetic celebration of quaint, simple people. It was the artists' effort to merge with that populace and erase any differences between artist and tribe.

This desire for community had a way of weakening the presentations. Depression artists repeatedly acted as though the only legitimate perspectives were those of "the people." By contrast, the views of artists or other intellectuals lacked authenticity and were thus somehow inferior.

Of course some artists, like Joe Jones or Jack Conroy, were not far removed from "the people," and others thought that as artists they could manage more felicitous expressions than could "the people." But there was a strong element of self-deprecation about the other social artists, a belittling denial of their own experiences. In writing for the *New Masses* in 1932, Sherwood Anderson demonstrated this sentiment. Capitalism was failing, he wrote, and if that meant that artists also had "to be submerged, let us be submerged. Down with us." With the old political and esthetic guard dispossessed, he believed that the new leaders would "come out of the masses." Josephine Herbst had similar feelings about artists and intellectuals, and a year later shared her views with writer Katherine Anne Porter. "The trouble with us and our kind," Herbst told Porter, "is that under this system we are such isolated people . . . we have too little contact with struggling people." Such contact was important not so much because it stimulated the intellectual's own thinking, but because "the people" had better and more direct ideas. As Herbst explained to Porter in yet another letter, "My head gets foggy if I hang around the intellectuals but if I go out where the farmers are talking turkey it all gets fairly simple. . . ."[4] Repeatedly one encounters a similar lack of self-confidence, a paralyzing humility that weakens much of the social culture of the 1930s. The reader (and the viewer—though less frequently) gets the sense that if one *really* wants to talk turkey, it would be best to ignore Herbst or Anderson altogether and take up with their hitchhikers or farmers. The creation of a piece—the act of writing or painting or photographing—involves a necessary intellectual arrogance, the gall to say that one has come up with an approximation of some truth. But this wincing self-effacement of the 1930s diminishes one's confidence in the writer or artist and casts considerable doubt upon the veracity of his writing or pictures. With greater credence in themselves and less thralldom to "the people," Herbst, Anderson, and the others may well have created stronger works.

Another part of their effort to end art's alienation from life was to focus upon people who were obviously part of life. For this reason, social art and literature of the Depression had few heroes among its books or pictures. Seldom were there any larger-than-life characters who, like Odysseus, performed mighty deeds and verged upon being gods themselves. Instead, thirties works are populated by a set of considerably more down-to-earth actors. Their problems are often small or even amusing (Grandpa

Joad cannot get the buttons of his fly to line up), or their dilemmas are poignant and familiar (Rothstein's sharecropper woman is obviously poor and pregnant, and anyone can understand why she looks worried). But while it is easy to empathize with these lifelike characters, they are ultimately unsatisfying, for they lack the ability *to act*. Like Marx, these artists saw that the environment can rob people of power, and they portrayed a host of life's victims. But when their characters become anything other than victims, it is not by the characters' own doing; instead, it is destiny that repeatedly leads them to comfort. This is not only monotonous, it rings untrue; certainly people can and do act in the world and direct their own lives. Social artists and writers of the Depression compromised the esthetic quality of their work when they forgot the other half of Marx's equation: though humans are products of a material and cultural environment, they also possess the power to change that environment.

Social art and literature of the 1930s was within the larger Western tradition of realism. Realism was a movement that emerged in mid-nineteenth-century Europe as an artistic reaction against the notion that art pertained not to this world but to some higher transcendent one. Like their realist forerunners, Depression social artists realized that to take a given thing as one's subject was to give significance to that thing. By using everyday people and objects, they suggested that common things and persons were of esthetic importance, that there was little distance between art and life. With these subjects from the objective world, realists attacked the Cartesian separation between mind and matter. What for Descartes had been a practically unbridgeable gulf, was for them a matter of intimate acquaintance. But as the social realists of the thirties went about making their images of ordinary things and people, they repeatedly encountered a dilemma. Were their works things *extracted from* the world or *new to* the world? As artists, should they be *capturers* of things, or *creators* of them?

Most often Depression artists said that they chose capturing over creating. Steinbeck wanted to be "simply a recording consciousness," transcribing life into his stories. Other novelists like Asch and Anderson found fiction insufficiently transcriptive and left it for the "purer" recording of their travel reports. In the same vein, Gilbert Seldes and Dorothea Lange had both accepted Francis Bacon's charge to contemplate only "things as they are, without substitution or imposture."[5] With this belief, Bacon had been something of a bellwether for his Enlightenment contemporaries, helping lead others to his view of the mind as the *discoverer* of a rational world order rather than the *creator* of rational visions of the world. From the Enlightenment on, there has been in the West a lingering suspicion that to be creative, or even unabashedly interpretative, is to lie—or at least be frivolous. The novel, for example, was for years considered a trifling art form, weaker than nonfiction and a genre appropriate for "mere" women. Similarly, viewers continue to evince something akin to righteous outrage when they discover that a still photographer has taken an active role in composing a picture like Rothstein's "Duststorm." To be truthful and to be accurate are laudable aspirations. But the bias towards them can keep intellectuals from recognizing the necessary role of creativity in work of the mind. That very prejudice inhibited the work of writers and artists of the thirties like Nathan Asch, who waited with increasing impatience for his book to write itself.

One of the most common ways in which realists achieve veracity in their images of the world was to include details of the world. But like salt in the stew, too much detail can ruin a piece, producing such clutter that the theme is lost in a jumble of small observations. This happened with Depression works, and often the product emerges as something like one of those community murals in which each person conceives and executes his own vision on a single large canvas; the finished product is chock-full of meanings but has lost any overall meaning. Philip Evergood's paintings had this problem; his orchestra, for example (Chapter 5, figure 5), is really a set of small individual portraits that crowd each other on the canvas. Marion Post Wolcott's photo of migrant living quarters (Chapter 3, figure 10) is likewise cluttered, and consequently ambiguous about her intentions in making the photograph. Such details are nearly fatal for James T. Farrell's fiction; the reader becomes saturated with Farrell's minutiae of Irish Catholics in Chicago. Fortunately, others knew how deadly detail can be. Ben Shahn reprimanded Diego Rivera for painting murals that were too busy, and Shahn's roommate, Walker Evans, produced magnificently clean and concise photographs. But social artists of the thirties more commonly acted like the travel reporters and loaded up their works with a heavy burden of detail.

As a genre, documentary photography seems to be the most enduring esthetic accomplishment of the Depression's social art. There are, to be sure, solid individual achievements among the other genres. *The Grapes of Wrath*, for instance, still moves audiences nearly fifty years after the

Joads made their trek. Likewise, James Rorty's prose has some memorable moments, and Ben Shahn's portraits retain considerable vitality. But the photographs of Lange, Evans, and the others are more consistently powerful and more consistently appealing. Perhaps some of this is because the photographs are "easy"—they are accessible single images that seem to take less of the viewer's time than one must devote to a novel or a painting. But it is also because the photographers were most comfortable with the problems of being realists, for they confidently created visions of the real world. They began with actual scenes of thirties America and then unabashedly staged or manipulated those settings to achieve the visions in their minds' eyes. Their medium was arguably the most objective of the four, yet they also realized that as creators they were, of necessity, separated from the objective world and not of it; their techniques allowed them to be simultaneously close to and apart from their subjects. Willing to arrange the scenes before them, they seldom lost their messages in a sea of detail. Of the Depression's social artists, the documentary photographers most closely accomplished the end of alienation, and they comfortably shaped their images from what the world offered them. Combining the objective world *and* their visions of it, their achievements remain compelling and enduring.

Hope Is Not a Method

If the social art and literature of the thirties is a mixed bag of esthetic shortcomings and achievements, its political qualities are less ambiguous. These works were about the world, often created with the intention of changing that world, but with no plans for effecting change. Some years ago a major family-planning agency launched a campaign encouraging people to take active control of their reproductive lives. As part of the campaign, the agency coined a slogan: "Hope is not a method." Behind that maxim was the idea that one must *act*, one must have some coherent method for avoiding pregnancy. Merely *wishing* to avoid conception is insufficient. In an important way, social change is like contraception; hope by itself can accomplish neither. In both instances, passivity will achieve little, and the truly concerned person must do something.

Social artists and writers desperately wanted a better world than the one of the Depression. But seldom did they suggest methods to bring about that improvement. Instead, they hoped that the future would be better and, in most cases, became confident that it would. Novelists like Steinbeck placed their faith in a pleasantly deterministic fate that led inevitably to greater peace and happiness for most Americans. Lange and the photographers celebrated their characters' stalwart endurance and good humor, traits that might carry people through future difficulties but would do little to help them avoid those difficulties. Travelers such as Asch believed that the future just *had* to be an improvement over the present, and suggested that achieving the future was not so much a matter of action as it was a matter of following the right sort of leadership—perhaps the New Deal or perhaps the Communist Party. Evergood and his painter colleagues felt that salvation for art (and, by implication, for society) came from without; at some point conditions changed, and the old and corrupt were swept away to be replaced by the new and virtuous. There was thus a terrific optimism in these four genres. But it is a strangely baseless optimism. Certainly the promulgation of step-by-step plans for the future is not one of art's stronger suits. Praise and protest come more easily for art than do programs, and a given art work is probably more adept at evoking emotions or meting out moral judgments. This is especially true for the visual arts, for without a verbal syntax it is extremely difficult to accomplish much more than a gestural expression.[6] But still—if social art is to be effective, it must do two things. It must channel hope or anger *toward* some end, and not merely arouse those emotions. Furthermore, it must at least hint of ways in which its hoped-for ends can be achieved and maintained. These are "how" things, matters of method and process, and the Depression's social artists ignored them.

In some ways, they were scared hopeful. Many of their hopes were antidotes for their despair over the Depression. Initially they had been quite angry over the devastation, and their works loudly protested the rampant suffering. But the tempestuous atmosphere of evictions, strikes, and forced migrations was also bewildering, so bewildering that more than a few of them fled. Lange headed for Taos, Kent for Greenland, Adamic for Yugoslavia, and Asch away from Hollywood. When they actually faced the Depression, they sang a realist esthetic and brought life's harsh realities into their works. But having faced and complained about the fearful conditions, they eventually turned to fear's brighter twin, hope. Social realist painters convinced themselves that they had found security and independence through new patrons, while traveling reporters diligently pursued hard facts in the faith that empirical evidence would provide soothing alternatives to the decade's uncertainties. Similarly, documentary photographers sought out Americans who managed to preserve a comforting dignity and strength, and social novelists took solace in writing of a fate that eventually and inevitably improved the human lot. Having feared that nothing could be done, they came to hope that nothing need be done. Initially angry as well as upset, by decade's end most had lost their earlier bitterness and become quite sanguine. To be certain, some retained a critical social perspective; Ben Shahn made peace posters during the Vietnam war, and John Steinbeck never became an apologist for Main Street. But as the thirties passed, their feelings of consolation and confidence prevailed, and their reprimands and admonitions waned. It was not so much that they became tired of editorializing nor that they committed political apostasy from earlier radical commitments. It is rather that within their dual inspiration, the drive for social solace prevailed over their desire to offer social criticism.

Timely Art and Changing Times

By the late 1940s or early 1950s, the major manifestations of Depression art and writing had passed. Steinbeck had left his Okies to write about the inner turmoil of California youth, Lange's work reached a plateau and she never returned to her earlier level of productivity, Nathan Asch wrote short stories for the *New Yorker,* and Philip Evergood produced more and more paintings of pure fantasy. In some sense, this passing was "natural," part of the ordinary evolution that brings people to new pursuits. But social art of the 1930s was a type of expression that was almost bound to change, for it was essentially reactive work. When they created, the social novelists, documentary photographers, travel writers, and social realist painters each worked in response to the Depression. This gave to their work a cohesion that transcended genre boundaries, making it possible for a writer like Agee and a photographer such as Evans to collaborate, or for the novelist Steinbeck to draw inspiration from Lange's images. They believed themselves to be engaged in much the same enterprise, and as each strove to interpret the vital present, they used real-life images to achieve immediacy. But since their impulses derived so much from the outside setting, they had little choice but to move on when that Depression itself passed. Social art and literature of the thirties was timely art, and when the times changed, so did the art.

Many of their hopes for the future involved the vision of a vast community, one that could involve all sorts of people, including artists, in constructing a new order. A community of sorts came into being when America mobilized for World War II in the early 1940s. But it was more a destructive than a constructive one, and a community that became increasingly dubious about including social artists in its campaigns. The Depression had challenged the artists with repeated hardships, and warfare proved demanding in its own way. A number of them threw their enthusiastic support behind the Allied cause; having spent much of the thirties engaged in crusades against capitalism's evils, by the late thirties and early forties many reached the conclusion that fascism was an even greater evil and worthy of a global crusade. In this, of course, they received the coaching of the Communist Party and its affiliates, which under the Popular Front of the mid-thirties had encouraged writers and artists to take public stands against fascism. With war's arrival, official America finally proved willing to fight fascism, and many social artists lent their skills to the cause. Even before the United States technically entered the fray, Richard Wright offered his services to the army, hoping to mobilize black opinion for the war. Wright's fellow novelist Edward Newhouse also turned to the army, and with considerable success, for he rose from private to major in the Air Corps. Joseph Hirsch found more direct application for his own talents, serving as a pictorial war correspondent and producing some seventy-five works from the African, Italian, and Pacific theaters. Margaret Bourke-White and Erskine Caldwell managed to be in Russia at the time of massive German aerial bombardments; they ignored the danger to send back spirited and characteristically sensational battle dispatches.

Official America thus welcomed Caldwell, Bourke-White, Hirsch, and Newhouse into its ranks. But other social writers and artists of the thirties found less eager acceptance. Having protested government policies and acquired persistently critical outlooks, they now discovered that those forms of expression and habits of mind did not engender official favor. Dorothea Lange found work with the Office of War Information, a propaganda bureau, but her somber photographs of imprisoned Japanese-Americans proved to be poor propaganda, and the authorities promptly suppressed them. Soon after Pearl Harbor, the Office of Strategic Services came into being under the leadership of William J. Donovan, and brought to its German desk novelist Josephine Herbst, who had traveled extensively in Germany and was accomplished in the language. Before long, however, the agency eased Herbst from her position, for her persistently strong sympathies for the Spanish loyalists were in direct conflict with Donovan's support of the Franco regime. Philip Evergood and William Gropper had similar experiences. The army's War Artists Program recruited painters to record the war, and the two artists eagerly accepted appointments to the African theater. Evergood resigned a teaching post, both began their preparations, but within months, the army booted them out of the program. Because of their earlier radical activities, they had earned a place on an anti-red blacklist, and the army considered them insufficiently patriotic to fight fascism with their paintbrushes.[7]

Joining the fight was thus a frustrating and even futile effort for some. For others, the fighting itself proved disheartening, replacing the confidence that had been building in the late thirties with a new set of questions about the future. Disillusioned after his European war experiences, Steinbeck proved unable to weave those episodes into the fabric of his fiction. He also lost the warm sympathy that had marked his earlier writing, and his postwar author's voice became decidedly colder, more caustic and moralistic. Photographer Carl Mydans took his lumps as a war correspondent, suffering the biting cold of Finland and the near-fatal hostility of a French mob that mistook him for a German parachutist. To cap his experiences and his despair, he spent nearly two years interned in a Japanese prison camp in the Philippines. During the seemingly interminable months, he came to a dark "feeling of futility" and believed that his world had "no purpose and no future." The horrors of the war even registered upon Margaret Bourke-White. She was on hand when the Nazi death camps were liberated, and though Bourke-White was able to steel herself enough to photograph the grisly scenes, she did so only by drawing a protective veil across her mind. The gruesomeness registered, but later, when the images emerged from her darkroom and she felt "as though I was seeing these horrors for the first time." (Given the thickness of her skin, though, the war also proved to be an adventure for Bourke-White. Her work made her something of a hero for American girls, and her exploits were paraded before the juvenile readers of *Calling All Girls* and *Real Fact Comics*.)[8]

Many of the artists' prewar hopes for unity had been based upon the presumed demise of capitalism. Their vision was that once people put aside the goal of private property and worked for the good of all, then catastrophes like the Depression would no longer occur. But as the peculiar conditions of the Depression passed, so too passed the circumstances that had given birth to their anticapitalism. For the most part, social authors and artists were not committed radicals, and they lacked a sustaining social vision that could continue to inspire their work. They were mostly middle-class men and women, or aspirants to middle-class standing; the Depression brought them face-to-face with suffering on a scale they had never before encountered, or reminded them of miseries they had hoped to have left behind. Capitalism seemed responsible for a good deal of the suffering against which they railed, but most of them were eventually willing to make their peace with it. When the Depression eased and New Deal measures became accepted, capitalism learned to dress itself up with the cosmetics of welfare and bread-and-butter unionism, effectively masking the hunger and labor repression that had inspired so many thirties protests. Social artists and writers of the Depression had complained about the distress they saw, and when the signs of social injustice became less transparently obvious, their grumbling dwindled. Furthermore, they had fewer reasons to complain about their own conditions. Though the passing of the 1930s brought an end to federal programs upon which some of them depended, by the postwar years most had left behind the strained circumstances of their early years and were settled into moderately comfortable lives.

As society remained fundamentally unchanged, so too did the artist's relationship to his audience. Rather than the broad brotherhood of viewers and readers that they had imagined, their works remained commodities that touched only a small, often well-to-do, audience. Reaching larger groups and establishing close artist-audience contact appeared possible only through the movies or the emerging medium of television, fields where the alienating necessity of turning a profit seemed incompatible with the artists' earlier messages. Furthermore, fewer Americans were interested in the types of messages that Shahn and the others had presented during the Depression. There were still far too many Americans who were intimately familiar with the hunger that Shahn protested or the police brutality that Evergood attacked in *American Tragedy*. But as hunger retreated from its high-water mark of the thirties, and as people in power acquired tools other than police nightsticks to achieve their goals, the interest in protest art shrunk. Lacking a sizable audience for their protests, and increasingly unable even to conjure one up after the Depression, social artists and writers understandably moved on to other topics.

Moreover, by the 1950s, those prospects of losing the self in a community became less appealing. It increasingly seemed that, rather than adding a vital dimension to life, groups actually detracted from it. Where individualism had apparently given rise to the agonies of the Depression, conformity increasingly seemed the villain of the postwar years. The war had done much to alienate Carl Mydans from group experiences, for as a prisoner of the Japanese, he had been squeezed together with some 3,500 people in a tiny prison camp. Such mass experiences, perhaps more than any other factor, were the most disturbing aspect of the war for social artists and writers. Combat threw people together in vast organizations— prison camps, military units, civil defense corps—where the individual mattered little and corporate needs became paramount. Earlier, during the thirties, these artists and writers had been fascinated with and even enthusiastic over just such communities. Steinbeck eagerly described his phalanx man, Evergood painted the artists as part of a larger social march to the future, and Asch sought to lose himself in "the people." But even before the decade's end, their zeal for community had begun to fade. Painter George Biddle spoke of the artist as manipulating a gullible set of "the people," others became disenchanted with the group-think of American Communists, and photographer John Vachon gloried in the eccentricities of an individualistic Nebraska whore. Other artists increasingly shared Vachon's affection for independent minds and unconventional characters by the 1940s and 1950s, when masses of "the people" seemed more capable of demanding mindless homogeneity than of providing creative inspiration. Lange, Steinbeck, and the others abandoned their collectivist sympathies of the Depression, for they were less concerned with the glories of community than they were worried over the terrors of conformity. Like Edmund Wilson, who in 1932 had called upon "intellectuals of every kind, to identify their cause with that of the workers," they now thought they had indulged themselves in "some awful collectivist cant." Novelist Benjamin Appel, who had once been content to immerse himself in the collective voice of "the people," now believed that he and others of his generation had been guilty of "reducing the irreducible individual to pygmysize." Lorena Hickok had made her first tentative steps toward this position when she visited unemployed people in the late 1930s, and, to her joy, "one by one . . . they emerged—individuals." As early as 1941, Steinbeck began his own departure from phalanxes and moved toward an individualistic focus, claiming that in problems such as world hunger, it was meaningless "to know a million Chinese are starving unless you know one Chinese is starving."9

Ben Shahn best illustrated these postwar concerns about individuality and conformity. During the later thirties, his interest in themes of social justice evolved into a fascination with individuals' idiosyncrasies. As Shahn later noted, the content of his paintings developed "from what is called 'social realism' into a sort of personal realism." His concerns continued to grow so that by the academic year 1956–57 he felt compelled to deliver a lecture "On Conformity" as part of Harvard's Charles Eliot Norton Lecture Series. Shahn had done his homework, reading the works of sociologists like David Riesman and William H. Whyte, men who shared his anxiety that Americans had become indistinguishable from one another and from the merchandise they consumed. Shahn misread Riesman, however, concluding that the sociologist was an apologist for conformity; Shahn defended individualism and swore he could never "believe in Statistical Man or Riesman Man." In the thirties, Shahn had been inclined to see economic suppression as the greatest of human problems, but by the cold-war years, conformity seemed the greatest threat. Salvation now seemed to lie not so much in mass movements as in the person who purposefully took a stance far from the masses—the nonconformist. Perhaps the greatest nonconformist was the independent artist, that woman or man who resisted the terrific pressures that led people to evaluate themselves and the world through others' eyes. The individual artist and his creativity were of monumental importance in Shahn's view, preserving independent expression in a world of clones. The creative impulse was an individual thing, depending upon emotion, deep sympathy, or beauty and so could never be collective. For Shahn, the creative moment is "always specific and never generalized."10

Conformist pressures came not only from the larger society, but also from the art world itself. Modernist inclinations appeared to be dominating the artistic scene, and the remaining realists increasingly saw themselves as a beleaguered minority. Depression painters like Evergood had described the twenties as a modernist wasteland, full of effete abstractionist works executed without the virile assurance seemingly necessary to confront the actual world. Yet for all such complaints about the 1920s, modernism's American flowering came only later, in the years following World War II. The process began in earnest during the late thirties and early forties, when European artists like Marc Chagall and Piet Mondrian arrived in the United States, refugees from war-torn Europe. Seldom interested in realism, they were instrumental in bringing the American art community to share their modernist concerns. Moreover, a number of social realists found themselves drifting away from representational expression and toward the more abstract forms they had earlier rejected so vehemently. Louis Guglielmi, for instance, emerged from the military (where he served in a camouflage section) to produce canvases that more nearly resembled Stuart Davis's jazz abstractions than Guglielmi's own earlier pieces. By the mid-fifties, the art community seemed to have embraced modernism so completely that those who continued to consider themselves realists came to feel as though they were the pariahs of the American art world, suffering the rejections of gallery directors and museum curators who were determined to foster abstractionism while shutting realist works out of the art market. Embattled realists such as Reginald Marsh, Joseph Hirsch, and the Soyer brothers went on the attack in 1953. They founded their own journal (appropriately entitled *Reality*), called for art that explored objective human forms rather than subjective abstract shapes, and attacked the curatorial crowd for its "irresponsibility, snobbery and ignorance."[11]

Reception of the *Reality* manifesto pointed to yet another postwar influence that helped blunt Depression-style social criticism. By 1953, the cold war was well under way, and the American political climate was so charged with its hostilities that critical perspectives, even esthetic ones like the *Reality* proclamation, came under intense suspicion. When Museum of Modern Art officials read the manifesto, their response was to send *Reality*'s editorial board a warning, *by special messenger*, that the proclamation smacked of dangerous Communist sympathies. For a time during the thirties, social artists and writers had possessed leftist dreams, and a few had held outright Communist ones. But with the passing of the thirties, many found such visions harder to affirm, and, as *Reality*'s editors learned, even dangerous to affirm.

The wartime Russian-American alliance failed to redeem the Soviets in many Americans' eyes, and postwar tensions between the superpowers led to a considerable domestic prejudice against leftist Americans. For those intellectuals who continued to hold progressive beliefs, political repression in the United States became a serious concern. Starting in the late thirties, Congressional conservatives made art a special target for their right-wing suspicions, scrutinizing government art programs in search of radical influences. With their hands upon the purse strings of agencies like the WPA's Federal Art and Theatre Projects, conservatives managed to exercise a form of political censorship over artists working within those agencies. This did not always involve informed persecution of radical sentiments, as Federal Theatre administrator Hallie Flanagan learned during her testimony before the infamous Dies Committee. Flanagan made passing reference to sixteenth-century dramatist Christopher Marlowe, and Representative Joe Starnes interrupted her, demanding to know whether or not this Marlowe fellow was a Communist.[12] Despite such comic moments, when artists might be able to laugh at their tormentors, offical antiradicalism continued to grow with the postwar years, and the House Committee on Un-American Activities hauled in progressive artists like Pete Seeger, grilling them on their beliefs and the political content of their works. Although intellectuals and artists might scoff at Representative Starnes, Senator Joseph McCarthy, or other redhunters in local government and the private sector, they could not take such inquisitors lightly. Actual prosecution for political unorthodoxy was not all that frequent, but the mere hint of radical associations or beliefs easily could be enough to cost one a job or deny one access to galleries or publishers. Even a relatively apolitical person like Margaret Bourke-White came under suspicion. For years during the cold war, the Federal Bureau of Investigation considered her a security risk. The agency built a large dossier on Bourke-White, enlisting the Post Office, Customs Bureau, and her neighbors and colleagues to collect information on her. At one point, FBI director J. Edgar Hoover targeted Bourke-White as a candidate for internment.[13] The FBI was not the only agency to conduct such surveillance, and throughout the early fifties, there was an insidious if uncoordinated suppression of those ideas that had been close to the heart of much Depression social criticism. In such circumstances, other intellectuals like Joe Jones and John Spivak muted their earlier condemnations of American capitalism, producing less strident works in the atmosphere of pervasive political suppression.

At one time, it had been considerably easier to dream of a home among "the people." For a while "the people" had represented a cultural sanctuary that could endure despite the insanity of civilization's apparent capitalist collapse. But by the 1950s, "the people" had changed. Where they had once seemed capitalism's victims and even its critics, they now seemed closer to being rabid McCarthyites, demanding political conformity and attacking all who seemed in the least bit critical of the United States. By this time, Shahn and the others were almost content to be alienated. Where once they had sought community, they became content to be gadflies nipping at society's flanks.

Notes

Chapter One

1. James Agee, "Summer Evening," in *The Collected Poems of James Agee*, ed. Robert Fitzgerald (Boston: Houghton Mifflin, 1968), 154–55.
2. D. W. Gotshalk, *Art and the Social Order* (1947; reprint, New York: Dover, 1962), 206.
3. Warren Susman, "The Thirties," in *The Development of an American Culture*, ed. Stanley Coben and Lorman Ratner (Englewood Cliffs, N.J.: Prentice-Hall, 1970), 179–218. Richard Pells, *Radical Visions and American Dreams: Culture and Social Thought in the Depression Years* (New York: Harper and Row, 1973). Susman develops the "culture" versus "civilization" dichotomy at length, see pp. 188–89. Charles C. Alexander explores nationalism in the thirties in *Here the Country Lies: Nationalism and the Arts in Twentieth-Century America* (Bloomington: Indiana University Press, 1980), 152–91.
4. William Alexander, *Film on the Left: American Documentary Film from 1931 to 1942* (Princeton: Princeton University Press, 1981), 17. Gerald Rabkin, *Drama and Commitment: Politics in the American Theatre of the Thirties* (Bloomington: Indiana University Press, 1964), 179, 249. Malcolm Goldstein, *The Political Stage: American Drama and Theater of the Great Depression* (New York: Oxford University Press, 1974), 51–61.
5. For the distinction between film production and the creation of a painting or novel, see Raymond Fielding, *The March of Time, 1935–1951* (New York: Oxford University Press, 1972), 89. For the collective creativity of drama groups, see Rabkin, *Drama and Commitment*, 74–83, and Goldstein, *The Political Stage*, 76–92. Bill Nichols discusses the void between film and other thirties social culture in "The Documentary Film in America," *Canadian Review of American Studies* 16 (Summer 1985): 231–35.
6. Malcolm Cowley, "Thirty Years Later: Memories of the First American Writers' Congress," *American Scholar* 35 (Summer 1966): 500. Malcolm Cowley, *The Dream of the Golden Mountains: Remembering the 1930s* (New York:

Viking, 1980), 48. For a discussion of this myth, see Charles C. Alexander, *Here the Country Lies*, 152–56.

7. Malcolm Cowley, "Fable for Russian Children," *New Republic* 89 (November 25, 1936): 120ff.

8. Edmund Wilson, *The Shores of Light: A Literary Chronicle of the Twenties and Thirties* (New York: Farrar, Straus and Young, 1952), 493–96, 498–99.

9. For another Depression intellectual's three-stage art history, this one by William Phillips, see Terry A. Cooney, "Cosmopolitan Values and the Identification of Reaction: *Partisan Review* in the 1930s," *Journal of American History* 68 (December 1981): 583–84.

10. Henry F. May, *The End of American Innocence: A Study of the First Years of Our Own Times, 1912–1917* (New York: Alfred A. Knopf, 1959), 302–17.

11. Charles Rosen and Henri Zerner, "What Is, and Is Not, Realism," *New York Review of Books* 29 (February 18, 1982): 21; and "Enemies of Realism," *New York Review of Books* 29 (March 4, 1982): 29.

12. Christopher Lasch, *The New Radicalism in America, 1889–1963: The Intellectual as a Social Type* (New York: Random House, 1965), xiv–xv. Harold Stearns, ed., *Civilization in the United States: An Inquiry by Thirty Americans* (New York: Harcourt, Brace and Company, 1922), iii–vii. Joseph Wood Krutch, *The Modern Temper: A Study and a Confession* (1929; reprint, New York: Harcourt, Brace and World, 1956), 169.

13. John Steinbeck, "A Primer on the Thirties," *Esquire* 50 (June 1960): 90. Harold Clurman, *The Fervent Years: The Story of the Group Theater and the Thirties* (1945; reprint, New York: Alfred A. Knopf, 1950), 114. Anita Brenner, "The Clinical Eye," *Nation* 136 (May 17, 1933): 568.

14. Alfred Kazin, *Starting Out in the Thirties* (1965; reprint, New York: Random, 1980), 82–83. For a Vietnam-era activist with similar feelings, see Jane Alpert, *Growing Up Underground* (New York: William Morrow and Company, 1981), 130. For the *Pins and Needles* song, see Morgan Y. Himelstein, *Drama Was a Weapon: The Left-Wing Theater in New York, 1929–1941* (New Brunswick, N.J.: Rutgers University Press, 1963), 78. Edmund Wilson, *The Thirties: From Notebooks and Diaries of the Period* (New York: Farrar, Straus and Giroux, 1980), 303.

Chapter Two

1. Erskine Caldwell and Margaret Bourke-White, *Say, Is This the U.S.A.* (New York: Duell, Sloan and Pearce, 1941), 8–14.

2. Unsigned biographical sketch of Nathan Asch, in *American Stuff: An Anthology of Prose and Verse by Members of the Federal Writers' Project* (New

York: Viking Press, 1937), 293; Rose C. Field, "Aliens in America" (review of Nathan Asch's *The Valley*), *New York Times*, September 8, 1935, sec. 6, pp. 7ff; unsigned biographical sketch of Sholem Asch, *Saturday Review of Literature* 32 (October 8, 1949): 20. Nathan Asch, "Cross-Country Bus," *New Republic* 78 (April 25, 1934): 301–4. For Asch's increasing concern with Depression themes, see his article, "Hints to the Starving," *New Masses* 7 (January 1932): 8.

3. Asch, "Hints to the Starving," 8.

4. Nathan Asch, "Cross-Country Bus," 301. Asch, "Overland Reporter" (review of John L. Spivak's *America Faces the Barricades*), *New Republic* 84 (September 4, 1935): 108. The articles Asch incorporated into his travel book appeared in *New Masses*, *Partisan Review*, and *New Republic*. The book itself was *The Road: In Search of America* (New York: W. W. Norton, 1937). For discussions of Clifford Odets and Hollywood, see Malcolm Goldstein, *The Political Stage: American Drama and Theater of the Great Depression* (New York: Oxford University Press, 1974), 317–21; and Gerald Rabkin, *Drama and Commitment: Politics in the American Theatre of the Thirties* (Bloomington: Indiana University Press, 1964), 174–99. William Alexander discusses Asch's work in the Film and Photo League in *Film on the Left: American Documentary Film from 1931 to 1942* (Princeton: Princeton University Press, 1981), 19, 38, 44.

5. Asch, "Cross-Country Bus," 303–4, 301; "Overland Reporter," 108.

6. Asch, *The Road*, 29, 269, 232, 85.

7. The union "natives" organizing in Marked Tree did not think it extraordinary that they should come under fire, but neither did they think it "banal." Asch, *The Road*, 58ff. Asch underscored his emphasis on facts rather than news in his untitled review of James Rorty's *Where Life Is Better*, *New Republic* 86 (February 26, 1936): 86. For more strictly journalistic concerns, see Raymond Fielding, *The March of Time*, *1935–1951* (New York: Oxford University Press, 1978), 34.

8. *The Road*, 7, 195, 58. Asch, review of Rorty's *Where Life Is Better*, *New Republic* 86 (February 26, 1936): 86.

9. *The Road*, 58, 269.

10. *The Road*, 198, 85, 231, 202–6.

11. *The Road*, 219, 166, 132–36.

12. *The Road*, 139–41, 113, 139, 116–17.

13. *The Road*, 80, 230–32.

14. *The Road*, 10–11.

15. Harold Clurman, *The Fervent Years: The Story of the Group Theater and the Thirties* (1945; reprint, New York: Alfred A. Knopf, 1950), 83. Anita Brenner, "Rorty Reports America," *Nation* 142 (February 12, 1936): 194. Edward New-

house, "All They Do Is Talk," *New Yorker* 16 (July 13, 1940): 56–57. Jack Conroy, "A Proposed Symposium," *Carleton Miscellany* 6 (Winter 1965): 37.

16. Major reports by these authors include Theodore Dreiser, ed., *Harlan Miners Speak* (New York: Harcourt, Brace and Company, 1932), and *Tragic America* (New York: Horace Liveright, 1932); Sherwood Anderson, *Puzzled America* (New York: Charles Scribner's Sons, 1935); Benjamin Apple, *The People Talk* (New York: E. P. Dutton and Company, 1940; New York: Johnson Reprint Corporation, 1972); Erskine Caldwell, *Call It Experience: The Years of Learning How to Write* (New York: Duell, Sloan and Pearce, 1951), 90–192; and Margaret Bourke-White and Erskine Caldwell, *You Have Seen Their Faces* (New York: Modern Age Books, 1937), *North of the Danube* (New York: Viking, 1939), *Say, Is This the U.S.A.*, and *Russia at War* (London: Hutchinson, 1942). These writers were literary realists of some feather, and as Harvey Swados notes, journalistic backgrounds were common in the group. It is therefore understandable—though hardly "inevitable" as Swados holds—that they should turn to reporting with the crisis. See Harvey Swados, ed., *The American Writer and the Great Depression* (Indianapolis: Bobbs-Merrill, 1966), xxxi–xxxii.

17. James Rorty's report is *Where Life Is Better: An Unsentimental American Journey* (New York: Reynal and Hitchcock, 1936). James Agee, together with photographer Walker Evans, accepted the 1936 *Fortune* assignment that grew into their book *Let Us Now Praise Famous Men* (Boston: Houghton Mifflin, 1941). Robert Fitzgerald, "A Memoir," in *The Collected Short Prose of James Agee*, ed. Robert Fitzgerald (Boston: Houghton Mifflin, 1968), 3–57.

18. League of Professional Groups for Foster and Ford, *Culture and the Crisis: An Open Letter to the Writers, Artists, Teachers, Physicians, Engineers, Scientists, and Other Professional Workers of America* (New York: League of Professional Groups, 1932). Sherwood Anderson, *Sherwood Anderson's Memoirs*, ed. Ray Lewis White (1942; reprint, Chapel Hill: University of North Carolina Press, 1969), 527n. "For a National Writers' Congress," *New Masses* 23 (May 4, 1937): 25. Theodore Dreiser, Introduction, *Harlan Miners Speak*, 1–16. Dreiser to Franklin D. Roosevelt, August 23, 1938, September 1, 1938, and September 19, 1938, *Letters of Theodore Dreiser*, ed. Robert H. Elias (Philadelphia: University of Pennsylvania Press, 1959), 3:812–15. W. A. Swanberg, *Dreiser* (New York: Charles Scribner's Sons, 1965), 513–15.

19. Anna Louise Strong's report is *My Native Land* (New York: Viking Press, 1940), and *I Change Worlds: The Remaking of an American* (New York: Garden City Publishing Company, 1937) is her autobiography. John L. Spivak gave his assessment in *America Faces the Barricades* (New York: Covici-Friede, 1935). See also Spivak's autobiography, *A Man in His Time* (New York:

Horizon Press, 1967). Mauritz A. Hallgren wrote *Seeds of Revolt: A Study of American Life and the Temper of the American People During the Depression* (New York: Alfred A. Knopf, 1933). Lorena Hickok's work finally found publication as *One Third of a Nation*, ed. Richard Lowitt and Maurine Beasley (Urbana: University of Illinois Press, 1981). Jonathan Daniels entitled his travel report *A Southerner Discovers the South* (New York: Macmillan, 1938).

20. Gilbert Seldes, *The Years of the Locust: America, 1929–1932* (Boston: Little, Brown and Company, 1933). Louis Adamic, *My America, 1928–1938* (New York: Harper and Brothers, 1938). J. Saunders Redding, *No Day of Triumph* (New York: Harper and Row, 1942).

21. Asch, Spivak, and Strong published articles about their travels in *New Masses*, Hallgren and Rorty in *Nation*, Adamic in *Harper's*, Anderson in *Today*, Agee in *Fortune*, and Caldwell in *Atlantic Monthly*. Asch also published in *Partisan Review* and *New Republic*. Hallgren was on the staff of *Nation*, but as an editor rather than a reporter. Anderson's *Puzzled America* trip was an assignment for *Today*, but he had been formulating and promoting the project for years before the journal agreed to underwrite his expenses. Agee's trip was a *Fortune* assignment, but the essay he submitted was so much his own product and so little to the editors' liking that they refused to publish it and eventually released it to him. (Agee, *Let Us Now Praise Famous Men*, xii–xiv; see also William Stott, *Documentary Expression and Thirties America* [New York: Oxford University Press, 1973], 261–66.)

22. Like Agee and Dreiser, Robert and Helen Lynd were concerned with thirties conditions in a specific place and produced *Middletown in Transition* (1937), a sequel to their earlier study of Muncie, Indiana, *Middletown* (1929). Arthur Raper studied southern tenant farmers and presented his findings in *Preface to Peasantry* (1936), while Thomas Minehan took the Depression's homeless, wandering youths as his subject in *Boy and Girl Tramps of America* (1934). Ann Banks, ed., *First Person America* (New York: Random House, 1980) is a recent collection of FWP life-history narratives. For further discussion of the Federal Writers' Project, see Jerre Mangione, *The Dream and the Deal: The Federal Writers' Project, 1935–1943* (Boston: Little, Brown, 1972), 45–48, 244; William F. McDonald, *Federal Relief Administration and the Arts: The Origins and Administrative History of the Arts Projects of the Works Progress Administration* (Columbus, Ohio: Ohio State University Press, 1969), 657–62; and Monty Noam Penkower, *The Federal Writers' Project: A Study in Government Patronage of the Arts* (Urbana: University of Illinois Press, 1977), 25–26, 243.

23. In his brief treatment of social reporters, Richard Pells sees some similar personal motivations, but also argues that they possessed a nationalistic desire

to affirm American values. Richard Pells, *Radical Visions and American Dreams: Culture and Social Thought in the Depression Years* (New York: Harper and Row, 1973), 195–201.

24. Seldes, *The Years of the Locust*, 12. Anderson to Baroness Marie Koskus, December 15, 1930, *Letters of Sherwood Anderson*, ed. Howard Mumford Jones and Walter B. Rideout (Boston: Little, Brown and Company, 1953), 232. Strong, *My Native Land*, 123. Rorty, *Where Life Is Better*, 13.

25. Dreiser, *Tragic America*, 16–17. Caldwell, *Some American People* (New York: Robert M. McBride and Company, 1935), 118–23. Agee to James Harold Flye, August 18, 1932, and August 14, 1932, *Letters of James Agee to Father Flye* (New York: George Brazillier, 1962), 58, 56. Anderson to Edward H. Risley, Jr., February 24, 1938, *Letters*, 395. Rorty, "The Silent Land," *Nation* 132 (May 13, 1931): 533.

26. Adamic, "The Land of Promise: An Immigrant of 1913 Looks at America in 1931," *Harper's* 163 (October 1931): 624; Adamic, *My America*, 36, 117. Adamic frequently transcribed sections of his diary into *My America*. For Van Wyck Brooks's concerns and their echoes in the thirties, see Charles C. Alexander, *Here the Country Lies: Nationalism and the Arts in Twentieth-Century America* (Bloomington: Indiana University Press, 1980), 35–40, 156–62, 197–206.

27. Adamic, *My America*, 279–82, 289–90, 113, 416.

28. Edmund Wilson, *The American Jitters: A Year of the Slump* (1932; reprint, Freeport, New York: Books for Libraries, 1968), 303. Edmund Wilson, *The Thirties*, ed. Leon Edel (New York: Farrar, Straus and Giroux, 1980), xvii. Edmund Wilson, *The Triple Thinkers: Twelve Essays on Literary Subjects* (1938; reprint, New York: Farrar, Straus and Giroux, 1977), 210. Daniel Aaron has noted this same thirties inclination toward reportorial motifs. He does not like the genre and attributes it not so much to personal impulses as to the Communist Party's emphasis upon journalism, an emphasis that he believes destroyed the writers' talents. See Aaron's *Writers on the Left: Episodes in American Literary Communism* (New York: Harcourt, Brace and World, 1961), 393.

29. Seldes, *The Years of the Locust*, title page, 6, 11.

30. Rorty, *Where Life Is Better*, 157, 49–50, 13, 271–73. For a discussion of Pare Lorentz, see Alexander, *Film on the Left*, 93–94.

31. Dreiser, *Tragic America*, 14; Spivak, *America Faces the Barricades*, 49; Seldes, *The Years of the Locust*, 18; Hallgren, "Easy Times in Middletown," *Nation* 132 (May 6, 1931): 499. Hallgren knew of Robert and Helen Lynd's *Middletown*, and that it was a study of Muncie, Indiana. However, he chose to study nearby South Bend, Indiana and called it "Middletown, America" ("Easy Times in Middletown," 497).

32. Adamic, *My America*, 339. Caldwell, *Call It Experience*, 58. Caldwell, *Some*

American People, 9; *Call It Experience,* 163; *Tobacco Road* (1932; reprint, Savannah, Ga.: Beehive Press, 1974), viii.

33. Anderson to Charles Bockler, November 12, 1930, and December 13, 1930, *Letters,* 225, 230; Anderson to Ralph Church, December 19, 1930, *Letters,* 233. Dreiser to Dorothy Dudley Harvey, April 7, 1932, *Letters of Theodore Dreiser,* 2:583. Dreiser, *Tragic America,* 167. Although they eschewed fiction in the larger sense, Rorty, Caldwell, and Anderson did some fictionalizing of names and places in their reports.

34. Spivak, *A Man in His Time,* 170; Caldwell, *Tobacco Road,* viii. Asch, "Cross-Country Bus," 304; Agee, *Let Us Now Praise Famous Men,* 234. Agee's use of the camera metaphor implied a more precise copying of actuality than did Asch's, see the section on James Agee in this chapter.

35. Warren Susman, "The Thirties," in *The Development of an American Culture,* ed. Stanley Coben and Lorman Ratner (Englewood Cliffs, N.J.: Prentice-Hall, 1970), 188, 213. Sherwood Anderson, "Explain! Explain! Explain Again!" *Today* 1 (December 2, 1933). Sherwood Anderson, "Listen, Mr. President—," *Nation* 135 (August 31, 1932): 191–93. J. Saunders Redding, *No Day of Triumph,* 139, 100. James Rorty, *Our Master's Voice: Advertising* (New York: John Day Company, 1934), 75, 280.

36. Rorty, *Where Life Is Better,* 9–10; Adamic, *My America,* 281–93; Hickok, *One Third of a Nation,* ix–x; Anderson, "Nobody's Home," *Today* 3 (March 30, 1935): 20–21.

37. Anderson to Roger Sergel, June 18, 1932, *Letters,* 260. Rorty, *Our Master's Voice,* 280; Rorty, *Where Life Is Better,* 15–17, 56, 106–7, 119, 309–15. Strong, *I Change Worlds,* 10; Strong, *My Native Land,* 12.

38. Alfred Kazin stressed the journalistic nature of the social reporters' work, labeling it a "literature of Fact." He was their contemporary and, though critical of their seeming abandonment of imagination, was still sympathetic toward anyone who managed to write in the crisis. (Kazin, *On Native Grounds: An Interpretation of Modern American Literature* [New York: Reynal and Hitchcock, 1942], 485–519). Richard Pells repeats Kazin's themes of nationalism and concentration on fact, stressing the reporters' desires for order (Pells, *Radical Vision and American Dreams,* 195–201).

39. Strong, *I Change Worlds,* 155, 384, 375.

40. Strong, *I Change Worlds,* 126, 385. Strong, *My Native Land,* 6. John Dos Passos quoted in Townsend Ludington, *John Dos Passos: A Twentieth Century Odyssey* (New York: E. P. Dutton), 271.

41. Spivak, *A Man in His Time,* 11–24, 166, 284. Spivak, *America Faces the Barricades,* 287.

42. Hallgren, *Seeds of Revolt,* 350; and Hallgren, "Easy Times in Middletown," 499.

43. Spivak, *America Faces the Barricades*, 23. Spivak called the cabin an "outhouse," referring to its size and shape, a figurative use William Stott took literally when he assumed that the woman actually did live in an outhouse (Stott: *Documentary Expression and Thirties America*, 176). Hallgren, *Seeds of Revolt*, 115–17, 497–99. Strong, *My Native Land*, 154.

44. Strong, *My Native Land*, 22–23. Spivak, *America Faces the Barricades*, 32. Hallgren, *Seeds of Revolt*, 153–55. Lawrence W. Levine discusses the pervasive sense of shame in Depression America in "American Culture and the Great Depression," *Yale Review* 74 (Winter 1985): 202–5.

45. Strong, *My Native Land*, 293, 80; Spivak, *America Faces the Barricades*, 287; Hallgren, *Seeds of Revolt*, 349–51.

46. Spivak, *A Man in His Time*, 465.

47. Anderson to Charles Bockler, December 13, 1930, and November 12, 1930, *Letters*, 230, 225; Anderson, "A Writer's Notes," *New Masses* 8 (August 1932): 10. Anderson to Paul Rosenfeld, July 14, 1933, *Letters*, 293.

48. Anderson to Maxwell Perkins, October 6, 1934, *Letters*, 307–8. Anderson to John Anderson, autumn 1935, *Letters*, 320. Anderson to Theodore Dreiser, January 12, 1936, *Letters*, 344. Anderson to Theodore Dreiser, January 12, 1936, *Letters*, 344; Anderson to John Hall Wheelock, March 24, 1930, *Letters*, 217.

49. Adamic, *My America*, 113, 337–38, 301, 341, xiii.

50. Gilbert Seldes, *Mainland* (New York: Charles Scribner's Sons, 1936), dedication, no page number. Daniels, *A Southerner Discovers the South*, 293, 344.

51. Anderson, *Puzzled America*, xv; Anderson, "Explain! Explain! Explain Again!" 3. Adamic, *My America*, 44, 605. Hickok, *One Third of a Nation*, 61. Daniels, *A Southerner Discovers the South*, 68. Gilbert Seldes, "Have Americans Lost Their Nerve?" *Scribner's Magazine* 92 (September 1932): 151. Seldes, *The Years of the Locust*, 231–43; Seldes, *Mainland*, 404, 395.

52. Anderson, *Puzzled America*, 40, 164, 153, 65, 5–20; Anderson, "New Paths for Old," *Today* 1 (April 7, 1934): 12–13ff; Anderson, "At the Mine Mouth," *Today* 1 (December 30, 1933): 21; Anderson, " 'I Want to Work,' " *Today* 1 (April 28, 1934): 10.

53. Hickok, *One Third of a Nation*, 96, 223, 362–63. Adamic, *My America*, 299–300. Seldes's dark assessments in *The Years of the Locust*, 60–61, 207–8, became considerably brighter in *Mainland*, 395–415.

54. Anderson, "Blue Smoke," *Today* 1 (February 23, 1934): 7; Anderson, *Puzzled America*, 282–87. Seldes, *Mainland*, 7; Daniels, *A Southerner Discovers the South*, 346. Adamic thought the "long road" that his leaders would take was one that carefully threaded its way between both Marxism and fascism (*My America*, 549–662).

55. Rorty, *Where Life Is Better*, 129, 117, 33.

56. James Rorty, "Anti-Fascist Statement," *New Masses* 8 (April 1933): 12–13. Rorty, *Where Life Is Better*, 281, 321. Rorty, "Spivak, Star Reporter," *Nation* 141 (August 7, 1935): 163. Malcolm Cowley, *The Dream of the Golden Mountains: Remembering the 1930s* (New York: Viking, 1980), 116. For Edmund Wilson's report of the same evening of Rorty's poetry reading, see *The Thirties*, 340.

57. Asch, untitled review of Rorty's *Where Life Is Better*, 86. Asch, *The Road*, 7. Dreiser to Dallas McKown, June 9, 1932, and Dreiser to Evelyn Scott, June 17, 1938, *Letters of Theodore Dreiser*, 2:588 and 3:799. For Dreiser's departure from determinism see his introductory essay in *Harlan Miners Speak*, 4–16.

58. Redding, *No Day of Triumph*, 340. Caldwell, *Call It Experience*, 132–33, 235; Erskine Caldwell quoted in Robert Van Gelder, *Writers and Writing* (New York: Charles Scribner's Sons, 1946), 37.

59. Rorty, *Where Life Is Better*, 53–57, 13. Redding, *No Day of Triumph*, 288. Caldwell, *Some American People*, 25–30.

60. Caldwell, *You Have Seen Their Faces*, 169; Asch, "Cross-Country Bus," 301; Asch, *The Road*, 10–11; Redding, *No Day of Triumph*, 256–57, 340.

61. Agee, *Let Us Now Praise Famous Men*, 232–34.

62. *Let Us Now Praise Famous Men*, 233.

63. *Let Us Now Praise Famous Men*, 236.

64. Agee, "They That Sow in Sorrow Shall Reap," originally in the *Harvard Advocate*, 1931, here from *Collected Short Prose of James Agee*, ed. Fitzgerald, 83; Agee to James Harold Flye, August 14, 1932, and August 18, 1932, *Letters of James Agee to Father Flye*, 55–58. Laurence Bergreen believes that Agee's despair at this time was less social than it was personal; Agee was contemplating marriage. Laurence Bergreen, *James Agee: A Life* (New York: E. P. Dutton, 1984), 125.

65. Agee quoted in Fitzgerald, "A Memoir," *Collected Short Prose of James Agee*, 21. Agee to Flye, August 23, 1935, *Letters of James Agee to Father Flye*, 77. Agee, *Let Us Now Praise Famous Men*, 244–45.

66. Agee to Flye, February 17, 1936, *Letters of James Agee to Father Flye*, 87–88; Agee, *Let Us Now Praise Famous Men*, 249, 250. Agee, "Plans for Work: October, 1937," submitted by Agee with his application for a Guggenheim fellowship, here from *Collected Short Prose of James Agee*, ed. Fitzgerald, 140.

67. Agee quoted in Bergreen, *James Agee: A Life*, 163. Agee to Flye, August 12, 1938, *Letters of James Agee to Father Flye*, 104–5; *Let Us Now Praise Famous Men*, 12, 82.

68. Asch, *The Road*, 79; Agee, *Let Us Now Praise Famous Men*, 314–15.

69. *Let Us Now Praise Famous Men*, 203, 289, 210, 313, 397. Historians have had

an understandably difficult time with Agee, misreading his attitude toward action in the world, his delineation of imagination and description, and his relationship to other writers of the period. Richard Pells acknowledges the uniqueness of Agee's accomplishments, but misreads Agee and argues that Agee believed that one could satisfactorily combine imagination and description into a "total understanding" of a problem. Pells also stresses that *Let Us Now Praise Famous Men* was a call for social action in the world, which it was not. See Pells, *Radical Visions and American Dreams,* 246–51. Warren Susman notes Agee's emphasis on the theme of existence but mistakenly argues that Agee was "innocent" of ideological considerations (Susman, "The Thirties," 217–18). In fact, Agee simply laid those considerations aside for the moment. Harvey Swados minimizes the differences between the Agee-Evans team and their colleagues, saying that their book "expresses in quintessential form everything most ardent and unafraid about the creative men of those years" (Swados, *The American Writer and the Great Depression,* p. xxxii). Warren Eyster is closer to the mark when he notes that Agee employed some of the same material as a James T. Farrell or an Erskine Caldwell, but that Agee's perspective is much more poetic than theirs (Eyster, "Conversations with James Agee," *The Southern Review* 17 [April 1981]: 347–48). William Stott's reading of *Let Us Now Praise Famous Men* is astute. Stott sees that Agee was willing to accept contradictions, and that Agee set aside, in a mood of "doom and desperation," the task of improving the world to concentrate upon depicting it (Stott, *Documentary Expression and Thirties America,* 290–314).

70. Charles A. Beard, "Written History as an Act of Faith," *American Historical Review* 39 (January 1934): 220.

Chapter Three

1. Letter from John Vachon to John Collier [1942], Roy E. Stryker Papers, Archives of American Art, New York.
2. Examples of this approach are Michael Lesy, *Wisconsin Death Trip* (New York: Pantheon, 1973); George Talbot, *At Home: Domestic Life in the Post-Centennial Era, 1876–1920* (Madison: State Historical Society of Wisconsin, 1976); and Marsha Peters and Bernard Mergen, " 'Doing the Rest': The Uses of Photographs in American Studies," *American Quarterly* 29 (1977): 280–303.
3. Susan Sontag's *On Photography* (New York: Farrar, Straus and Giroux, 1977) is an intriguing, intelligent, and helpful exploration of the nature of photography; see pp. 6–7 for Sontag's discussion of the relationship between art and

truth. Joel Snyder and Neil Walsh Allen, "Photography, Vision and Representation," *Afterimage* 3 (January 1976): 8–13. Alan Trachtenberg contends that the desire to project a personal vision is an intimate part of the photographer's creative impulse; see his essay, "Images and Ideology: New York in the Photographer's Eye," *Journal of Urban History* 10 (1984): 453–64.

4. Dorothea Lange, "The Making of a Documentary Photographer," interview by Suzanne Riess (Berkeley: University of California Regional Oral History Office, 1968), 36, 45–52, 87–90.

5. Lange, "Documentary Photographer," 136, 141, 147. Dorothea Lange interview with Richard K. Doud (hereafter cited as Lange-Doud interview), May 22, 1964, Archives of American Art, New York, p. 5.

6. Lange, as quoted by her son, Daniel Dixon, in "Dorothea Lange," *Modern Photography* 16 (December 1952): 73–75. Lange, "Documentary Photographer," 144–45.

7. Lange, quoted in Dixon, "Dorothea Lange," 75.

8. Karin Becker Ohrn, *Dorothea Lange and the Documentary Tradition* (Baton Rouge: Louisiana State University Press, 1980), 24, 244 (n.36).

9. Lange, quoted in Dixon, "Dorothea Lange," 73. Lange, "Documentary Photographer," 148, 150, 146–47, 155. Lange's chronology of these events, recollected later in her life, is not always clear. My reconstruction is in essential agreement with that in Milton Meltzer, *Dorothea Lange: A Photographer's Life* (New York: Farrar, Straus, Giroux, 1978), 72–83. For another version, see Ohrn, *Dorothea Lange and the Documentary Tradition*, 21–24.

10. Dorothea Lange, "The Assignment I'll Never Forget: Migrant Mother," *Popular Photography* 46 (February 1960): 42, 128. See also Willard Van Dyke, "The Photographs of Dorothea Lange—A Critical Analysis," *Camera Craft* 41 (October 1934): 464, and James C. Curtis, "Dorothea Lange, Migrant Mother, and the Culture of the Great Depression," *Winterthur Portfolio* 21 (Spring 1986): 1–20.

11. Lange-Doud interview, p. 22. Lange, "Documentary Photographer," 158. John Steinbeck used a copy of "Drought Refugees from Oklahoma Camping by Road" on the cover of his pamphlet "Their Blood is Strong" (San Francisco: Simon J. Lubin Society of California, 1938). Rather than courage and determination, William Stott sees in this woman's face a look of despair and pleading; see Stott's *Documentary Expression and Thirties America* (New York: Oxford University Press, 1973), 59.

12. Margaret Bourke-White, *Portrait of Myself* (New York: Simon and Schuster, 1963), 18.

13. Margaret Bourke-White, "Blast Furnaces," *World's Work* 58 (September 1929): 43. Bourke-White, *Portrait of Myself*, 49, 90–92.

14. Margaret Bourke-White, "Photographing This World," *Nation* 42 (February

19, 1936): 217–18. Margaret Bourke-White and William McGarry, "Your Business as the Camera Sees It," *Nation's Business* 26 (April 1938): 96.

15. Bourke-White, *Portrait of Myself*, 134, 110.

16. Bourke-White, *Portrait of Myself*, 112.

17. Erskine Caldwell, *Tobacco Road* (Savannah: Beehive Press, 1974, 1932), viii. For more on the distinct styles of Lange and Bourke-White, see Ohrn, *Dorothea Lange and the Documentary Tradition*, 178.

18. Lewis Hine, quoted in *Documentary Photography*, by the editors of Time-Life Books (New York: Time-Life Books, 1972), p. 56. Walker Evans and John Collier, Jr., two documentary photographers, discovered Brady and Eugene Atget (a French documentary precursor) after they began working in the documentary mode. Evans, interview with Leslie Katz (hereafter cited as Evans-Katz interview), *Art in America* 59 (March–April 1971): 85; Collier to Roy E. Stryker, "Thursday Night," September 1941, p. 3, Stryker Papers. Jack Delano thought he alone had invented the documentary approach. Jack and Irene Delano, interview with Richard K. Doud (hereafter cited as Delano-Doud interview), June 12, 1965, Archives of American Art, New York, p. 20. Berenice Abbott was the most obvious exception to this general unawareness of earlier documentary photographers, for she knew Atget personally and modeled her work after his. See Abbott's "Eugene Atget, Forerunner of Modern Photography," *U.S. Camera* 1 (November 1940): 20ff., and (December 1940), 68–71. Paul Von Blum argues that documentary photography was a continuation of Hine's work, *The Critical Vision: A History of Social and Political Art in the U.S.* (Boston: South End Press, 1982), 44. Documentary photographers did produce images that were similar to Hine's, but of course this is not to say that they knew they were operating within his tradition. Commercial success seldom accompanied documentaries of any form, and even the long-running *March of Time* newsreel was never profitable. Raymond Fielding, *The March of Time, 1935–1951* (New York: Oxford University Press, 1978), 74–75, 301.

19. Russell and Jean Lee, interview with Richard K. Doud (hereafter cited as Lee-Doud interview), June 2, 1964, Archives of American Art, New York, p. 2. Lee to Stryker, January 4, 1962, Stryker Papers. John Collier, interview with Richard K. Doud (hereafter cited as Collier-Doud interview), January 18, 1965, Archives of American Art, New York, pp. 1–2. John Collier, career resumé, Stryker Papers.

20. Delano-Doud interview, pp. 2–20. Gene Thornton, *Masters of the Camera: Stieglitz, Steichen and Their Successors* (New York: Holt, Rinehart and Winston, 1976), 23. Ben Shahn, interview with Richard K. Doud (hereafter cited as Shahn-Doud interview), April 14, 1964, Archives of American Art, New York, p. 3.

21. Beaumont Newhall, *The History of Photography from 1839 to the Present*

Day, revised and enlarged edition (New York: Museum of Modern Art, 1964), 148. J. Ghislain Lootens, "The Story of Carl Mydans," *U.S. Camera* 1 (December 1939): 22–23. Carl Mydans, interview with Richard K. Doud (hereafter cited as Mydans-Doud interview), April 29, 1964, Archives of American Art, New York, pp. 1–6. Marion Post Wolcott, undated autobiographical sketch, Stryker Papers. Marion Post Wolcott, interview with Richard K. Doud (hereafter cited as Post Wolcott-Doud interview), January 18, 1965, Archives of American Art, New York, pp. 1–6. For more on Post Wolcott's career, see Sally Stein, "Marion Post Wolcott: Thoughts on Some Lesser Known FSA Photographs," *Marion Post Wolcott: FSA Photographs* (Carmel, Calif.: Friends of Photography, 1983), 3–10.

22. Eliot Elisofan, "Playgrounds for Manhattan," *U.S. Camera* 1 (April–May 1940): 20ff. Robert Disraeli, untitled autobiographical sketch in *Saturday Review of Literature* 10 (June 16, 1934): 755. Yet another documentary photographer was Theo Jung, a former illustrator. While employed in the Federal Emergency Relief Administration making graphs and charts, this amateur photographer moved away from the pictorial photographs of shadows and fire escapes that had earlier fascinated him, and began making pictures of impoverished people. He lent some of those photos to a campaign for social security legislation, and when the RA photo administrator saw the pictures, he hired Jung. Theo Jung, interview with Richard K. Doud (hereafter cited as Jung-Doud interview), January 19, 1965, Archives of American Art, New York, pp. 2–6.

23. Evans-Katz interview, pp. 83–84. *Walker Evans: Artist in Residence* (Hanover, N.H.: Hopkins Center, Dartmouth College, 1972), n.p. Abbot, "Eugene Atget, Forerunner of Modern Photography," passim. Abbott quoted in Avis Berman, "The Unflinching Eye of Berenice Abbott," *Art News* 80 (January 1981): 92. Michael G. Sundell, "Berenice Abbott's Work in the 1930s," *Prospects* 5 (1980): 269–92.

24. Ohrn, *Dorothea Lange and the Documentary Tradition,* 30. Carl Mydans, "A Tireless Perfectionist," in *The Photographs of Margaret Bourke-White,* ed. Sean Callahan (New York: Bonanza Books, 1972), 25. For Ansel Adams's biography, see Nancy Newhall, *Ansel Adams: The Eloquent Light* (San Francisco: Sierra Club, 1963). John Neary, "Eliot Porter," *American Photographer* 7 (December 1981): 44–46. Archibald MacLeish, *The Land of the Free* (New York: Harcourt, Brace and Company, 1938), 89. For a discussion of photo magazines and the thirties, see Warren Susman, "The Thirties," in *The Development of an American Culture,* ed. Stanley Coben and Lorman Ratner (Englewood Cliffs, N.J.: Prentice-Hall, 1970), 191. James L. McCamy, *Government Publicity: Its Practices in Federal Administration* (Chicago: University of Chicago Press, 1939), 81. Lee-Doud interview, p. 34.

25. For a discussion of documentary's directness, immediacy, and authenticity,

see Stott, *Documentary Expression in Thirties America*, 77. Linda Nochlin also believes that westerners find realism attractive in confused times; Nochlin, *Realism* (Baltimore: Penguin Books, 1971), 42–43. Alfred Kazin lived through the thirties and realized how frequently the camera served as a symbol of objectivity. Kazin, *On Native Grounds: An Interpretation of Modern American Prose Literature* (New York: Reynal and Hitchcock, 1942), 381–86.

26. F. Jack Hurley, *Portrait of a Decade: Roy Stryker and the Development of Documentary Photography in the Thirties* (Baton Rouge: Louisiana State University Press, 1972), 36–40.

27. Emphasis has often been upon Stryker rather than the photographers who worked for him. Hurley's approach in *Portrait of a Decade* is through Stryker. Peter Pollock in *The Picture History of Photography*, revised and enlarged edition (New York: Harry N. Abrams, 1969), 346–51, approaches documentary photographers through Stryker and the RA-FSA bureaucracy. In *Masters of the Camera: Stieglitz, Steichen and Their Successors*, 22–23, Gene Thornton suggests that it was government patronage that initiated those photographic impulses that found room to develop within RA-FSA and the Federal Art Project. Similarly, in analyzing the photographic agency, John Durniak kept his "Focus on Stryker," *Popular Photography* 51 (September 1962): 6off.

28. Roy E. Stryker, interview with F. Jack Hurley (hereafter cited as Stryker-Hurley interview), July 28–29, 1967, Mississippi Valley Collection, John Willard Brister Library, Memphis State University, pp. 8–16. Stryker to Jonathan Garst, November 30, 1939, Stryker Papers.

29. Shahn-Doud interview. Roy E. Stryker, interview with Thomas H. Garver (hereafter cited as Stryker-Garver interview), July 1, 1968, in Garver, introduction, *Just Before the War: Urban America from 1935 to 1941 as seen by Photographers of the Farm Security Administration* (New York: October House, 1968), unpaginated. Stryker to Edna Bennett, August 29, 1962, Stryker Papers.

30. Shahn-Doud interview, pp. 3–7. Post Wolcott, autobiographical sketch. Collier-Doud interview, p. 13. Lange-Doud interview, p. 8. Mydans-Doud interview, p. 15.

31. Lee to Stryker, September 9, 1940, September 24, 1940, and September 6, 1942, Stryker Papers. Collier to Stryker late 1942 or early 1943, and February 11, 1943, Stryker Papers. Through his article "Life on the American Frontier—1941 Version," *U.S. Camera* 4 (October 1941), Lee hoped to promote national unity, pp. 40–41.

32. Collier-Doud interview, p. 10.

33. Delano to Stryker, received September 18, 1940. Rothstein to Stryker, Janu-

ary 16, [1939]. Lee to Stryker, December 9, 1936, January 2, 1937, and January 14, 1937. Lee to Stryker [late summer or early fall, 1937], and September 5, 1937. Post Wolcott to Stryker, January 1939. All in Stryker Papers.

34. Post Wolcott-Doud interview, p. 8.

35. Lee, quoted in Ohrn, *Dorothea Lange and the Documentary Tradition*, 78.

36. Post Wolcott to Stryker, [January 1939], Stryker Papers. Collier to Stryker, "Tuesday Night," [September 1941], Stryker Papers. Shahn-Doud interview, p. 3.

37. For Lange's attitude toward mechanization, see Dorothea Lange and Paul Schuster Taylor, *An American Exodus: A Record of Human Erosion* (New York: Reynal and Hitchcock, 1939). William Alexander examines the relationship between Lange and Lorentz in *Film on the Left: American Documentary Film from 1931 to 1942* (Princeton: Princeton University Press, 1981), 101–6. Lee to Stryker, February 14, 1939, Stryker Papers. For Lee's photograph "North Dakota" (1937), see Roy E. Stryker and Nancy Wood, *In This Proud Land: America, 1935–1943, as Seen in the FSA Photographs* (Boston: New York Graphic Society, 1973), 103. For an analysis of the drought that echoes Rothstein's contention that humans rather than fate were responsible for the tragedy, see Donald Worster, *Dust Bowl: The Southern Plains in the 1930s* (New York: Oxford University Press, 1979).

38. Lange's "Billboard" (a black maid answering the phone and saying, "They's mostly out since they got that new Ford V-8"), near Los Angeles, August 1936, is in Garver, *Just Before the War*, n.p. Post Wolcott's "Behind the Bar," Birney, Montana, 1941, is in Stryker and Wood, *In This Proud Land*, 177.

39. Russell Lee to Ed Locke, September 15, 1937, Stryker Papers. Sheldon Rodman, *Portrait of the Artist as an American. Ben Shahn: A Biography with Pictures* (New York: Harper and Brothers, 1951), 99. Lange, "Documentary Photographer," 152. Collier-Doud interview, p. 27. Some selections from the Photo League's works are in *New Masses* 31 (May 16, 1939): 10. For a discussion of the Photo League, see Anne Tucker, "Photographic Crossroads: The Photo League," *Afterimage* 5 (April 1978), special supplement, 2, 6–8. Leo Hurwitz, Paul Strand, and Ralph Steiner were central figures in the early League; Steiner was the least political of the three, with sentiments that were closer to those of Lange and the other documentary photographers. Alexander, *Film on the Left*, 13–17.

40. Evans-Katz interview, pp. 84, 87. Edwin Locke to Stryker, February 4, 1937, Stryker Papers. Locke worked with Evans in the Memphis area during the flood of late winter and early spring 1937.

41. Ansel Adams to Alfred Stieglitz, May 1934, Adams to Willard Van Dyke, Spring (?) 1934; quoted in Nancy Newhall, *Ansel Adams*, 98 and 126.

42. Weston to Adams, December 3, 1934; Adams to Weston, November 7, 1938,

quoted in Newhall, *Ansel Adams,* 111 and 136. Adams's interest in social themes continued at the same level in his study of the victims of racial prejudice during World War II. When he visited the Manzanar relocation center, where Japanese-Americans were imprisoned more to satisfy the prejudices of West Coast Anglos than for any security reasons, Adams made a number of photographs that eventually became the basis for his *Born Free and Equal, Photographs of the Loyal Japanese-Americans at Manzanar Relocation Center, Inyo County, California* (New York: U.S. Camera, 1944). But rather than showing an oppressed minority that needed the sympathy of a picture-viewing audience, as William Stott has suggested (*Documentary Expression and Thirties America,* 214), Adams presented the internees as the fortunate recipients of government benevolence, placed in an environment that "strengthened the spirit of the people" (*Born Free and Equal,* 25, 9). Lange visited the camp at virtually the same time, and her photographs stand in marked contrast to Adams's. Where he showed placid people in beautiful surroundings, Lange's bent-backed laborers struggled in a place plagued with dust storms. (Lange's photography was under the auspices of the War Relocation Authority, and much of it appears in Maisie and Richard Conrat, *Executive Order 9066: The Internship of 110,000 Japanese-Americans* [Cambridge: MIT Press, 1972.]) Unlike Adams, Lange felt that Manzanar was "shameful." She realized that Adams's Manzanar book was one of his few excursions into social issues, and told an interviewer that Adams "felt pretty proud of himself for being such a liberal [laughter] in the book." (Lange, "Documentary Photographer," 190–91.) For a discussion of their different perspectives, see Karin Becker Ohrn, "What You See Is What You Get: Dorothea Lange and Ansel Adams at Manzanar," *Journalism History* 4 (Spring 1977): 14–32ff.

43. Adams has not been alone in regarding documentary photography as largely a protest movement. In his article, "The F.S.A. Photographers," *U.S. Camera Annual 1939* (New York: U.S. Camera, 1938), 42–46, Edward Steichen stressed the photographers' reformist orientation. Steichen's *The Bitter Years: 1935–1941. Rural America as seen by the Photographers of the Farm Security Administration* (New York: Museum of Modern Art, 1962) implies that the photographs depict chiefly a dark vision of the decade. Peter Pollock feels that documentary photography is concerned mostly with the "grim facts of the political and social scene," while its images are "harbingers of what may beset the nation again if the people are not wary" (*The Picture History of Photography,* p. 62). Similarly, Beaumont Newhall goes little beyond the reform-sympathy aspect of documentary photography in his *History of Photography* (142–51). Susan Sontag has continued to stress the documentarians' reform motives (*On Photography,* 62). Among newer treatments that give an ex-

panded reading of documentary motives is Stryker and Wood, *In This Proud Land,* a work intended to counteract Steichen's emphasis on the photographers' darker pictures. Hank O'Neal's *A Vision Shared: A Classic Portrait of America and Its People, 1935–1943* (New York: St. Martin's, 1976) is the best collection of the RA-FSA photographs, and its scope is large enough to include photos other than the most famous ones. O'Neal worked closely with the surviving photographers in compiling his book, allowing them to select pictures for publication. Many show humor and determination as well as pain and suffering.

44. Dixon, "Dorothea Lange," 68. Bourke-White, "Photographing This World," 218. See also her *Portrait of Myself,* 112. Jung-Doud interview, p. 3. Edwin Locke, "Documentary Photography," undated manuscript [late 1930s or early 1940s], Stryker Papers. Dorothea Lange and Daniel Dixon, "Photographing the Familiar," *Aperture* 1, no. 2 (1952): 15, 9. See also Lange-Doud interview, p. 14.

45. Berenice Abbott, "Documenting the City," *The Complete Photographer* 4 (April 20, 1942): 1393; Abbott, "Photography, 1839–1937," *Art Front* 3 (April-May 1937): 25; and Abbott, "Photographer as Artist," *Art Front* 2 (September-October 1936): 6. Of course the problem of just what constitutes "reality" is a long-standing one, and our perception of "reality" can be wrong and it can change over time. In the above article, Abbott wrote that in Brady's photographs there was "no posing of dead men, no stage setting for battle scenes," the opposite of what we now know to have been the case. Eight months after the publication of "Photographer as Artist," Abbott was much more inclined to accept posing. She praised early photographers who "posed their sitters or arranged a composition of landscape they were photographing," and believed that in her own day "the best contemporary photographers practice the same creative control of their machine, only with a more highly developed knowledge of its potentialities and with the benefit of the workers who preceded them." See "Photography 1839–1937," 25. In her later years, Abbott became a science photographer, producing illustrations of the "realities" that physics describes. See Hank O'Neal, *Berenice Abbott, American Photographer* (New York: McGraw Hill, 1982).

46. Abbott, "Documenting the City," 1393.

47. Abbott, "Documenting the City," 1403.

48. Shahn-Doud interview, p. 5. Evans-Katz interview, p. 87. Lange-Doud interview, p. 10. John Szarkowski, introduction, *Walker Evans* (New York: Museum of Modern Art, 1971), 18.

49. Bourke-White, *Portrait of Myself,* 133. Margaret Bourke-White and Erskine Caldwell, *You Have Seen Their Faces* (New York: Arno, 1975, 1937), 89–190.

Jack and Irene Delano similarly violated a black church (Irene Delano to "Toots," April 21, 1941, Stryker Papers), but, unlike Bourke-White, they did not brag about the affair (Delano-Doud interview, pp. 29–31).

50. Lange, "Documentary Photographer," 158–59. Lange to Stryker, May 16, 1929, Stryker Papers. Hurley, *Portrait of a Decade*, 142–43. Delano-Doud interview, p. 22. Lee to Stryker, May 11, 1939 and June 21, 1939, Stryker Papers.

51. Eliot Elisofan, "Playgrounds for Manhattan," 68. Vachon to Stryker [late 1940], Stryker Papers. Delano-Doud interview, p. 17.

52. James C. Curtis and Sheila Grannen, "Let Us Now Appraise Famous Photographs: Walker Evans and Documentary Photography," *Winterthur Portfolio* 15 (Spring 1980): 9–20.

53. Arthur Rothstein, interview with Richard K. Doud (hereafter cited as Rothstein-Doud interview), May 25, 1964, Archives of American Art, New York. Arthur Rothstein, "Memorandum to Roy Stryker," undated manuscript [early 1960s], Stryker Papers. O'Neal, *A Vision Shared*, 20–22.

54. Arthur Rothstein, "Direction in the Picture Story," *The Complete Photographer* 4 (April 10, 1942): 1356–57.

55. Because of an unauthorized editorial change, historians for a number of years have assumed that Rothstein actually did stage the photograph as the original article stated, "Direction in the Picture Story," 1360. Recently, however, Rothstein has corrected the error. See Arthur Rothstein, "Setting the Record Straight," *Camera* 35 22 (April 1978): 50–51.

56. In his letter to Rothstein, April 13, 1936, Stryker said that he liked the "dust pictures," Stryker Papers. When the furor over the skull broke, Locke issued statements to the press denying that the skull was a movable prop, wrote Rothstein telling him to stick close to the story and "if you still have that goddam skull hide it for Christ's sake." Locke to Rothstein, August 20, 1936, Stryker Papers.

57. Examples of color photographs from the Library of Congress, Farm Security Administration Collection, are Russell Lee, "On the Main Street of Cascade, Idaho," July 1941, LC USF35–212; Russell Lee, "Musicians During Intermission at a Square Dance," McIntosh County, Oklahoma, June 1939, LC USF35–315; and John Collier, "Lincoln, Nebraska," [1938], LC USF35–266.

58. Berenice Abbott, "Changing New York," in *Art for the Millions: Essays from the 1930s by Artists and Administrators of the WPA Federal Art Project*, ed. Francis V. O'Connor (Greenwich, Conn.: New York Graphic Society, 1973), 158–61. Berenice Abbott, *Changing New York*, text by Elizabeth McCausland (New York: E. P. Dutton, 1939). Abbott, "Eugene Atget, Forerunner," p. 76, passim. Abbott quoted in Avis Berman, "The Unflinching Eye of Berenice Abbott," 93.

59. Lee to Locke, summer 1937, probably August, Stryker Papers. Evans-Katz interview, p. 87. Lee-Doud interview, pp. 32–33. John Vachon, "Standards of the Documentary File," undated c. 1939 manuscript, Stryker Papers.

60. Collier to Stryker, sometime in 1942, Stryker Papers. Robert Disraeli, "The Farm Security Administration," *Photo Notes* (May 1940): 3. Lange quoted in Ohrn, *Dorothea Lange and the Documentary Tradition*, 37.

61. Elisofan, "Playgrounds for Manhattan," 69. Shahn-Doud interview, pp. 8–9. Lee to Locke, September 15, 1937, Stryker Papers. Post Wolcott-Doud interview, p. 12. Edwin Locke, "FSA," *U.S. Camera* 1 (1941), 27.

62. Collier to T. Anthony Caruso, October 30, 1954, Stryker Papers. Collier to Stryker, sometime in 1942, from Ephrata, Pennsylvania, Stryker Papers. Lee to Stryker, May 30, 1940, Stryker Papers. For a discussion of the larger Depression fascination with anthropology, see Susman, "The Thirties," 183–90.

63. Delano-Doud interview, p. 53.

64. Edward Weston, *The Daybooks of Edward Weston*, ed. Nancy Newhall (New York: Horizon Press, 1961 and 1966), 2:256–57. Delano-Doud interview, pp. 56, 27. Stryker-Garver interview, n.p.

65. Joan Murray, "Marion Post Wolcott: A Forgotten Photographer from the FSA Picks Up Her Cameras Again," *American Photographer* 4 (March 1980): 89. Post Wolcott-Doud interview, pp. 5, 16–18. Delano to "Toots," late 1940 or early 1941 (?), Stryker Papers. Jean Lee's description is in the Lee-Doud interview, p. 35, where Russell agrees with her portrayal.

66. Bourke-White, *Portrait of Myself*, 110, 133–34. Margaret Bourke-White, "Dust Changes America," *Nation* 140 (May 22, 1935): 597.

67. Russell Lee, "Life on the American Frontier—1941 Version," *U.S. Camera* 4 (October 1941): 39–54ff. Rothstein-Doud interview, p. 28. Vachon to Stryker, April 19, 1940, [Spring] 1942, and [late October or early November] 1938, Stryker Papers.

68. Ben Shahn, interview with John D. Morse, "Ben Shahn: An Interview," *Magazine of Art* 37 (April 1944): 137. Ben Shahn, *The Shape of Content* (Cambridge: Harvard University Press, 1957, 1963), 25–52, passim. Ben Shahn, interview with Harlan Phillips (hereafter cited as Shahn-Phillips interview), October 3, 1965, 39–40. Ben Shahn, "Portrait of a Social Artist: Professor Eric Goldman Talks with Ben Shahn, Artist and Author," tape recording (North Hollywood, Calif.: Center for Cassette Studies, 1972, recorded 1965).

69. Shahn, *The Shape of Content*, 38.

70. Shahn-Phillips interview, pp. 39–40. Ben Shahn quoted in John Charles Carlisle, "A Biographical Study of How the Artist Became a Humanitarian Activist: Ben Shahn, 1930–1946," (Ph.D. diss., University of Michigan, 1972), 110. Shahn, *The Shape of Content*, 40–41.

71. Shahn, *The Shape of Content*, 38. Bernarda Bryson Shahn, *Ben Shahn* (New York: Harry N. Abrams, 1972), 288.
72. Shahn, *The Shape of Content*, 47.

Chapter Four

1. Richard Wright, "Long Black Song," in *Uncle Tom's Children* (New York: Harper and Row, 1938), 210, 213–14.
2. For a discussion of the historicity of social novels, see Warren French, *The Social Novel at the End of an Era* (Carbondale: Southern Illinois University Press, 1966), 7.
3. Alfred Kazin, *Starting Out in the Thirties* (Random House, 1980, 1965), 13. John Steinbeck, "A Primer on the Thirties," *Esquire* (June 1970): 85–93. Edgar M. Branch, *James T. Farrell* (New York: Twayne, 1971), 26.
4. For "shock treatment" interpretations, see Maxwell Geismar, *Writers in Crisis: The American Novel Between Two Wars* (Boston: Houghton Mifflin, 1942), 84; and Alfred Kazin, *On Native Grounds: An Interpretation of Modern American Prose Literature* (New York: Reynal and Hitchcock, 1942), 364.
5. Walter B. Rideout, *The Radical Novel in the United States 1900–1954: Some Interrelations of Literature and Society* (Cambridge: Harvard University Press, 1956), 207–9.
6. Sometimes the two are inappropriately grouped together under the proletarian label. See for example Rideout, *The Radical Novel in the United States*, 295–98; and Howard Mumford Jones and Richard M. Ludwig, *Guide to American Literature and Its Backgrounds Since 1890*, 4th ed. (Cambridge: Harvard University Press, 1972), 200–201.
7. See Richard Pells, *Radical Visions and American Dreams: Culture and Social Thought in the Depression Years* (New York: Harper and Row, 1973), 169–80, for a detailed discussion of the critics' criteria for proletarian literature.
8. Lawrence W. Levine, "American Culture and the Great Depression," *Yale Review* 74 (Winter 1985): 208–9. Ernest Hemingway, *To Have and Have Not* (New York: Charles Scribner's Sons, 1937), 225.
9. Faulkner, Wolfe, Hemingway, the proletarian camp, and the social novelists were all active in the thirties, but engaged in essentially different pursuits. Their contemporaneousness, though, has led some to see more connections than actually existed between these contemporaries. Daniel Aaron acknowledges that the best of the social novelists did not become proletarian writers, but also argues that they subordinated their craft to aid Gold and Hicks as those two critics argued for proletarian literature. Daniel Aaron, *Writers on the Left: Episodes in American Literary Communism* (New York: Harcourt,

Brace and World, 1961), 392–93. Richard Pells aligns the social novelists with Hemingway, Wolfe, and Faulkner, and concludes that the social novelists followed them to reject the thirties collectivist tendencies and take up the defense of individualism. Pells, *Radical Visions and American Dreams*, 194–95ff. With the exception of Dos Passos, however, there was little sympathy for individualism among the social novelists. Maxwell Geismar analyzed Steinbeck along with Hemingway, Wolfe, and Faulkner. He argued that the Depression brought them all to explore their American roots in an outpouring of nationalistic literature. This analysis does the novelists considerable disservice and reflects more of the climate in which Geismar wrote (just prior to World War II) than of the novels themselves. Geismar, *Writers in Crisis*, 285.

10. Dahlberg quoted in Fred Moramarco, "An Interview with Edward Dahlberg," *Western Humanities Review* 20 (Summer 1966): 249. James T. Farrell, "Some Observations on Naturalism, So Called, in Fiction," in *Reflections at Fifty* (New York: Vanguard Press, 1954), 150–51. Algren quoted in H. E. F. Donohue, *Conversations with Nelson Algren* (New York: Hill and Wang, 1964), 95.

11. Alfred Kazin overestimates the novelists' commitment to naturalism and argues that they never abandoned it. *On Native Grounds*, 371, 392.

12. See Nelson Blake, *Novelists' America: Fiction as History, 1910–1940* (Syracuse: Syracuse University Press, 1969), 136; Warren French, *The Social Novel at the End of an Era*, 42–86; and David W. Noble, David A. Horowitz, and Peter N. Carroll, *Twentieth Century Limited* (Boston: Houghton Mifflin Company, 1980), 265.

13. See Richard N. Current et al., *American History: A Survey*, 6th ed. (New York: Alfred A. Knopf, 1983), 279; and Edwin Rozwenc and Thomas Bender, *The Making of American Society*, 2d ed. (New York: Alfred A. Knopf, 1978), vol. 2, 401.

14. Steinbeck to Carl Wilhelmson, late 1930, in *Steinbeck, A Life in Letters*, ed. Elaine Steinbeck and Robert Wallsten (New York: Viking, 1975), 29 (hereafter cited as *Steinbeck Letters*).

15. Steinbeck's first three novels were *The Cup of Gold* (1929), *The Pastures of Heaven* (1932), and *To a God Unknown* (1933). For a discussion of these three novels, see Warren French, *John Steinbeck*, 2d ed., rev. (Boston: Twayne, 1975), 45–62.

16. Steinbeck to Robert O. Ballou, June 1, 1933, in *Steinbeck Letters*, 76. Steinbeck to George Albee, 1933, in *Steinbeck Letters*, 73.

17. Steinbeck to Carlton A. Sheffield, June 21, 1933, in *Steinbeck Letters*, 76. Steinbeck to Sheffield, June 30, 1933, in *Steinbeck Letters*, 78. Richard Astro, *John Steinbeck and Edward F. Ricketts: The Shaping of a Novelist* (Minneapolis: University of Minnesota Press, 1973), 11, 55.

18. John Steinbeck, "Argument of Phalanx," undated short essay written some time between 1934 and 1936, quoted in Astro, *John Steinbeck and Edward F. Ricketts*, 63–65. Steinbeck to Carlton A. Sheffield, June 21, 1933, in *Steinbeck Letters*, 76, 77. Steinbeck to George Albee, 1933, in *Steinbeck Letters*, 80.

19. Steinbeck, "Argument of Phalanx," in Astro, 63–65. Steinbeck to George Albee, 1933, in *Steinbeck Letters*, 81.

20. Steinbeck to George Albee, 1933, in *Steinbeck Letters*, 81. Steinbeck to Carlton A. Sheffield, June 21, 1933, in *Steinbeck Letters*, 64, 76, 77. Steinbeck to George Albee, 1933, in *Steinbeck Letters*, 84.

21. Steinbeck to Carlton A. Sheffield, June 21, 1933, in *Steinbeck Letters*, 76.

22. John Steinbeck, *In Dubious Battle* (New York: Viking, 1936), 144–45.

23. Other accounts do not acknowledge Steinbeck's determinism. Warren French claims the fight is dubious because it is a clash of two armies, neither of which has completely meritorious positions (*John Steinbeck*, 80). In *John Steinbeck: Nature and Myth* (New York: Thomas Y. Crowell Company, 1978), 74, Peter Lisca argues that this battle was fortunately dubious, for while the growers would defeat the strikers this time, capitalism would eventually make concessions to labor in order to head off Communist advances.

24. Steinbeck to George Albee, January 15, 1935, in *Steinbeck Letters*, 98. Steinbeck, *In Dubious Battle*, 253. Maxwell Geismar assumes that this was to be a Marxist battle, *Writers in Crisis*, 261, 267.

25. Steinbeck to Mavis McIntosh, February 4, 1935, in *Steinbeck Letters*, 105. Steinbeck to George Albee, January 15, 1935, in *Steinbeck Letters*, 98. Steinbeck, letter to Henry May, *Occident* (Fall 1936): 5.

26. Jackson J. Benson, *The True Adventures of John Steinbeck, Writer* (New York: Viking, 1984), 362.

27. Steinbeck to Elizabeth Otis, February 1938, in *Steinbeck Letters*, 158. Steinbeck to Otis, March 7, 1938, in *Steinbeck Letters*, 161.

28. Reworked *San Francisco News* articles, together with a new epilogue and illustrations, appeared as the pamphlet, John Steinbeck, "Their Blood is Strong" (San Francisco: Simon J. Lubin Society of California, 1938). Steinbeck to Elizabeth Otis, March 7, 1938, in *Steinbeck Letters*, 162.

29. Steinbeck to Elizabeth Otis, May 2, 1938, in *Steinbeck Letters*, 163. For a discussion of Steinbeck's title, *L'Affaire Lettuceberg*, see Peter Lisca, *The Wide World of John Steinbeck* (New Brunswick, N.J.: Rutgers University Press, 1958), 147.

30. Steinbeck to Mavis McIntosh and Elizabeth Otis, June 1938, quoted in Lisca, *The Wide World of John Steinbeck*, 147.

31. John Steinbeck, *The Grapes of Wrath* (New York: Viking, 1939), 33, 577.

32. Steinbeck, *The Grapes of Wrath*, 100, 264, 606, 204–6.

33. Steinbeck, *The Grapes of Wrath*, 618–19. Steinbeck to Pascal Covici, January 16, 1939, in *Steinbeck Letters*, 178.

34. James T. Farrell, "End of a Literary Decade," *The American Mercury* 48 (December 1939): 413.

35. Dion Quintin Kempthorne, "Josephine Herbst: A Critical Introduction" (Ph.D. diss., University of Wisconsin–Madison, 1973), 7–53. Josephine Herbst, "A Year of Disgrace," *The Noble Savage* 3 (1961): 128–60. Josephine Herbst, untitled autobiographical essay in *Authors Today and Yesterday*, ed. Stanley Kunitz (New York: H. W. Wilson, 1933), 309–10. Elinor Langer's *Josephine Herbst: The Story She Could Never Tell* (Boston: Little, Brown, 1984) is the first full biography of this important literary figure. For more on Herbst's involvement in the Spanish Civil War, see 219–31.

36. Josephine Herbst, *Pity Is Not Enough* (New York: Harcourt, Brace, 1933), 346, 310–12. Josephine Herbst, autobiographical essay in *Authors Today and Yesterday*, 309.

37. Robert Cantwell, *Laugh and Lie Down* (New York: Farrar and Rinehart, 1931), xii.

38. Townsend Ludington, *John Dos Passos: A Twentieth Century Odyssey* (New York: E. P. Dutton, 1980), 229. John William Ward, "Lindbergh, Dos Passos and History," *Carleton Miscellany* 6 (Summer 1965): 23–26. Malcolm Cowley, "Dos Passos: The Poet and the World," *New Republic* 70 (April 27, 1932): 300–305; also in Malcolm Cowley (Henry Dan Piper, ed.), *Think Back on Us: A Contemporary Chronicle of the 1930s* (Carbondale, Ill.: Southern Illinois University Press, 1967), 216. John Dos Passos, *The Best Times: An Informal Memoir* (New York: New American Library, 1966), 205–6. The three volumes of *U.S.A.* are *The 42nd Parallel* (1930), *1919* (1932), and *The Big Money* (1936).

39. Edward Newhouse, *This Is Your Day* (New York: Lee Furman, 1937), 92. James T. Farrell, quoted in Branch, *James T. Farrell*, 15. James T. Farrell, introduction, *Studs Lonigan*, the complete trilogy (New York: Modern Library, 1938), xii; *Young Lonigan* (1932), 35–36; *The Young Manhood of Studs Lonigan* (1934), 25; and *Judgment Day* (1935), 465.

40. For a treatment of marginal men in Depression culture, see Warren Susman, "The Thirties," in *The Development of an American Culture*, ed. Stanley Coben and Lorman Ratner (Englewood Cliffs, N.J.: Prentice-Hall, 1970), 204–5.

41. Richard Wright, *American Hunger* (New York: Harper and Row, 1977), 7.

42. Richard Wright, *Native Son* (New York: Harper and Brothers, 1940), 9. Richard Wright, "How 'Bigger' Was Born," in *Native Son*, xiv–xv.

43. Daniel Aaron, introduction to Jack Conroy, *The Disinherited* (New York: Hill and Wang, 1963, 1933), x–xi. Jack Conroy, *A World to Win* (New York: Civici,

Friede, 1935), 32–33. Edward Dahlberg, *Bottom Dogs* (London: G. P. Putnam's Sons, 1929), 285. Tom Kromer, *Waiting for Nothing* (1935; reprint, New York: Hill and Wang, 1968), 186.

44. Erskine Caldwell, "Blue Boy," *The Anvil* (March–April 1935) in *Writers in Revolt: The Anvil Anthology*, ed. Jack Conroy and Curt Johnson (New York: Lawrence Hill and Company, 1973), 31–34. Erskine Caldwell, *Tobacco Road* (1932; reprint, Savannah, Ga.: Beehive Press, 1974), 195.

45. Donohue, *Conversations with Nelson Algren*, 55–56, 95. Nelson Algren, *Somebody in Boots* (1935; reprint, New York: Vanguard Press, 1965), 230.

46. Edward Dahlberg, *From Flushing to Calvary* in Edward Dahlberg, *Bottom Dogs, From Flushing to Calvary, Those Who Perish, and Hitherto Unpublished and Uncollected Works* (New York: Thomas Y. Crowell, 1976), 474–75. Farrell, *The Young Manhood of Studs Lonigan*, 211.

47. Kromer, *Waiting for Nothing*, 174–77. Conroy, *A World to Win*, 30–32. Walter B. Rideout thinks that this violence came more from the authors' own hard knocks than any literary design, *The Radical Novel in the United States*, 178–79. Nelson Algren, "If You Must Use Profanity," *The American Mercury* 31 (April 1934): 432.

48. James T. Farrell, "For White Men Only," in *Guillotine Party and Other Stories* (New York: Vanguard Press, 1935), 243. John Steinbeck, *The Pastures of Heaven* (1932; reprint, Cleveland: World Publishing Company, 1946), 128–43. Wright, *Native Son*, 300, 336.

49. Alfred Kazin, in *On Native Grounds*, 372–73, regards this as violence for its own sake, a product of what he believes to be a self-indulgent naturalism in the social novels.

50. Kromer caught tuberculosis and quit writing, marital problems kept Algren away from novels until the forties, Dahlberg became a critic and essayist, and Caldwell abandoned fiction for travel reporting.

51. Ann Banks, *First-Person America* (New York: Random House, 1980), 82. Jack Conroy, *A World to Win*, 347–48. Conroy quoted in Daniel Aaron, introduction to Jack Conroy, *The Disinherited* (1933; reprint, New York: Hill and Wang, 1963), xii. Edward Newhouse, untitled autobiographical essays in *Wilson Bulletin* 11 (May 1937): 588; and Stanley J. Kunitz and Vineta Colby, eds., *Twentieth Century Authors*, first supplement (New York: H. W. Wilson, 1955), 713. For an example of Newhouse's new direction in fiction, see his story, "Three-Letter Man," *New Republic* 92 (September 22, 1937): 184–85.

52. Farrell, *Judgment Day*, 448.

53. Donohue, Conversations with *Nelson Algren*, 87. Steinbeck to Louis Paul, February 1936, in *Steinbeck Letters*, 120.

54. Josephine Herbst, "The Starched Blue Sky of Spain," *The Noble Savage* 1 (1960): 79–80. Dos Passos to Robert Cantwell, January 25, 1935, in *The Four-*

teenth Chronicle: Letters and Diaries of John Dos Passos, ed. Townsend Ludington (Boston: Gambit, 1973), 463. John Steinbeck, "A Primer on the Thirties," 91. Steinbeck to Elizabeth Otis, March 26, 1940, in *Steinbeck Letters,* 201.

55. Josephine Herbst, "Literature in the U.S.S.R.," *New Republic* 66 (April 29, 1931): 305–6. Josephine Herbst, *The Executioner Waits* (New York: Harcourt, Brace, 1934), 178, 316. Those signing the "Call for an American Writers' Congress" (*New Masses* 14 [January 22, 1935]: 20) were Nelson Algren, Erskine Caldwell, Robert Cantwell, Jack Conroy, Edward Dahlberg, James T. Farrell, Josephine Herbst, Edward Newhouse, and Richard Wright.

56. John Dos Passos, "The Writer as Technician," in *American Writers' Congress,* ed. Henry Hart (New York: International Publishers, 1935), 81–82. Josephine Herbst, "Yesterday's Road," *New American Review* 3 (1968): 103. James T. Farrell, *A Note on Literary Criticism* (New York: Vanguard Press, 1936), 128, 137. James T. Farrell, "Literature and Ideology" (1942), in *The League of Frightened Philistines and Other Papers* (New York: Vanguard Press, 1945), 92–93. Dos Passos to Edmund Wilson, December 23, 1934, in *The Fourteenth Chronicle,* ed. Ludington, 459. Langer, *Josephine Herbst,* 192, 184–85.

57. Josephine Herbst, "The Ruins of History," *The Nation* 182 (April 14, 1956): 304.

58. Wright, *American Hunger,* 39–40, 62, 77. Wright, quoted in Constance Webb, *Richard Wright: A Biography* (New York: G. P. Putnam's Sons, 1968), 208.

59. Wright, *American Hunger,* 26. Richard Wright, "Blueprint for Negro Writing," *New Challenge* 2 (Fall 1937): 53–56; also in Ellen Wright and Michel Faber, eds., *Richard Wright Reader* (New York: Harper and Row, 1978), 45, 44.

60. Farrell, "End of a Literary Decade," 409.

61. Farrell, *The Young Manhood of Studs Lonigan,* 369–70. Joseph Warren Beach, *American Fiction, 1920–1940* (New York: Russell and Russell, 1960, 1941), 298–302, sees that Farrell had liberation in mind but argues that the freedom comes through writing rather than education.

62. James T. Farrell, *Father and Son* (New York: Vanguard Press, 1940), 109. Farrell to Laurence Pollinger, March 10, 1939, quoted in Branch, *James T. Farrell,* 96.

63. Townsend Ludington, *John Dos Passos,* 261–62, 270, 310–11. John Dos Passos, *The Big Money* (1936; reprint, New York: New American Library, 1969), 468, 168. Dos Passos to Edmund Wilson, March 23, 1934, in *The Fourteenth Chronicle,* 435–36.

64. Dos Passos to Edmund Wilson, December 23, 1934, in *The Fourteenth Chronicle,* 459–60.

65. In contrast, Richard Pells argues that this preference for individualism was widespread. See Pells, *Radical Visions and American Dreams*, 195, 225.

66. Cantwell, *The Land of Plenty*, 369.

67. Wright, *American Hunger*, 63. Wright, *Native Son*, 307.

68. Herbst, "A Year of Disgrace," 150. Herbst, untitled autobiographical essay in *Authors Today and Yesterday*, ed. Kunitz (1933), 309. Herbst, "The Ruins of History," 303.

69. Josephine Herbst, *Rope of Gold* (New York: Harcourt, Brace, 1939), 240, 406.

70. Wright, *Native Son*, 353.

71. Richard Wright, "Joe Louis Uncovers Dynamite," *New Masses* 17 (October 8, 1935), 18. Cantwell, *The Land of Plenty*, 102.

72. Donohue, *Conversations with Nelson Algren*, 248.

73. Richard Wright, "Bright and Morning Star," in *Uncle Tom's Children* (New York: Harper and Row, 1940), 215. Alfred Kazin disagrees with this interpretation and sees the social novelists as pessimists who could only indulge in "the aimless bombardment of rage." *On Native Grounds*, 397.

74. This did not escape their more perceptive contemporaries. See Edmund Wilson's characterization of Dos Passos's trilogy in his letter to Dos Passos, July 22, 1936, in Edmund Wilson, *Letters on Literature and Politics, 1912–1972*, ed. Elena Wilson (New York: Farrar, Straus and Giroux, 1977), 279. For Malcolm Cowley's characterization of Robert Cantwell's writing, see Cowley's *The Dream of the Golden Mountains: Remembering the 1930s* (New York: Viking, 1980), 127.

Chapter Five

1. Rockwell Kent, *This Is My Own* (New York: Duell, Sloan and Pearce, 1940), 234–40.

2. Philip Evergood, "Sure, I'm a Social Painter," *Magazine of Art* 36 (November 1943): 255. John I. H. Baur, *Philip Evergood* (New York: Frederick A. Praeger, 1960), 1–34. (Much of this book is in Evergood's own words, transcribed from interviews Baur had with the artist.) Kendall Taylor, "Philip Evergood and the Humanist Intention," *American Art Review* 18 (May 1978): 105.

3. Philip Evergood, "Art in Our Time," *Educational Leader* 23 (July 1954): 15–18. Kendall Taylor, *Philip Evergood: Selections from the Hirshhorn Museum and Sculpture Garden* (Washington: Smithsonian Institution Press, 1978).

4. Evergood quoted in Baur, *Philip Evergood*, 47–48; Evergood, "Art in Our Time," 14–15.

5. Philip Evergood, "Social Art Today: II," *American Contemporary Art* 1 (December 1944): 5–6; "Art in a Democracy," transcription of a radio speech

broadcast over station WQXR, New York City, April 29, 1938, Edith Bry Papers, Archives of American Art, New York.

6. Philip Evergood, foreword to Charlotte Willard, intro., *Moses Soyer* (Cleveland: World Publishing Company, 1962), 14. Evergood, "Social Art Today: II," 5–6.

7. Courbet's painting *Painter's Studio* (1857) shows the artist as a workman with his tools and also as the central figure in a social system based upon Charles Fourier's doctrines. See Linda Nochlin, *Realism* (Baltimore: Penguin, 1971), 128–30.

8. Philip Evergood, "Take Your Choice," *Reality* 2 (1954): 6. Philip Evergood answers to a list of eighteen questions submitted to artists who were at the moment on the mural section of the Works Progress Administration/Federal Art Project (WPA/FAP), *Art Front* 3 (1937): 9.

9. Philip Evergood, answers to questions, 9.

10. Philip Evergood, "Social Surrealism," *New Masses* 54 (February 13, 1945): 22. Philip Evergood, letter written upon the opening of an exhibition of his work on October 11, 1942, quoted in Herman Baron's unpublished history of the American Contemporary Art (ACA) Gallery, Herman Baron Papers, Archives of American Art, New York, 66–68. For John I. H. Baur's evaluation of *Dance Marathon* (he thinks its figures are repulsive), see his *Revolution and Tradition in Modern American Art* (Cambridge: Harvard University Press, 1958), 42.

11. Evergood, answers to questions, 9.

12. Evergood, quoted in Kendall Taylor, "The Philip Evergood Papers," *Archives of American Art Journal* 18 (No. 3): 4. Evergood, quoted in Baur, *Philip Evergood*, 52.

13. Evergood, answers to questions, 10; "Social Art Today: II," 6.

14. Philip Evergood, "Building a New Art School," *Art Front* 3 (April–May 1937): 21.

15. Philip Evergood, "Should the Nation Support Its Arts?" *Direction* 1 (April 1938): 5; "Art in a Democracy."

16. Richard D. McKinzie, *The New Deal for Artists* (Princeton: Princeton University Press, 1973), concentrates upon the bureaucracies and policies of the New Deal art agencies. McKinzie's focus implies that agency matters were the social realists' primary concerns, and that the New Deal was the inspiring force behind their art.

17. Nochlin, *Realism*, 20, 42–48. Works of the European realists and the American Ash Can school (see below) are important reminders that realism is not always a dismal genre. Joshua C. Taylor, *America as Art* (Washington, Smithsonian Institution Press, 1976), 240, argues that realism usually takes for its topics the darker and less optimistic aspects of life, however.

18. Those social realists who took instruction from Ash Can painters were Stuart

Davis, William Gropper, Joseph Hirsch, Reginald Marsh, Rockwell Kent, and Moses Soyer. Raphael Soyer felt Henri's influence through his brother, Moses.

19. For overviews of twentieth-century American art, see Milton W. Brown, *American Painting from the Armory Show to the Depression* (Princeton: Princeton University Press, 1955); Frances T. Feldman, "American Painting During the Great Depression" (Ph.D. diss., New York University, 1963); and Lloyd Goodrich and John I. H. Baur, *American Art of Our Century* (New York: Frederick A. Praeger, 1961).

20. Townsend Ludington, *John Dos Passos: A Twentieth Century Odyssey* (New York: E. P. Dutton, 1980), 251. George Biddle devoured art critic Anita Brenner's work on the Mexican school; see Biddle, *An American Artist's Story* (Boston: Little, Brown and Company, 1939), 263. Judd Tully, "20th Century Raphael," *Horizon* 25 (July–August 1982): 26.

21. For a discussion of federal murals and their social significance, see Karal Ann Marling, *Wall-to-Wall America: A Cultural History of Post Office Murals in the Great Depression* (Minneapolis: University of Minnesota Press, 1982), 38–39. Francis V. O'Connor, ed. and intro., *Art for the Millions: Essays from the 1930s by Artists and Administrators of the WPA Federal Art Project* (Boston: New York Graphic Society, 1973), 305.

22. Goodrich and Baur, *American Art of Our Century*, 49.

23. James M. Dennis, *Grant Wood: A Study in American Art and Culture* (New York: Viking, 1975), 197.

24. For one such lumping, see Charles C. Alexander, *Here the Country Lies: Nationalism and the Arts in Twentieth-Century America* (Bloomington: Indiana University Press, 1980), 179. Matthew Baigell, in *The American Scene: American Painting of the 1930s* (New York: Praeger, 1974), tries to group both regionalists and social realists into the category, "American Scene" painters. Social realism and regionalism were common enough forms of expression during the thirties, especially among younger painters. But the bulk of painting during the Depression remained much the same as most American painting throughout the twentieth century, a domestic naturalism rendering up landscapes, still lifes, or historical scenes. Lloyd Goodrich, in the foreword to Frederick S. Wight's *Jack Levine* (Boston: Institute of Contemporary Art, 1955), and David Shapiro, *Social Realism: Art as Weapon* (New York: Frederick Ungar, 1973), 4, both conversely argue that social realism was the period's *dominant* art form. For another interpretation, see O'Connor, *Art for the Millions*, 23.

25. Evergood, answers to questions, 10; Joe Jones in *Gropper 1940* (New York: ACA Gallery, 1940); Moses Soyer, "The Second Whitney Biennial," *Art Front* 1 (February 1934): 7. Thomas Hart Benton, *An Artist in America* (New York:

McBride, 1937), 263–65. For an analysis of the debate, see Karal Ann Marling, "Thomas Hart Benton's *Boomtown:* Regionalism Redefined," *Prospects* 6 (1981): 92–95.

26. Moses Soyer, "Three Brothers," *Magazine of Art* 32 (April 1939): 201–7ff; Alfred Werner, intro., *Moses Soyer* (South Brunswick, N.Y.: A. S. Barnes, 1970), 17–48.

27. Moses Soyer, "Contemporary American Art," partially complete essay (c. 1939), 4–7. Moses Soyer, "A Dedication," undated manuscript. Both in Moses Soyer Papers, Archives of American Art, New York.

28. Moses Soyer, "Contemporary American Art," 6–7; "A Dedication."

29. For biographical material on Peter Blume, see Frank Getlein, text, *Peter Blume* (New York: Kennedy Galleries, 1968), unpaginated. Peter Blume, "After Superrealism," *New Republic* 80 (October 31, 1934): 339; "The Artist Must Choose," *First American Artists' Congress* (New York: Editorial Committee of the First American Artists' Congress Against War and Fascism, 1936), 27–29.

30. Joseph Hirsch, statement in *Americans 1942: 18 Artists from 9 States*, ed. Dorothy C. Miller (New York: Museum of Modern Art, 1942), 62. Stuart Davis, "American Artists' Congress" (c. 1939), in *Art for the Millions*, ed. Francis V. O'Connor, 249. Louis Guglielmi, "After the Locusts" (c. 1936–38), in O'Connor, 113. For a reproduction of Gropper's *Art Patrons*, see *Art Digest* 14 (March 1, 1940): 12.

31. Audrey McMahon, "A Dialogue," in *The New Deal Art Projects: An Anthology of Memoirs*, ed. Francis V. O'Connor (Washington: Smithsonian Institution Press, 1972), 310–11.

32. Guglielmi, "After the Locusts," 113; "I Hope to Sing Again," *Magazine of Art* 37 (May 1944), 176. Ben Shahn, interview with Harlan Phillips, October 3, 1965, Archives of American Art, New York transcribed, pp. 33, 20. Evergood, "Should the Nation Support Its Art?," 2–3. Soyer, "Three Brothers," 207. Stuart Davis, "Why An Artists' Congress?" *First American Artists' Congress*, 3. Guglielmi, "After the Locusts," 113.

33. Philip Evergood, letter October 11, 1942, quoted in Baron's unpublished history of the ACA Gallery, Herman Baron Papers, 66–68. Moses Soyer, "A Dedication." Guglielmi, "After the Locusts," 113. Ben Shahn to Mr. Pelsue, undated letter, Archives of American Art. George Biddle, *An American Artist's Story*, 309.

34. Biddle, *An American Artist's Story*, 315–16. Rockwell Kent, *It's Me, O Lord: The Autobiography of Rockwell Kent* (New York: Dodd, Mead, 1955), 478, and *This Is My Own*, 243.

35. Biddle, *An American Artist's Story*, 261, 291. John Reed Club, exhibition catalogue for exhibit, "The Social Viewpoint in Art," quoted in *Creative Art*

12 (March 1933): 218. Joe Jones quoted in "Joe Jones Tries to 'Knock Holes in Walls,'" *Art Digest* 7 (February 15, 1933): 9. Guglielmi, "I Hope to Sing Again," 176.

36. Jack Levine, "Form and Content," *College Art Journal* 9 (Autumn 1949): 57–58. Moses Soyer, "Contemporary American Art," 6–7. Louis Guglielmi, statement in *American Realists and Magic Realists,* ed. Dorothy C. Miller and Alfred H. Barr, Jr. (New York: Museum of Modern Art, 1943), 38. Jones in "Joe Jones Tries to 'Knock Holes in Walls,'" 7.

37. Daniel Aaron argues for a similar occurrence for many Depression writers. See his *Writers on the Left: Episodes in American Literary Communism* (New York: Harcourt, Brace and World, 1961), 150.

38. Moses Soyer, "A Dedication"; Jack Levine, "Street Scene" (October 13, 1939), in O'Connor, *Art for the Millions,* 120.

39. Moses Soyer, "A Dedication"; "About Moses Soyer," *Art Front* 1 (February 1935): 6. Joe Jones quoted in *Joe Jones,* catalogue of an exhibition at ACA Gallery, November 10–30, 1940 (New York: ACA Gallery, 1940), unpaginated. Jack Levine, "Man Is the Center," *Reality* 1 (Spring 1953): 5. The social realists' "humanism" was distinct from the New Humanism, a contemporary literary movement associated with Irving Babbitt and Paul Elmer More.

40. Guglielmi, "After the Locusts," 113.

41. Biddle, *An American Artist's Story,* 258.

42. Diane Kelder, introduction to her collection, *Stuart Davis* (New York: Praeger, 1971), 3–14. John R. Lane, *Stuart Davis: Art and Art Theory* (New York: The Brooklyn Museum, 1978), 33–40.

43. Stuart Davis, "Abstract Painting Today" (c. 1939), in O'Connor, *Art for the Millions,* 127. Davis, 1932 daybook entries, *Stuart Davis,* ed. Kelder, 56, 59–60. Davis, "Abstract Painting Today," 126; daybook entry, June 2, 1940, from Davis Papers, quoted in Lane, *Stuart Davis,* 34.

44. Louis Guglielmi, statement in Miller and Barr, *American Realists and Magic Realists,* 38–39. Guglielmi, "Accomplishments #3" (c. 1945); Guglielmi, undated manuscript; Guglielmi to S. Carl Fracassini, c. April 1951; all in Louis Guglielmi Papers, Archives of American Art, New York.

45. Guglielmi, "I Hope to Sing Again," 175; statement in Miller and Barr, *American Realists and Magic Realists,* 38–39.

46. For a discussion of expressionism, see John I. H. Baur, *Revolution and Tradition in Modern American Art,* 41–42. Raphael Soyer, quoted in Lloyd Goodrich, *Raphael Soyer* (New York: Harry N. Abrams, 1972), 84. Ben Shahn, "Portrait of a Social Artist: Professor Eric Goldman Talks with Ben Shahn, Artist and Author," recorded 1965 (North Hollywood, Calif.: Center for Cassette Studies, 1972), tape recording. Levine, "Street Scene," 120.

47. Moses Soyer, "Three Brothers," 204; Hirsch, statement in Miller, *Americans 1942,* 60; Levine, "Street Scene," 120.

48. Soyer, "Three Brothers," 204. "Joe Jones of Missouri, a 'Success Story,'" *Art Digest* 10 (January 15, 1936): 15. Sheldon Rodman, *Portrait of the Artist as an American. Ben Shahn: A Biography with Pictures* (New York: Harper and Brothers, 1951), 99. Feldman, "American Painting During the Great Depression," 163. Kent, *It's Me, O Lord*, 484, 572. Gerald M. Monroe, "The American Artists' Congress and the Invasion of Finland," *Archives of American Art Journal* 15 (November 1, 1975): 17–18.

49. For an exaggerated account of the Communists' power, see Goodrich and Baur, *American Art of Our Century*, 100. Lane, *Stuart Davis*, 34. Raphael Soyer, *Diary of an Artist* (Washington, D.C.: New Republic Press, 1977), 222. For discussions of Communist influence in the Congress and Union, see Gerald M. Monroe, "The American Artists' Congress and the Invasion of Finland," and "The Artists' Union of New York" (Ed.D. diss., New York University, 1971), 138–41. Shahn-Phillips interview, 27–28.

50. Lewis Mumford, "Opening Address," First American Artists' Congress (New York: American Artists' Congress, 1936), 1–2. Soyer, *Diary of an Artist*, 226. Biddle, *An American Artist's Story*, 315. Biddle's remark—that bombs rather than paintings might better aid the Spanish Loyalists—suggests that he was unfamiliar with Pablo Picasso's *Guernica* (1937), a powerful abstract painting that eloquently protests the brutal fascist bombing of a Spanish village. Perhaps Biddle missed or ignored the painting because of his antipathy for abstractionism.

51. Moses Soyer, "The Children's Exhibition," *Art Front* 2 (March 1934): 12.

52. See Evergood's *Lynching Party* (1935) in Lucy R. Lippard, *The Graphic Work of Philip Evergood: Selected Drawings and Complete Prints* (New York: Crown Publishers, 1966), plate 42; Joe Jones's *American Justice* (c. 1934), in *American Magazine of Art* 27 (January 1934): 17; William Gropper's *Southern Landscape* (c. 1937), in *Gropper* (New York: ACA Gallery, 1938), unpaginated.

53. For Hirsch's *Landscape with Tear Gas*, see Miller, *Americans 1942*, 63.

54. David Shapiro makes such a suggestion in *Social Realism*, 15 and 28 (n.1).

55. For Evergood's *Toiling Hands*, see Baur, *Philip Evergood*, 1974 ed., plate 125. For reproductions of Gropper's *Homework* and *Roadworkers*, see the 1938 ACA publication, *Gropper*.

56. Levine, "Street Scene," 120.

57. For *The Millionaire*, see Miller, *Americans 1942*, 89.

58. For George Biddle's *Starvation* (c. 1934–35), see Baigell, *The American Scene*, plate 30. Joe Jones's *Luncheon* and *Who Could Ask for More?* are reproduced in the ACA Gallery's 1940 catalogue, *Joe Jones*.

59. Paul Richard, "The Roots of Alexandre Hogue," *Washington Post*, August 26, 1985, sec. C. *Mother Earth Laid Bare* is in the Gilcrease Museum, Tulsa, Oklahoma. Examples of the social realists' Dust Bowl works are Joe Jones,

American Farm, reproduced in Matthew Baigell, *The American Scene,* plate 29; George Biddle, *Sand,* in *America Today: A Book of 100 Prints Chosen and Exhibited by the American Artists' Congress* (New York: Equinox Cooperative Press, 1936), 59; William Gropper, *Last Cow, Art Digest* 13 (June 1939): 21. Philip Evergood's *Sorrowing Farmers* appears in Lippard, *The Graphic Work of Philip Evergood,* plate 154.

60. Joseph Hirsch, *Seller of Apples,* in *The Graphic Work of Joseph Hirsch,* ed. Sylvan Cole (New York: Associated American Artists, 1970); Jones, *Man Power* and *Nothing Better to Do* are in the 1940 ACA catalogue.

61. Raphael Soyer, *Diary of an Artist,* 237.

62. Lloyd Goodrich in Goodrich and Baur, *American Art of Our Century,* 91, suggests that the Soyers refrained from critical comment. Milton Brown similarly places the Soyers close to the politically conservative Regionalists, when in fact the Soyers had strong disagreements with the Regionalists; see Brown, *American Painting from the Armory Show to the Depression,* 182–85.

63. Goodrich, *Reginald Marsh,* 14–36, 295–97. Philip Evergood, "There Is a Difference in Bums," undated manuscript in Herman Baron Papers, Archives of American Art. For examples of Reginald Marsh's beach bodies and adjusted bums, see his *Coney Island Beach* (1935) and *East Tenth Street Jungle* (1934), in Lloyd Goodrich, *Reginald Marsh,* 120, 64.

64. Guglielmi, "After the Locusts," 113–14; statement in Miller and Barr, *American Realists and Magic Realists,* 38; "I Hope to Sing Again," 175–77. For a reproduction of *Wedding on South Street,* see *Architectural Record* 81 (February 1937): 9.

65. Ben Shahn, "American Painting at Mid-Century: An Unorthodox View" (1951), in Martin H. Bush, *Ben Shahn: The Passion of Sacco and Vanzetti* (Syracuse, N.Y.: Syracuse University Press, 1968), 60; Hirsch, statement in Miller, *Americans 1942,* 62; Moses Soyer, "Contemporary American Art," 6–7.

66. Moses Soyer, "About Moses Soyer," 6; Rockwell Kent, "An Interview with Rockwell Kent," conducted by Paul Cummings, February 26–27, 1969, *Archives of American Art Journal* 12 (January 1972): 10; *It's Me, O Lord,* 126.

67. Marquis W. Childs, "Three St. Louis Artists," *American Magazine of Art* 28 (August 1935): 483–85. Jones, quoted in 1940 ACA Gallery catalogue, *Joe Jones,* unpaginated. Herman Baron, unpublished history of the ACA Gallery, 28–37. Jones, quoted in "Joe Jones Tries to 'Knock Holes in Walls,'" 8; Baron, unpublished history of the ACA Gallery, 33–34.

68. For a discussion of the various New Deal art agencies, see Richard D. McKinzie, *The New Deal for Artists.* Shapiro, in *Social Realism,* 9, and Brown, in *American Painting from the Armory Show to the Depression,* vi, contend that the programs were responsible for both the form and content of

social realism. Lloyd Goodrich in Goodrich and Baur, *American Art of Our Century*, 98–101, argues that social realists usually came to their genre before joining a New Deal program. For a discussion of the artists' lobbying efforts for a program like WPA/FAP, see O'Connor, *Art for the Millions*, 27–28. Rockwell Kent, *This Is My Own*, 303–12; "The Artist Tells the Whole Story," *New Masses* 25 (November 16, 1937): 5–11.

69. Kent, *It's Me, O Lord*, 520. Kent, *This Is My Own*, 198. Evergood, "Should the Nation Support Its Art?" 2–3; Davis, "Federal Art Protection and the Social Education of the Artist," 164. Evergood, "Art in a Democracy."

70. Kent, *This Is My Own*, 297. Moses Soyer, "Contemporary American Art," 6–7; Guglielmi, "Accomplishments #3"; Guglielmi, "I Hope to Sing Again," 177. William Gropper quoted in Philip Evergood, "William Gropper," *New Masses* 50 (February 29, 1944): 26–27. Biddle, *An American Artist's Story*, 313–15. If by "proletarian art" we mean an art that arises from the workers themselves, then social realism does not fit the term.

71. Joe Jones, quoted in *Joe Jones*, unpaginated. For a discussion of the public's reception of political art, see Linda Nochlin, "Museums and Radicals: A History of Emergencies," *Art in America* 59 (July 1971): 35–37. Sheldon Rodman, *Portrait of the Artist as an American. Ben Shahn: A Biography with Pictures* (New York: Harper and Brothers): 51.

72. David Shapiro disagrees. He contends that social realism was revolutionary art that could not mature, and so faded, because there was no American revolution to nurture it. See *Social Realism*, 27–28.

73. For material on Hirsch, see "Biographical Notes on Contributing Artists," Third Annual Art Auction, Joint Anti-Fascist Refugee Committee, Herman Baron Papers, Archives of American Art. Philip Evergood, "William Gropper," 27.

74. For a discussion of esthetic isolation, see Matthew Baigell, *The American Scene*, 174.

75. Guglielmi, "Accomplishments #3." For a reproduction of Guglielmi's *Terror in Brooklyn* (1941), see his article, "I Hope to Sing Again." For *Evergood's Flight of Fancy* (1947), see Baur, *Philip Evergood* (1960), plate 41.

76. For Evergood's *Art on the Beach* (c. 1936), see Baur, *Philip Evergood* (1960), plate 6. E. W. Benson refers to Gropper's *Burlesque* (c. 1936) as depicting a "hot-moma type of footlight Venus"; see Benson's article, "Two Proletarian Artists: Joe Jones and Gropper," *American Magazine of Art* 29 (March 1936): 189.

77. A reproduction of Hirsch's *Two Men* appears in *American Magazine of Art* 32 (May 1939): 262. Baur, *Philip Evergood*, 48.

78. Gropper, "Gropper Visits Youngstown," *Nation* 145 (July 3, 1937): 14–15, and "Out West," *Nation* 145 (July 24, 1937): 96.

Chapter Six

1. John Dos Passos, introduction to the 1932 editon of his 1921 novel, *Three Soldiers* (New York: Modern Library, 1932), ix.

2. Joseph Hirsch, statement in *Americans 1942: 18 Artists from 9 States*, ed. Dorothy C. Miller (New York: Museum of Modern Art, 1942), 62. Rockwell Kent, *This Is My Own* (New York: Duell, Sloan and Pearce, 1940), 172.

3. "Farm Security Administration Picture Comments," from viewers attending the First International Photographic Exposition, New York, New York, April 18–29, 1938. Roy E. Stryker Papers, Archives of American Art, New York. Comments 326, 343.

4. Sherwood Anderson, "A Writer's Notes," *New Masses* 8 (August 1932): 10. Josephine Herbst to Katherine Anne Porter, October 10, 1933, and August 16, 1934, quoted in Elinor Langer, *Josephine Herbst: The Story She Could Never Tell* (Boston: Little, Brown, 1984), 150.

5. John Steinbeck to George Albee, January 15, 1935, in *Steinbeck: A Life in Letters*, ed. Elaine Steinbeck and Robert Wallsten (New York: Viking, 1975), 98. Gilbert Seldes, *The Years of the Locust (America, 1929–1932)* (Boston: Little, Brown and Company, 1933), title page. Robert McElvaine thinks that there was less alienation between intellectual and ordinary Americans in the thirties than there had been in the twenties. Robert S. McElvaine, *The Great Depression: America, 1929–1941* (New York: Times Books, 1984), 198–202.

6. For more on the visual arts and words, see John Brumfield, "Words and Pictures," *Center Quarterly* 4 (1983): n.p.

7. Dion Quinton Kempthorne, "Josephine Herbst: A Critical Introduction" (Ph.D. diss., University of Wisconsin-Madison, 1973), 52. Philip Evergood to Deborah Calkins, July 26, 1943, Evergood Papers, Archives of American Art, New York.

8. Warren French, *John Steinbeck*, 2d ed., rev. (Boston: Twayne, 1975), 10, 28. Letter from the publisher, *Time* 45 (February 12, 1945): 9. Margaret Bourke-White, *Portrait of Myself* (New York: Simon and Schuster, 1963), 259. Sean Callahan, ed., *The Photographs of Margaret Bourke-White* (New York: Bonanza Books, 1972), 21.

9. Edmund Wilson to Theodore Dreiser, May 2, 1932, and to Maxwell Geismar, June 10, 1942, in Edmund Wilson, *Letters on Literature and Politics 1912–1972* (New York: Farrar, Straus and Giroux, 1977), 223, 285. Benjamin Apple in "A Proposed Symposium," *Carleton Miscellany* 6 (Winter 1965): 20. Lorena Hickok, *One Third of a Nation: Lorena Hickok Reports on the Great Depression* (Urbana: University of Illinois Press, 1981), ix–x. John Steinbeck, *The Forgotten Village* (New York: Viking, 1941), preface.

10. Ben Shahn, *The Shape of Content* (Cambridge: Harvard University Press, 1957), 40–41, 76–84.

11. John H. Baker, "O. Louis Guglielmi: A Reconsideration," *Archives of American Art Journal* 15 (1973): 18–19. *Reality* 1 (Spring 1953): 1.
12. Judd Tully, "20th Century Raphael," *Horizon* 25 (July-August 1982): 26. Hallie Flanagan, *Arena: The History of the Federal Theatre* (New York: Benjamin Blom, 1965, 1940), 342.
13. For a discussion of the amazingly vicious surveillance of Bourke-White, see Robert E. Snyder, "Margaret Bourke-White and the Communist Witch Hunt," *Journal of American Studies* 19 (1985): 5–25.

Bibliographical Note

What follows is a selective evaluation of books, manuscripts, interviews, and collections that this study draws upon. The goal is not to list all the sources employed, nor is it to comment upon every item cited in the notes. Instead, this is a review of some of the more important primary and secondary works and may serve as a guide for those who want to continue exploring the themes of social criticism and social solace in Depression America.

There are no satisfactory general histories of America's social art and literature of the Depression years. Richard Pells's *Radical Visions and American Dreams: Cultural and Social Thought in the Depression Years* (New York: Harper and Row, 1973) is the most thorough single examination of intellectual development of the thirties, and no one interested in exploring the decade's creative impulses should ignore this study. Its best sections are on social theorists and literary critics, and the portions on art and literature are limited to discussions of major works. Robert S. McElvaine, *The Great Depression: America, 1929–1941* (New York: Times Books, 1984) is a good broad survey of Depression America and adds important considerations to Pells's treatment of cultural and intellectual trends. Warren Susman's essay "The Thirties," in *The Development of an American Culture,* ed. Stanley Coben and Lorman Ratner (Englewood Cliffs, N.J.: Prentice-Hall, 1970), 179–218, is another mandatory stop for anyone exploring the decade. Susman's essay is a catalogue of almost everything that might conceivably fall under the rubric of thirties culture, social or otherwise, and is full of intriguing but undeveloped ideas that deserve book-length studies. Alfred Kazin's *On Native Grounds: An Interpretation of Modern American Prose Literature* (New York: Reynal and Hitchcock, 1942) is dated and gives nationalism an unwarranted role in the Depression's social literature. It is, however, a penetrating analysis of the decade's fiction and essays and does a good job of placing them within the tradition of American literary naturalism and realism.

Kazin's memoir, *Starting Out in the Thirties* (Boston: Little, Brown, 1965) is important for its recollections and for its treatment of realism. Another essential memoir is Malcolm Cowley's *The Dream of the Golden Mountains* (New York: Viking, 1980); this is a collection of Cowley's recollections that have been spread in a number of journal articles and interviews. Edmund Wilson was another important literary figure of the Depression. His most revealing work on the thirties can be found in *The American Jitters: A Year of the Slump* (Freeport, N.Y.: Books for Libraries, 1968, 1932); *The Thirties: From Notebooks and Diaries of the Period*, edited by Leon Edel (New York: Farrar, Straus and Giroux, 1980); and *Letters on Literature and Politics, 1912–1972*, edited by Eleana Wilson (New York: Farrar, Straus and Giroux, 1977).

Communism was an important factor in the creative environment of the thirties, and in *Writers on the Left: Episodes in American Literary Communism* (New York: Harcourt, Brace, 1961), Daniel Aaron carefully details the Party's efforts to cultivate writers; in Aaron's interpretation, most authors were content to grow within the Party's garden. Caroline Bird's *The Invisible Scar: The Great Depression* (New York: Simon and Schuster, 1966) is too chatty and journalistic to be of much value, and Charles C. Alexander's *Nationalism in American Thought, 1930–1945* (Chicago: Rand McNally, 1969) has at its heart the untenable assertion that nationalism can explain *every* aspect of American culture between the Crash and the end of World War II. His next book, *Here the Country Lies: Nationalism and the Arts in Twentieth-Century America* (Bloomington: Indiana University Press, 1980), has a more limited and defensible definition of nationalism—the effort to cultivate mature American-produced arts.

Many of these themes I have traced also echoed through drama of the thirties. Jane DeHart Mathews's *The Federal Theatre, 1935–1939: Plays, Politics and Relief* (Princeton: Princeton University Press, 1967) intelligently probes the development of a federal art bureaucracy while also analyzing the creative products of that bureaucracy. Malcolm Goldstein's *The Political Stage: American Drama and Theater of the Great Depression* (New York: Oxford University Press, 1974) is more inclusive and of more help to the reader interested in the content of Depression plays. Other important books on the Depression stage are Gerald Rabkin, *Drama and Commitment: Politics in the American Theatre of the Thirties* (Bloomington: Indiana University Press, 1964), and Harold Clurman's memoir, *The Fervent Years: The Story of the Group Theater and the Thirties* (1945; reprint, New York: Alfred A. Knopf, 1950).

Few scholars have chosen to combine literary and pictorial materials in their treatments. William Stott is an exception to the rule, and his *Documentary Expression in Thirties America* (New York: Oxford University Press, 1973) brings together social reporters and documentary photographers in one book. Stott's treatment is strong on demonstrating the prevalence of documentary expression in the thirties, but weak in explaining why it had such an appeal for writers and photographers.

The Depression's artists and writers created according to their own inspirations and did not strive to capture the visions or principles of the New Deal cultural agencies. Many of the people whom I discuss, however, were enrolled in those agencies, and for a sense of the places in which they worked, one should consult William R. McDonald, *Federal Relief Administration and the Arts: The Origins and Administrative History of the Arts Projects of the Works Progress Administration* (Columbus, Ohio: Ohio State University Press, 1969); Jerre Mangione, *The Dream and the Deal: The Federal Writers' Project, 1935–1943* (Boston: Little, Brown, 1972); and Monty Noam Penkower, *The Federal Writers' Project: A Study in Government Patronage of the Arts* (Urbana: University of Illinois Press, 1977).

Anthologies cannot replace primary sources, but they can provide handy introductions to materials that are hard to come by in some locales. *Years of Protest: A Collection of American Writings of the 1930s,* edited by Jack Salzman and Barry Wallstein (New York: Bobbs-Merrill, 1967), is the best edited and most creatively arranged anthology available. More than just a collection of literature, it also includes paintings and photographs and places them among the writings with which they have the most in common. Harvey Swados's *The American Writer and the Great Depression* (New York: Bobbs-Merrill, 1966) is a thorough introduction to the decade's social literature and contains helpful headnotes. For popular culture of the thirties, one should see Warren Susman, ed., *Culture and Commitment, 1929–1945* (New York: George Braziller, 1973); and for news and politics, examine Daniel Aaron and Robert Bendiner, eds., *The Strenuous Decade: A Social and Intellectual Record of the 1930s* (Garden City, N.Y.: Doubleday, 1970).

The body of secondary literature on social fiction of the Depression is quite large. Perhaps the single most helpful general treatment is Walter B. Rideout, *The Radical Novel in the United States, 1900–1954: Some Interrelations of Literature and Society* (Cambridge: Harvard University Press, 1956), which gives the novels some insightful readings and places them within the perspective of their predecessors. But Rideout too firmly ties the social novels to the more ideological proletarian ones, which tended to follow a Communist formula. Maxwell Geismar's *Writers in Crisis: The American Novel Between Two Wars* (Boston: Houghton Mifflin, 1942) overstates the radical convictions of Steinbeck and Dos Passos and places them in the inappropriate company of Faulkner, Wolfe, and Hemingway. Sometimes lists of books are helpful, and the chief value of Halford E. Luccock's *American Mirror: Social, Ethical and Religious Aspects of American Literature 1930–1940* (New York: Macmillan, 1941) is that it is an extensive annotated list including all the major novels of the thirties and a good number of the more obscure ones. *American Fiction 1920–1940* (New York: Russell and Russell, 1941), by Joseph Warren Beach, is a standard work, but it is almost useless for much of it is given over to demonstrating to bourgeois readers that the social novels have literary value because they take up themes of beauty and moral strength. Warren French, ed., *The Thirties: Fiction, Poetry, Drama* (Deland, Fla.: Everett Edwards, 1967) is a collection of intriguing essays that serves as a good introduction to the social novels and draws important parallels between them and the decade's drama and poetry.

There are certain social novels of the Depression that are essential stepping stones toward an understanding of the decade's social culture. To fully understand them, one should read these books in conjunction with other supporting documents that help to clarify the authors' intentions. John Dos Passos's *U.S.A.* trilogy (New York: Harcourt, 1939, 1930–1936) is a monumental literary achievement that reveals the author's path through Marxism and liberalism and on to conservatism. Dos Passos's writings in Townsend Ludington, ed., *The Fourteenth Chronicle: Letters and Diaries of John Dos Passos* (Boston: Gambit, 1973) help illuminate the twists and turns on that path. Ludington's biography, *John Dos Passos: A Twentieth Century Odyssey* (New York: E. P. Dutton, 1980), is loaded with detail—street addresses, for example—at the expense of probing the novelist's intellectual life. Another biography is *Dos Passos: A Life* (New York: Doubleday, 1984), by Virginia Spencer Carr.

Studs Lonigan (New York: Random House, 1938, 1932–1935), by James T. Farrell, is a key trilogy, and Farrell's *A Note on Literary Criticism* (New York: Vanguard Press, 1936) shows the sophisticated Marxist ideology that lay behind his often tedious novels. Josephine Herbst's memoirs reveal more than the roots of her Trexler trilogy; they are a fascinating portrait of the confidence and anxiety of a woman novelist in the thirties. Readers should see "The Ruins of History," *Nation* 182 (April 14, 1956): 302–4; "The Starched Blue Sky of Spain," *The Noble Savage* 1 (1960): 76–110; "A Year of Disgrace," *The Noble Savage* 2 (1961): 128–60; and "Yesterday's Road," *New American Review* 3 (1968): 81–104. Elinor Langer's biography, *Josephine Herbst: The Story She Could Never Tell* (Boston: Little, Brown, 1984) is a fair and perceptive treatment.

Because he touched upon so many common themes of the thirties, John Steinbeck is a good novelist with whom to begin one's reading. The most important of his thirties works are *In Dubious Battle* (New York: Covici-Friede, 1936) and, of course, *The Grapes of Wrath* (New York: Viking, 1939). Steinbeck has been the subject of more secondary studies than any other social novelist. Warren French, *John Steinbeck*, 2d ed., rev. (Boston: Twayne, 1975) is the best single study and contains a careful analysis of the various stages of Steinbeck's thought on determinism. Although it lacks the scholarly orientation of French's analysis, Peter Lisca's *John Steinbeck: Nature as Myth* (New York: Thomas Y. Crowell, 1978) is also helpful. Jackson J. Benson's *The True Adventures of John Steinbeck, Writer* (New York: Viking, 1984) is less skillfully executed and full of more details than necessary. Biological metaphors and his biologist friend Ed Ricketts were important influences upon Steinbeck's thinking, and Richard Astro's *John Steinbeck and Edward F. Ricketts: The Shaping of a Novelist* (Minneapolis: University of Minnesota Press, 1973) examines that influence. The most important published source for examining Steinbeck's creative processes, and for charting his often bizarre turns of thought, is the collection of his letters, *Steinbeck: A Life in Letters* (New York: Viking, 1975), edited by Elaine Steinbeck and Robert Wallsten.

Native Son (New York: Harper and Row, 1940) by Richard Wright is another of the more significant social novels. *American Hunger* (New York: Harper and Row, 1977) is the second portion of Wright's autobiography; it illuminates the special problems of a black man during the Depression, demonstrates Wright's infatuation and then dissatisfaction with the Communist Party, and helps trace the growth of *Native Son*.

Not all the social novelists were as skillful as these writers. Good places to begin moving beyond that first echelon are Jack Conroy, *The Disinherited* (New York: Covici-Friede, 1933), a technically flawed first novel that still achieves some haunting symbolism; Robert Cantwell, *The Land of Plenty* (New York: Farrar and Rinehart, 1934), a sentimental but common juxtaposition of the natural family with the family of workers; and Tom Kromer, *Waiting for Nothing* (1935; reprint, New York: Hill and Wang, 1968), a dreary and largely autobiographical account of near-hopeless drifting. Nelson Algren's recollections in H. E. F. Donohue, *Conversations with Nelson Algren* (New York: Hill and Wang, 1964), depict the painful experiences of a middle-class youth who found his career expectations shattered with the Depression, and who turned to social fiction as a release for his anger and frustration. Harry Hart, ed., *American Writers' Congress* (New York: International Publishers, 1936), contains important addresses by a number of the social novelists, including Dos Passos and Jack Conroy.

Documentary photographers of the Depression took an enormous number of photographs. The largest collection, those pictures that the FSA photographers made, is now housed in the Library of Congress; the file contains somewhere in excess of 200,000 negatives and prints. The several published selections from the collection are much more readily accessible to the average reader. The best selection is Hank O'Neal's *A Vision Shared: A Classic Portrait of America and Its People, 1935–1943* (New York: St. Martin's, 1976). O'Neal allowed the photographers themselves to choose photos for publication, and his book contains few of the standard, timeworn pictures.

Other useful photo books are Edward Steichen, ed., *The Bitter Years, 1935–1941* (New York: Museum of Art, 1962); Thomas H. Garver, intro., *Just Before the War: Urban America from 1935 to 1941 as seen by Photographers of the Farm Security Administration* (Balboa, Calif.: New Port Harbor Art Museum, 1968); and Roy Emerson Stryker and Nancy Wood, eds., *In This Proud Land: America, 1935–1943 as seen in the FSA Photographs* (Boston: New York Graphic Society, 1973). *Portrait of a Decade: Roy Stryker and the Development of Documentary Photography in the Thirties* (Baton Rouge: Louisiana State University Press,

1972), by F. Jack Hurley, is not a very helpful tool for probing the photographers' minds. It concentrates chiefly on the growth of the FSA bureaucracy and gives almost no attention to the photographers' reasons for making their pictures. The FSA people were not the only organized group of photographers active in the thirties, and the reader interested in their younger and more radical counterparts should see Anne Tucker, "Photographic Crossroads: The Photo League," *Afterimage* 5 (April 1978): special supplement. Although Susan Sontag gives little specific attention to documentary photography in *On Photography* (New York: Farrar, Straus and Giroux, 1977), her book is a contemplative and analytical examination of the mental processes involved in taking pictures.

We are fortunate that so many of the documentary photographers worked for the federal government. As part of their jobs, they were required to report back to Washington while on field trips. Those letters are part of the Roy E. Stryker Collection, Archives of American Art, New York, and important sources for the photographers' daily workings and the creative goals they hoped to achieve. Equally important is a set of oral interviews that Richard K. Doud had with the photographers in 1964 and 1965. The interviews are occasionally clouded with hindsight, but documentary photographers wrote few articles or autobiographies, and the interviews are the most revealing statements many have left us. Transcripts of the interviews are also available in the Archives of American Art, and the photographers' permissions are required before using them.

Margaret Bourke-White did write an autobiography, *Portrait of Myself* (New York: Simon and Schuster, 1963), which reveals someone considerably different from the other photographers, a woman less inclined than the others were to treat her subjects with respect or to portray them as dignified people. For reproductions of Bourke-White's photos, see Sean Callahan, ed., *The Photographs of Margaret Bourke-White* (New York: Bonanza Books, 1972).

The most complete window into Dorothea Lange's thinking is her extensive set of interviews with Suzanne Riess, "The Making of a Documentary Photographer" (Berkeley: University of California, Regional Oral History Office, 1968). Also useful for Lange's early and later life are Milton Meltzer's biography, *Dorothea Lange: A Photographer's Life* (New York: Farrar, Straus and Giroux, 1978), and Karin Becker Ohrn, *Dorothea Lange and the Documentary Tradition* (Baton Rouge: Louisiana State University Press, 1980). Howard M. Levin and Katherine Northrup, eds., *Dorothea Lange: Farm Security Administration Photographs, 1935–1939* (Glencoe, Ill.: Text-Fiche Press, 1980) is a two-volume set containing Lange's captions plus microfiche reproductions of her photographs.

In Walker Evans's "Interview with Leslie Katz," *Art in America* 59 (March–April 1971): 82–89, he tells how he decided to abandon writing for photography and espouses his principle that photography should never become a nostalgic medium. Walker Evans, *Walker Evans: American Photographs* (1938; reprint, New

York: East River Press, 1975) contains his major photographs of the 1930s, complete with some from his uncharacteristic excursion into candid photography. For Berenice Abbott's efforts to preserve images of New York's older buildings and its shrinking number of pushcart vendors, see her collection *Changing New York* (New York: E. P. Dutton, 1939), as well as Avis Berman's article, "The Unflinching Eye of Berenice Abbott," *Art News* 80 (January 1981): 86–95. *Berenice Abbott, American Photographer* (New York: McGraw-Hill, 1982), by Hank O'Neal, is also useful.

Only recently has Marion Post Wolcott begun to receive the attention she deserves; see for example *Marion Post Wolcott: FSA Photographs* (Carmel, Calif.: Friends of Photography, 1983). Ben Shahn's photos became less political and more concerned with eccentric people over the years, and the shift is evident in Margaret R. Weiss, ed., *Ben Shahn, Photographer: An Album from the Thirties* (New York: DeCapo Press, 1973). Paul Von Blum's *The Critical Vision: A History of Social and Political Art in the U.S.* (Boston: South End Press, 1982) examines both documentary photography and social realist painting; though informed with sympathetic political perspectives and filled with important illustrations, this is not a sophisticated or penetrating book.

There are no separate studies of the traveling reporters. The most detailed discussions of their works are in Kazin's *On Native Grounds* and Pells's *Radical Visions and American Dreams*, but both of these treatments place unwarranted emphasis upon the reporters' interest in nationalistic issues. To fully understand the travelers, it is best to go directly to their reports and then examine their motives for traveling that surface in other, more autobiographical writings. Nathan Asch's *The Road: In Search of America* (New York: W. W. Norton, 1937) displays in vivid detail the emotional uncertainties and intellectual expectations that lay behind his long bus ride. To put that report in context, one should consult his article based upon an earlier trip, "Cross-Country Bus," *New Republic* 87 (April 25, 1934): 301–4, and his autobiographical short story about the frustrations of working in Hollywood, "The Greatest Story," *New Masses* 14 (February 5, 1935): 17–19.

Sherwood Anderson's *Puzzled America* (New York: Charles Scribner's Sons, 1935) shows how a confused liberal set out to discover what was wrong with the country and came back from his travels no less sure of the nation's ailment but certain that the New Deal was its appropriate cure. In addition, his letters in Howard Mumford Jones and Walter B. Rideout, eds., *Letters of Sherwood Anderson* (Boston: Little, Brown and Company, 1953), show an author who was quite willing to abandon fiction in the early 1930s and turn to more reassuringly concrete writing like travel reporting.

Erskine Caldwell was the traveler with the most persistent wanderlust, and his autobiography, *Call It Experience: The Years of Learning How to Write* (New York:

Duell, Sloan and Pearce, 1951), describes his trips of the thirties as more agonizing and less reassuring than the other expeditions of his life.

James Rorty's *Where Life Is Better: An Unsentimental American Journey* (New York: Reynal and Hitchcock, 1936) is probably the best-written of the travel reports, and Rorty devoted a good portion of it to wrestling with the role ideology should play in his effort to make objective observations. Rorty wrote advertising copy before the Crash, and his essay "I Was an Ad-Man Once," *New Republic* 73 (January 25, 1933): 290–93, is a repudiation of that earlier life.

John Spivak observed America from a leftist perspective, and his report of his observations, *America Faces the Barricades* (New York: Covici-Friede, 1935), has a similar orientation. Spivak's radical hopes evaporated with the Nazi-Soviet pact and for an account of the devastating effect the agreement had upon his beliefs, see his autobiography, *A Man in His Time* (New York: Horizon Press, 1967).

Anna Louise Strong spent the better part of her life traveling from one revolutionary situation to another. Her *I Change Worlds: The Remaking of an American* (New York: Garden City Publishing Company, 1937) is a confession of her obsessive need to align herself with progressive movements. Strong described her travels in the United States in *My Native Land* (New York: Viking Press, 1940), where she rather oddly claimed that America had become the latest to join the international revolutionary movement.

Three Tenant Families: Let Us Now Praise Famous Men (Boston: Houghton Mifflin Company, 1941) is James Agee's recollection of his trip to visit Alabama sharecroppers, a piece of prose that approximates sophomoric poetry. Agee was much less concerned with empiricism than were the other travelers, and the collection *Letters of James Agee to Father Flye* (New York: G. Braziller, 1962) underscores the differences between Agee and the others. Agee's life might be described as a monument to self-destruction, and for an examination of that tendency, see Laurence Bergreen, *James Agee: A Life* (New York: E. P. Dutton, 1984).

Lewis Adamic is the last of the more significant travelers. His *My America, 1928–1938* (New York: Harper and Brothers, 1938) is both travel report and autobiography, an often anguished account of an immigrant's efforts to cope with an adopted country that had suddenly fallen into the grips of the Depression.

Unlike the works of the documentary photographers, the paintings of the social realists are not conveniently collected in any one place. If it is impossible for the reader to visit each of the galleries and collections that house their works, one can study reproductions in catalogues, books about the individual artists, and other art histories. There are a number of useful broad analyses of American art, and particularly helpful are Lloyd Goodrich and John I. H. Baur, *American Art of Our Century* (New York: Frederick A. Praeger, 1961), and Milton W. Brown, *American Painting from the Armory Show to the Depression* (Princeton: Princeton University Press, 1955).

Matthew Baigell mistakenly brings social realism and regionalism together into one genre in his *The American Scene: American Painting of the 1930s* (New York: Frederick A. Praeger, 1971), but the book has a number of good reproductions of important social realist paintings. Joshua C. Taylor does a much better job of distinguishing between social realism and regionalism. Taylor contends that both schools were trying to find "the people," but the difference was that the social realists were looking for "the masses" and the regionalists were looking for "the folk"; see Joshua C. Taylor, *America as Art* (Washington: National Collection of Fine Arts, Smithsonian Institution Press, 1976).

David Shapiro has conveniently collected several important essays by the social realists into his anthology, *Social Realism: Art as a Weapon* (New York: Frederick Ungar Publishing Company, 1973). In his introduction and headnotes, however, Shapiro overestimates the painters' militancy.

Richard D. McKinzie's *The New Deal for Artists* (Princeton: Princeton University Press, 1973) is a good bureaucratic history of the various federal art projects and helps explain why the painters preferred to work in some agencies rather than others. Several key essays on social painting, including ones by Jack Levine and Louis Guglielmi, appear in Francis V. O'Connor, ed., *Art for the Millions: Essays from the 1930s by Artists of the WPA Federal Art Project* (Greenwich, Conn.: New York Graphic Society, 1973).

Herman Baron ran the New York gallery that was a center of social realism, and his unpublished history of the ACA Gallery, Herman Baron Papers, Archives of American Art, has especially important analyses of the careers and works of Philip Evergood, Joe Jones, and William Gropper. For a discussion of realism in painting, see Linda Nochlin, *Realism* (Baltimore: Penguin, 1971).

Writings by and about the individual artists are perhaps the most valuable tools for getting at the origins of social realism. John I. H. Baur conducted a series of extensive interviews with Philip Evergood during the late 1950s, and these appear, together with Evergood's most important paintings, in Baur's *Philip Evergood* (New York: Frederick A. Praeger, 1960). The text of the 1974 edition of Baur's *Philip Evergood* is essentially the same, but the 1974 edition has more paintings, including Evergood's *Artist in Society*. For Evergood's belief that the Depression fundamentally altered the course of American art, see his essay, "Building a New Art School," *Art Front* 3 (April–May 1937): 21.

For Stuart Davis's similar analysis, see his essay, "Federal Art Protection and the Social Education of the Artist," c. 1938, reproduced in Diane Kelder, ed., *Stuart Davis* (New York: Frederick A. Praeger, 1971). Kelder's collection contains other significant writings by Davis, including selections from his notebooks of the twenties and thirties.

Rockwell Kent had a monumental ego, even for an artist, and his firm belief in his own worth led him to write two autobiographies in the space of only fifteen years. The first one is the more useful of the two and is chock-full of his reflections on art in the midst of social crisis—*Rockwell Kent, This Is My Own* (New York: Duell, Sloan and Pearce, 1940).

The most complete collection of William Gropper's work is August L. Freundlich, *William Gropper: Retrospective* (Los Angeles: The Ward Ritchie Press, 1968), and a good number of reproductions of Joe Jones's work appear in the exhibit catalogue, *Joe Jones* (New York: ACA Gallery, 1940). For a good biography of Reginald Marsh, as well as quality reproductions of his work, one should consult Lloyd Goodrich, *Reginald Marsh* (New York: Harry N. Abrams, 1972). Moses Soyer's article, "Three Brothers," *Magazine of Art* 32 (April 1939): 201–7ff., is a biography of Moses, Raphael, and their brother Isaac; accompanying it are some reproductions of their paintings of the thirties.

There comes a point in the act of creating or appreciating a painting when words and intellectual analysis fail and one must draw upon other faculties. No one realized this better than Ben Shahn. His *The Shape of Content* (Cambridge: Harvard University Press, 1963, 1957) is not only a telling description of his odyssey from social commentary to character portrayal during the Depression years, it is also a very thoughtful examination of the tug-of-war an artist experiences between the demands of his reason and the compulsions of his intuitions.

Index